Cancún
Riviera Maya

Fourth Edition

Travel better, enjoy more

ULYSSES
Travel Guides

Offices

Canada: Ulysses Travel Guides, 4176 St. Denis Street, Montréal, Québec, H2W 2M5, ☎(514) 843-9447, ⇌(514) 843-9448, info@ulysses.ca, www.ulyssesguides.com

Europe: Les Guides de Voyage Ulysse SARL, 127 rue Amelot, 75011 Paris, France, ☎01 43 38 89 50, ⇌01 43 38 89 52, voyage@ulysse.ca, www.ulyssesguides.com

U.S.A.: Ulysses Travel Guides, 305 Madison Avenue, Suite 1166, New York, NY 10165, info@ulysses.ca, www.ulyssesguides.com

Distributors

U.S.A.: Hunter Publishing, 130 Campus Drive, Edison, NJ 08818, ☎800-255-0343, ⇌(732) 417-1744 or 0482, comments@hunterpublishing.com, www.hunterpublishing.com

Canada: Ulysses Travel Guides, 4176 St. Denis Street, Montréal, Québec, H2W 2M5, ☎(514) 843-9882, ext.2232, ⇌514-843-9448, info@ulysses.ca, www.ulyssesguides.com

Great Britain and Ireland: Roundhouse Publishing, Millstone, Limers Lane, Northam, North Devon, EX39 2RG, ☎1 202 66 54 32, ⇌1 202 66 62 19, roundhouse.group@ukgateway.net

Other countries: Ulysses Travel Guides, 4176 St. Denis Street, Montréal, Québec, H2W 2M5, ☎(514) 843-9882, ext.2232, ⇌514-843-9448, info@ulysses.ca, www.ulyssesguides.com

National Library of Canada Cataloguing-in-Publication

Main entry under title:

　　　　Cancún and the Riviera Maya
　　　　(Ulysses travel guide)
　　　　Biennial.
　　　　[1999]-
　　　　Translation of: Cancún et la Riviera Maya.

　　　　ISSN 1495-2645
　　　　ISBN 2-89464-625-9

1. Riviera Maya Region (Mexico) - Guidebooks. 2. Cancún (Mexico) - Guidebooks. I. Series.

F1333.C36　　　　917.2'6704836　　　　C00-390045-2

© April 2004, Ulysses Travel Guides.
All rights reserved
Printed in Canada
ISBN 2-89464-625-9

At four o'clock we left Pisté, and very soon we saw rising high above the plain, the Castillo of Chichén. In half an hour we were among the ruins of this ancient city, with all of the great buildings in full view, casting prodigious shadows over the plain, and presenting a spectacle which, even after all we had seen, once more excited in us emotions of wonder.

John Lloyd Stephens
Incidents of Travel in Yucatán

Research and Writing
Denis Faubert
Alain Legault
Alain Théroux
Caroline Vien

Publisher
André Duchesne

English Editing
Cindy Garayt
Jennifer McMorran

Production Assistance
Mélanie Enard
Olivier Girard
Amber Martin

Page Layout
Isabelle Lalonde

Computer Graphics
André Duchesne

Cartographer
Isabelle Lalonde

Artistic Director
Patrick Farei (Atoll)

Illustrations
Myriam Gagné
Lorette Pierson
Marie-Annick Viatour

Photography
Philip Coblentz
(Brand X Pictures)

Acknowledgements: We gratefully acknowledge the financial support of the Government of Canada through the Book Publishing Industry Development Program (BPIDP) for our publishing activities. We would also like to thank the government of Québec for its SODEC income tax program for book publication.

Write to Us

The information contained in this guide was correct at press time. However, mistakes can slip in, omissions are always possible, places can disappear, etc. The authors and publisher hereby disclaim any liability for loss or damage resulting from omissions or errors.

We value your comments, corrections and suggestions, as they help us to keep each guide up to date. The best contributions will be rewarded with a free book from Ulysses Travel Guides. All you have to do is write us at the following address and indicate which title you would be interested in receiving.

Ulysses Travel Guides

4176 St. Denis Street
Montréal, Québec
Canada H2W 2M5

305 Madison Avenue
Suite 1166, New York
NY 10165

www.ulyssesguides.com
E-mail: *text@ulysses.ca*

Symbols

≡	Air conditioning
bkfst incl.	Breakfast included
⊗	Fan
⇄	Fax number
☺	Fitness centre
½b	Half board (lodging + 2 meals)
K	Kitchenette
≈	Pool
pb/sb	Both private and shared bathrooms*
sb	Shared bathroom*
ℝ	Refrigerator
ℜ	Restaurant
△	Sauna
✿	Spa
☎	Telephone number
tv	Television
🚢	Ulysses's favourite
⊛	Whirlpool

*Note that all establishments have private bathrooms unless otherwise indicated.

Attraction Classification

★	Interesting
★★	Worth a visit
★★★	Not to be missed

Hotel Classification

$	less than 50$
$$	$50 to $80
$$$	$81 to $130
$$$$	$131 to $180
$$$$$	more than $180

Unless otherwise indicated, the prices in the guide are
for one standard room, double occupancy in high season.

Restaurant Classification

$	less than $10
$$	$10 to $20
$$$	$21 to $30
$$$$	more than 30$

Unless otherwise indicated, the prices in the guide are for a
three-course evening meal for one person, not including drinks and tip.

All prices in this guide are in US dollars.

Table of Contents

List of Maps

Map Symbols

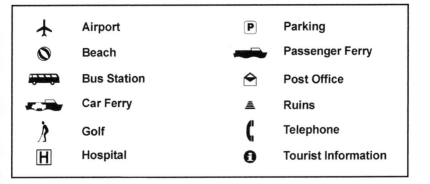

✈	Airport	Ⓟ	Parking
◎	Beach	🚤	Passenger Ferry
🚌	Bus Station	✉	Post Office
🚢	Car Ferry	⛬	Ruins
🏌	Golf	☏	Telephone
Ⓗ	Hospital	❶	Tourist Information

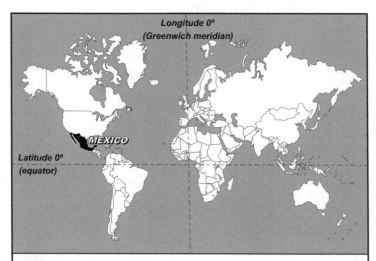

 Where is Cancún?

©ULYSSES

Mexico

Capital: Mexico City
Population: 100,368,000 inhab.
Currency: Mexican peso
Area: 1,967,183 km²

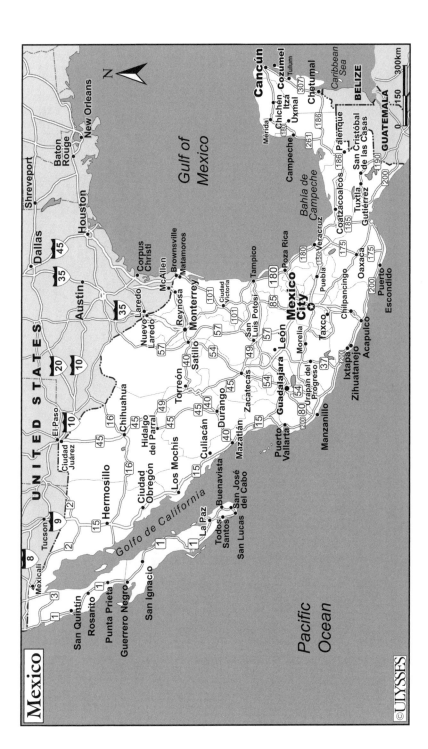

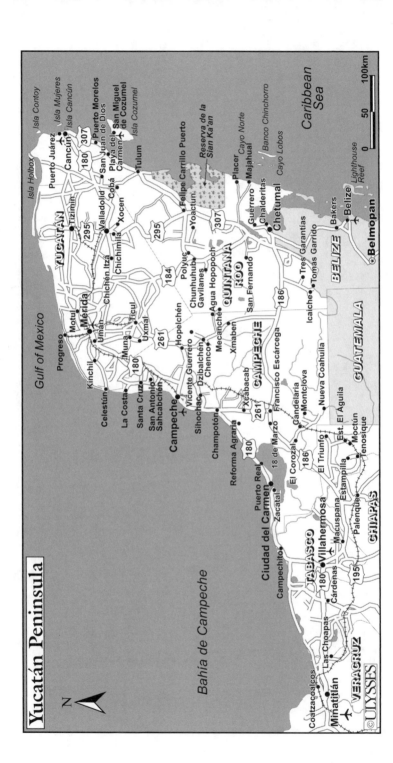

Yucatán Peninsula

Cancún and the
Riviera Maya are primarily renowned for their glorious white-sand beaches and modern infrastructures.

This is also a region in which diversity triumphs: from the uninhabited northern islands and the mangrove swamps of the Sian Ka'an biosphere reserve to natural wells known as cenotes and huge reefs that line the Caribbean coast. The beauty and variety of the underwater and terrestrial worlds are the region's greatest assets. Here, you can discover the heart and soul of the Yucatán Peninsula, its people and treasures, both past and present, including archaeological sites such as Chichén Itzá, remains of the great Mayan empire.

Tree-studded plains littered with thousand-year-old archaeological sites; outstanding beaches; tropical fish; lagoons and coral reefs like the one off Palancar on Cozumel... these are a few of the wonders to be found in this unique region, making it one of the most popular tourist destinations in the northern hemisphere. The Yucatán was clearly blessed by the gods (Mayan or Catholic—take your pick!).

This region is easy to explore. The Yucatán Peninsula is lined with flat, well-laid out roads linking interesting villages. Archaeological sites, some in progress, others still hidden by the jungle; swimming with dolphins; scuba diving... these are just some of the region's many attractions, each located close enough to each other that you can enjoy them all, on your own or with a guide, even during a short stay in the region.

The Chichén Itzá archaeological zone and Isla Mujeres are easy to reach from Cancún. Visitors can also take the Cancún-Tulum Corridor and go down the Riviera Maya to the vast Sian Ka'an biosphere reserve. The Cobá remains are easy to reach from Tulum. It is also easy to travel from Cancún to Cozumel or vice versa by boat or by plane.

Cancún is a highly developed seaside resort, tailor-made for night owls and action-seekers. But lovers of the great outdoors—and especially of aquatic activities—will find lots to do on the Riviera Maya. And the ocean, with its long golden-sand beaches bathed with beautiful, foaming, turquoise waters, is mystifying.

If there is one attraction that is not to be overlooked, though, it's the people. The Yucatán Peninsula was the cradle of the Mayan civilization, and the modern Maya are hardworking, patient and humble people with a slow-paced, studied way of life. Their shy, courteous manner conceals a serene empathy and a genuine kindness, a smile all their own.

Geography

A peninsula in southeast Mexico, the Yucatán, land of corn (maize) and henequen, is divided into three parts: the state of Campeche, to the west, remains untouched by mass tourism; the state of Quintana Roo, a long, narrow stretch of land along the eastern shore, is home to Cancún, Tulum, Cozumel and Isla Mujeres; to the north, the state of Yucatán extends out into the Gulf of Mexico and boasts the region's most important archaeological site, Chichén Itzá, as well as the colonial town of Mérida.

A large part of the peninsula is composed of lime-stone rocks perforated by sinkholes known as *cenotes*, some of which used to be the scene of Mayan sacrifices. Some *cenotes* have become very popular with scuba divers. Among the Yucatán's most fascinating attractions, the *cenotes* are the only visible bodies of water on the peninsula, whose few rivers and lakes are underground.

Cenotes

The reason there are so many *cenotes* in the Yucatán is that the peninsula is composed of limestone. The entire region is scattered with caves, some empty, others full of cool, crystal-clear water, a phenomenon found nowhere else in Mexico. The ancient Maya marvelled at these natural wells, and, after settling in the area, made them into sacred places. They built their villages near the *cenotes*, the main source of potable water in the region. They also believed that these natural wells, which they referred to as *dzonot* (a term that became "*cenotes*" in Spanish), were the refuge of the rain gods.

The caves riddling the peninsula are washed by underground rivers, which, repeatedly swollen by rainwater then shrunken by droughts, erode the limestone subsoil, causing the earth's crust to collapse. Eventually exposed, these amazing fissures, which vary in size from the northern to the southern part of the peninsula, are almost perfectly round, their sides marked by erosion.

Today, dog-paddling children and experienced divers alike are regular visitors to the Yucatán's *cenotes*, some of which have become major attractions, while others remain untouched by the tourist frenzy.

Most *cenotes* are good places to go swimming, but scuba diving in them requires more caution, as there is a risk of getting lost in the maze-like underwater caverns or of suddenly feeling claustrophobic. Exploring the nooks and crannies of a *cenote* is a thrilling experience, but one best left to experienced cave-divers.

The following are a few of the most popular *cenotes*:

Cenote Sagrado (sacred *cenote*): Located on the Chichén Itzá archaeological site, 201km from Cancún via Highway 180, this *cenote* is popular because of the amazing finds that archaeologists have made here. As indicated by its name, this place was an important Mayan religious site, where sacrifices were carried out. Sixty metres in diameter and 40m deep, it is unusable today, due to its stagnant waters.

Sin Nombre (nameless): This *cenote* lies about 100km south of Cancún on Highway 307, not far from Puerto Aventuras. To get there, follow the signs.

Xel-Há: This charming *cenote* is partially located

on a Postclassic Mayan site, in front of the Xel-Há national park, on the other side of Highway 307. Most tour operators don't show tourists this *cenote*, so you will have to get there on your own. No swimming.

Tankah: This *cenote* is located 137km south of Cancún (Highway 307), near Tulum. Access is gained by a small road, which is indicated on the highway by a wooden sign. Swimming permitted.

Fauna

Thanks to its special geographical location, lagoons, *cenotes* and brackish creeks, and because it is a peninsula, the Yucatán is an ideal habitat for a wide variety of animals.

Concerned about the unbridled destruction of the forest and other vegetation brought about by the region's tourist development, Mexican authorities are taking steps to preserve and showcase certain areas that lend themselves perfectly to ecotourism.
The two most important projects involve the coralline island of Contoy, located north of Isla Mujeres and home to nearly 80 species of birds, and the fascinating Reserva de la Biósfera Sian Ka'an, designated a UNESCO biosphere reserve in 1986 and located

Flamingo

a few kilometres south of Tulum.

The reserve is home to a variety of wild animals, including pumas, jaguars, manatees and crocodiles. Even the most unadventurous tourists will come across countless lizards, those placid little spies that blend into the landscape, only drawing attention to themselves when they scamper off.

The iguana, easily recognizable by its dark skin, is one of the most common reptiles on the island, but geckoes, as tiny as insects, and black iguanas also roam the peninsula, and can as easily be spotted atop a Mayan temple, watching a guide get bogged down in his own explanations, as on the table of a seaside restaurant.

Pelicans, which often travel in pairs, soar over the beach with a single flap of their wings, watching the tourists soaking up the sun. The gleaming, black frigate bird also flies about near swimming areas, spreading its long, narrow wings and practising its hovering skills, opening its forked tail periodically to maintain its delicate balance.

Terns, for their part, often make a racket near restaurants, fixing a menacing eye on those customers who don't immediately toss them a piece of bread.

Frigate bird

Unexpected meetings often provide astonishing ornithological discoveries: merging with the landscape, a perched male frigate bird will suddenly swell his scarlet throat to seduce a female and successfully attract the eyes of onlookers.

To ensure the success of your expedition, bring binoculars, insect repellent and a camera with a telephoto lens.

Tourists who venture inland might spot a toucan, the symbol of many southern countries. In the northernmost part of the peninsula, near Río Lagartos, there is a colony of flamingoes with an estimated population of nearly 30,000.

Other animal species, such as jaguars, snakes and anteaters, can be observed on short expeditions outside populated areas.

Marine Life

The underwater world off the shores of the state of Quintana Roo is a paradise of multicoloured coral and countless varieties of fish in all different shapes and sizes.

Scuba diving and snorkelling—the best way to observe the underwater world—are so popular that they account for more than 20% of the tourist activity on the island of Cozumel, renowned for its coral reefs, which cover many metres and attract divers from all over the world.

The limpid water, as mentioned above, makes it possible to observe a vast number of aquatic plants and animals in the sea and in various parks and reserves. Sport fishers flock have a ball here as well, as Isla Mujeres and Cozumel organize annual competitions during which many record catches are made.

The number of creatures inhabiting the region's waters is so vast that we couldn't possibly provide an exhaustive list here. Below, however, we have mentioned a few of the species you are likely to encounter on even the briefest excursion.

Cancún

Grouper, red snapper, barracuda and bluefin tuna are among the species that can be spotted, particularly

Marlin

during tours offered in the hotel zone.

Isla Mujeres

On the est coast of the island, Parque Nacional El Garrafón is home to a wide variety of animals. The park is a refuge for many species of fish, including angelfish, recognizable by their bright white and yellow stripes, and *sar*, usually found around staghorn and black coral, where they like to hide. The damselfish zealously protects its territory and won't hesitate to attack foolhardy swimmers who venture onto its turf, lured by the beauty of the sea anemones strewn across the ocean floor. Other, more imposing species, many sought-after by fishers, patrol the same waters—*ludjan*, grouper, red snapper, barracuda and tuna, among others.

Cozumel

A ferocious fish with a terrifying set of teeth, the great barracuda haunts the waters around the reef that bears its name, and can also be found near the San Juan reef. It is not always necessary to comb the ocean floor in scuba gear to see the wonders of the sea: by simply boarding the boat that plies the waters between Playa del Carmen and Cozumel, you're sure to see some flying fish or magnificent dolphins leaping joyfully out of the water.

Noteworthy species found in the Cozumel region include the wahoo, the blue shark or shortfin mako, the mahi-mahi, the tuna, the sailfish and swordfish, as well as the blue marlin, the star of Ernest Hemingway's novel *The Old Man and the Sea*.

Near the "little sea" (*Chakanaab* in Maya), tropical fish and coral are legion. You will spot a parrotfish through the branches of staghorn coral here; an angelfish, easy to overlook at just 2cm long, near some "diploria" coral there; and in the distance, but clearly visible in this limpid water, a 2kg marlin. From May to September, visitors have a chance to observe giant turtles laying their eggs in the area.

Flora

The Yucatán jungle is nothing like the Amazon forest. The landscape is characterized by a dense, low forest made up of coconut trees, banana trees and sapodillas, whose latex, called *chicle*, was once used to make chewing gum. Fruits found in this region include avocados, oranges, limes, grapefruits and papayas. Corn (maize) and beans are widely cultivated in this part of the country. Henequen, a type of agave used for sisal fibre, is grown mainly in the northwestern part of the peninsula, and is on the decline.

All along the roads, around the archaeological sites and in the parks, lovely silk-cotton trees display their

The Vanishing Coconut Tree

Over the past few years, a worrisome epidemic has struck coconut trees (*Cocos nucifera*) in tropical regions. This disease, known as LY, for Lethal Yellowing, first started attacking trees in Florida in the mid-1970s, then spread to the Mexican state of Quintana Roo, Haiti, Jamaica and most recently Belize.

Caused by a primitive bacterium transported by insects that inject it into the leaves of the coconut tree they are feeding on, the disease invades and obstructs the tree's vascular system. After turning yellow, the tree loses its leaves and branches until nothing is left but its bare trunk. A major project to reforest those areas already affected or at risk with a more resistant species is presently underway.

pretty reddish-orange flowers to passersby.

It is also worth noting the contribution made by landscape gardeners, who have put some natural colour back into Cancún, especially in the hotel zone, where concrete often predominates. Alongside the roads, on medians and in the parks, kilometres of imaginatively sculpted shrubs form a motionless, green menagerie of big birds and other animals.

Climate

The rainy season lasts from May to September, a period characterized by high temperatures and humidity, especially in June. During the rest of the year, the weather is mild and dry.

As in the Caribbean islands, Cancún and the Riviera Maya face the most formidable of enemies, namely the hurricanes that make their annual rounds from September to November, sometimes leaving desolate landscapes in their wake.

Hurricanes Gilbert (1988) and Roxanne (1995) hit the state of Quintana Roo hard, teaching a brutal lesson to inexperienced entrepreneurs who had built hotels and restaurants too close to the shore.

History

Prehistory

Many scientists now believe that the disappearance of the dinosaurs was caused by a gigantic meteor hitting the earth 65 million years ago, a theory supported by a research expedition carried out in January of 1997. For months after the collision, a thick cloud of dust hung in the sky, the temperature soared and floods swept the land, wiping out 70% of all species. In 1989, what is believed to be the point of impact was discovered in the Yucatán: an immense, circular crater known as the Chicxulub crater (named after a small village several kilometres north of Mérida), which measures between 180 and 300km; the diameter of the meteor that supposedly created it is estimated at 10 to 20km.

In the Quaternary period, during the glacial epoch, sea levels dropped for a brief period, enabling the inhabitants of the Asian continent to cross the Bering Strait to Alaska. For thousands of years, these nomadic peoples gradually occupied the continent from north to south, all the way to Tierra del Fuego. The oldest anthropological discovery in Mexico is Tepexpan man, who is 12,000 years old. Gradually giving up hunting and gathering, the tribes started settling and taking up farming and fishing

Portrait

around the year 7000 BC. The first villages were thus built along the shore.

The Archaic Period

Corn was first cultivated here around 5000 BC. Clay figurines dating back 5,000 years indicate a certain development in religion around this period.

The San Lorenzo Olmec civilization reached its apogee around 1200 BC. The Olmecs had their own hieroglyphic writing, a complex calendar and a system of numeration, and greatly influenced later civilizations through their art and social organization. Vestiges of their society include a number of colossal basalt heads up to 3m high and several large ceremonial sites.

Another important stage in Mexican history was the era of the dazzling city of Teotihuacán, a religious centre. This metropolis, located near Mexico City, originated around 200 BC. It is the largest pre-Columbian city discovered in the Americas to date. At its height, it was bigger than ancient Rome. Though it is not known who founded Teotihuacán, there is no doubt that the city's political, cultural and religious power extended tens of kilometres. It appears to have reached its peak between AD 300 and AD 650.

By AD 200, Mexican civilizations were already highly developed from an architectural, artistic and scientific point of view.

Astronomy and mathematics, in particular, seem to have been central to their concerns.

The Mayan Civilization

Mayan civilization reached its peak between AD 200 and AD 900. There are several cities dating from that era on the Yucatán Peninsula, including Uxmal and Cobá.

By the year 900, the commercial influence of the high plateau civilizations had superseded that of the Classical-era Mayas. Nevertheless, the Toltec and Mayan civilizations coexisted and intermingled. The Chichén Itzá archaeological site, among others, features ornamentation typical of both civilizations.

The decline of the great cities was swift, however, and the Aztecs stepped to the fore around the year 1300. Through their technical and commercial achievements, they succeeded in dominating their rivals.

The Aztecs

The Aztecs founded Tenochtitlán (now Mexico City). Their power stretched great distances, and their reign lasted about 150 years. They were conquered by the Spanish, who were led by Cortés and aided by enemy peoples.

The Spanish Conquest

The tale of the Spaniards' encounter with the New World has given rise to all sorts of speculation, but one thing is certain: it was one of the most important and troubling moments in the history of the world. The first contact with the Maya took place in 1512, when the priest Jerónimo de Aguilar and the navigator Gonzalo Guerrero, both of whom were shipwrecked, were taken prisoner by the Maya. Guerrero won the respect of his captors, learned their language and married Princess Zacil. The couple had three sons, who were the first *mestizos*.

In 1519, Hernán Cortés set out from Cuba with a fleet of about 10 boats and 500 men. He freed Aguilar and made him his interpreter. It took the conquistadors no more than two years to destroy the Aztec empire. In fact, on August 13, 1521, after three months of bitter fighting, the Spaniards and their native allies seized Tenochtitlán.

In 1522, Cortés had the city rebuilt. It was thenceforth named Mexico City (Ciudad de México) and became the capital of New Spain. The conquest of the Yucatan took more than two decades.

Missionaries

The first Franciscan missionaries arrived in Mexico in 1523 and quickly started building monasteries, soon

Chicle

In the late 19th century, American pharmacies started carrying a new product called "Adams New York Gum", a box containing little balls of a gummy substance known as chicle, which was to be chewed but not swallowed.

A kind of latex extracted from the sapodilla, a large tree that is very common in Central America and the Yucatán, this gum was imported and marketed in the United States by American inventor Thomas Adams around 1880. Although new to Americans, chicle already existed as "chewing gum"; in fact, the Maya and Aztecs had long since recognized its hygienic and digestive values, and knew how to collect it.

Chicle is obtained by cutting several large, deep X's into the bark of the sapodilla. The liquid then flows out and is collected by *chicleros*, after which it is boiled, cut into cubes and exported.

At the beginning of the century, Chicago businessman William Wrigley added mint and fruit flavours to the gum and dubbed his creation the Chiclet. The product was so successful that the tremendous demand for raw material from the Yucatán prompted a migration to the peninsula, especially in 1920. In the 1950s, however, a less expensive substitute for chicle, polyester, replaced the natural substance.

Though the industrial-scale collection of chicle is now a thing of the past, many sapodillas in the Yucatán still bear large scars. Tour buses sometimes stop to show tourists some roadside specimens. This happens, notably, during trips to Chichén Itza and around the Xcaret site. In the cities, the trees are scraggly; they are most common in Valladolid and at Playa del Carmen.

to be followed by the Augustinians and the Jesuits. In 10 years, during which time millions of natives were converted, scores of pre-Columbian monuments were demolished, numerous natives were enslaved and there was widespread plundering of their wealth and resources.

In his book *Relaciones de las cosas de Yucatán*, Bishop Diego de Landa recorded numerous observations on Mayan society. Historians believe that he is largely to blame for our inability to understand Pre-Columbian Mayan society.

Though the indigenous peoples accepted, albeit unenthusiastically, the Catholic religion imposed upon them, they adapted it to their own beliefs.

Even in the 19th century, the natives were stripped of their land and forced to work on haciendas. The meagre salaries they were allotted could only be spent in the *tiendas de raya* (hacienda stores). They had no choice but to accumulate debt, entering a vicious cycle that kept not only them, but also their children, who inherited their father's debts, prisoners of the system. Their plight did not end when Mexico became independent, after 11 years of war (1810-1821), as the land simply changed hands. Among the Mayas, the flames of revolt, fanned for too long, started to flare up.

The Caste War

After suffering such harsh mistreatment, the Mayas, weakened and bereft of hope, lashed out violently against their oppressors in 1847 in what later came to be known as the "Caste War." Following the execution of the Mayan leader Manuel Antonio Ay, in Tepich, 76km south of Valladolid, they massacred all the Whites who had not left the city. The killing continued in most of the towns in the northern Yucatán. Despite repeated calls for help, the city of Mérida was about to fall when it came time for the Mayas to return to their corn fields, which could no longer wait, as the rainy season had arrived. The Spanish colonists took merciless revenge. Men, women and children were indiscriminately slaughtered, imprisoned or sold as slaves. The Mayan population, already decimated by epidemics and poor living conditions,

dropped from 500,000 to 300,000 between 1846 and 1870. Some natives took refuge in the south of Quintana Roo and put up a fierce resistance. The Cruzobs, based in Santa Cruz (which would become Felipe Carillo Puerto), controlled the southeastern half of the Yucatán peninsula for over 40 years.

The Resistance

It was difficult for the government to control the peninsula, isolated as it was from the rest of the country. Toward the end of the 19th century, the Mexican government, under President Porfirio Díaz, began to take a serious interest in the Yucatán. It wasn't until 1901, however, during a campaign led by General Ignacio Bravo, that the federal army seized the capital, Santa Cruz Chan, which the Cruzobs had abandoned. The Mayas continued to wage a guerilla war until 1935, when the Cruzobs agreed to sign a peace treaty with the federal army.

The Revolution

The Revolution, which lasted 10 years and claimed the lives of a million Mexicans, broke out in 1910 as a result of Porfirio Díaz's fraudulent re-election. It was launched by Francisco de Madero and led by various revolutionary leaders. Madero, an ally of Pancho Villa, succeeded Díaz in 1911, but was overthrown during an uprising led by General Huerta, and assassinated in 1913. This event triggered a popular revolt, led for 10 years by Villa, Obregón, Carranza and Zapata. The Revolution was intended to put an end to the landowners' blatant unfairness and bring about a redistribution of wealth.

The Revolution also spawned a new constitution, parts of which are still in effect today. Schooling was provided for all children and the possessions of the Church were redistributed.

Carranza was recognized by the United States as President of Mexico in 1916. Nevertheless, the revolution continued. Zapata fought on relentlessly until his assassination in 1919. Pancho Villa, for his part, was killed in 1923. In 1917, a new constitution limited the presidential mandate to four years. Schools were built and rural properties were confiscated and distributed to peasants. Conflicts with the Church intensified.

Relations with the United States

Mexico's relations with the United States also suffered as a result of the Revolution. President Woodrow Wilson waited a long time before officially recognizing Venustiano Carranza as the new Mexican president and offering him assistance. Carranza was finally recognized by the United States as President of Mexico in 1916.

It wasn't until Lázaro Cárdenas became president (1934-1940), however, that the peasants of the peninsula began benefitting from these reforms.

Modern Mexico

At the beginning of the 20th century, the Yucatán was finally linked to the rest of Mexico by rail. Despite major economic problems, Mexico made progress between 1940 and 1970. An irrigation system was built, enabling the farming industry to develop. More and more roads were laid out. The state became the engine of economic development but Mexico's reduced ability to compete on world markets led to tough economic times.

The discovery of large petroleum deposits in Mexico, made it the world's fourth-largest oil-producing nation. At the same time, however, due to high inflation and economic mismanagement, the country found itself saddled with a budget deficit that led to a massive flight of capital. In 1982, President López Portillo hosted the North-South Conference in Cancún in an effort to free Latin American countries from the vicious circle of debt.

Conceived in the 1960s, the seaside resort of Cancún came to life in 1974, following the construction of an extensive infrastructure. The region has been developing at a faster pace since 1982; in fact, tourism is now the second most important sector of the economy on the Yucatán Peninsula.

Politics

Yucatán and Quintana Roo are two of the 31 states in the federal republic of Mexico, which also has a Federal District encompassing Mexico City and its surroundings.

Though the constitution allows for a multi-party system, until very recently Mexico was a "single-party democracy." Political pluralism became a reality in the 1980s, with the emergence of the National Action Party (PAN) and the Democratic Revolution Party (PRD), the two major opposition parties. These parties compete for government seats, alongside the Institutional Revolutionary Party (PRI), whose power remained uncontested for a long time.

In 1929, the Party of the Mexican Revolution was founded; it has been called the Institutional Revolutionary Party, or PRI, since 1945. Since its inception, the party has supplied the country with every single one of its presidents until the year 2000.

The U.S. is now Mexico's principal trading partner, accounting for over 65% of the country's exports. However, numerous agreements have been signed in an effort to increase the number of its trading partners, since all is not rosy between the two neighbours (President Salinas de Gortari signed a free-trade agreement, NAFTA, with Canada and the U.S. in 1992). Issues causing conflict include the presence of illegal Mexican workers in the United States and the U.S. government's refusal to recognize Spanish as a second language, despite its widespread use within its borders.

The winds of change were blowing during the elections of July 2000. The Institutional Revolutionary Party (PRI), which had been in power for 71 years, was ousted by the PAN and its charismatic leader, Vicente Fox. Mexicans can thus begin to look forward to a democratization of their institutions.

The Economy

Mexico has a fairly diversified economy. Mining, manufacturing, the petroleum industry (60 billion barrels of reserves), electronics, textiles and tourism are all highly developed sectors.

With 21.7 million visitors in 1996, Mexico ranks seventh in the world as a tourist destination. Tourism plays a large role in the Mexican economy, especially in the state of Quintana Roo. For years, in fact, it was the country's main source of revenue. The cities of Acapulco, Puerto Vallarta and Cancún alone welcome millions of visitors each year.

From 1976 to 1982, Mexico experienced massive

inflation, which slowed its development to a halt. Nevertheless, the tourist industry in Quintana Roo continued to flourish, since investors were confident that tourism could pull the region out of its predicament.

In October 1982, President José López Portillo organized a conference in Cancún aimed at finding ways of stopping the flight of capital. He nevertheless left his successor, Miguel de la Madrid Hurtado (elected in 1982), a nation suffering from massive inflation. The country's accession to the General Agreement on Tariffs and Trade (GATT) in 1986, a new debt conversion agreement signed in 1987, and a decrease in protectionism forced the Mexican people to cope with stringent economic measures and high unemployment.

In 1994, a new crisis led to a 60% drop in the value of the peso, and the country's economy still hasn't bounced back, despite drastic austerity measures and the aid obtained by President Ernesto Zedillo from the International Monetary Fund (IMF). The rate of inflation, which reached a record high of 160% in 1987, dropped below 10% in 2000, however.

The People

Mexico, land of mixed ancestry. The Mexican people, as a whole, form a *mestizo* society that prides itself on integrating the legacies of the past into the everyday.

For tourists, this fact becomes evident during a guided visit to a Mayan site, during which the guide, who has all the physical attributes of his Iberian descendants, will automatically and rather unaccountably identify himself with his supposed Maya ancestors, readily qualifying the Spanish conquest as barbarous.

For its part, the Mayan society of today has to struggle to assert its rights and shout its demands from the rooftops, especially in regards to the increasing exploitation of Mayan culture as a tourist attraction, which often results in buses making deliberate detours to picturesque little villages whose isolated inhabitants live in step with the past.

Mayan Society

Though little is known about the origins of the Maya, it is believed that several Mayan villages existed in 2000 BC. The first Maya to inhabit the Yucatán Peninsula seem to have settled in such places as Dzibilchaltún (in the northern part of the Yucatán), where stone temples were erected.

Scattered settlements started grouping together, leading to the development of great Mayan cities, where scientific discoveries and remarkable inventions were made. The towns and ceremonial centres reached a considerable size during the Classic Period, from AD 300 to about AD 900. Urban centres abounded, with large avenues, aqueducts and sewer systems, gigantic pyramids and palaces, and pelota courts the size of soccer fields.

The scientific and social achievements of the Maya were equalled only by their artistic accomplishments.

The gigantic stelae, sculptures, paintings and abstract decorations of the Mayan temples still make this civilization stand out from other cultures of the world.

All these achievements are that much more amazing when you consider that the Maya never used the wheel (except for children's toys) as they had no draught animals.

Many believe that Mayan cities were very precisely laid out according to units of time. Each ornament and each step of a temple represented a unit of time. The Mayan calendar is a combination of two calendars, making it possible to identify a specific day millions of years in the past or the future. Each day, laden with good or ill portents, was analyzed by the rulers, who made their decisions accordingly.

Chichén Itzá's heyday ended around the year 1200, when Mayapán reached its apogee. The decline of centralized power began around 1450, when this last great metropolis was abandoned.

Today, many descendants of the Maya live inland on the Yucatán Peninsula. They are easily recognizable by their small stature, dark complexion and flat profile. The women wear *huipiles*, a sort of light dress, made with a square piece of white cotton, embroidered at the neck and on the sleeves.

Arts and Culture

Music

Music occupies an important place in Mexicans' day to day life. In Cancún, there are many musicians in front of restaurant terraces, singing ballads about a lost or unrequited love, a sorrow, or a quarrel. These ballads are inspired by "Mexicanized" Spanish songs.

Mariachi music is definitely the style best-known abroad. Groups of musicians decked out in *ranchero* gear, mariachis have a proud, erect bearing. Each band has a guitarist, a violinist, a trumpet-player and a singer, and their songs are enriched by the cultures of Europe.

The traditional instruments are the trumpet, the guitar, the marimba and the harp.

On Isla Mujeres, where a "Musician's House" was recently established, popular local music is omnipresent during festivities and social events. Considered the father of the music of Isla Mujeres, troubadour Virgilio Fernández, who died in 1962 at the age of 60, sang about his island in songs with evocative names like *Mujer Isleña, Mi son pa Contoy*, and *Bahía Isleña*. Today, there are numerous bands on the island.

Since 1990, Cancún has hosted an annual jazz festival in May, featuring such greats as Etta James, Ray Charles, Carlos Santana and Tito Puente. The concerts are held on an outdoor stage at Ballenas beach.

Finally, several Mexican composers have made a name for themselves in the world of classical music. They include Manuel Ponce (1886-1948), Julian Carillo (1875-1965), Carlos Chávez (1899-1978) and Silvestre Revueltas (1899-1940).

Dance

Many of the dances found in Mexico date back to pre-Columbian times. Pagan dances, forbidden by the conquistadors, were advocated by missionaries, who no doubt viewed them as a means of integrating the Catholic

religion into the native culture.

Dance plays a prominent role in Mexican festivities. The list of dances includes the stag dance, the feather dance, the quetzal dance, the old folks' dance, the *Sonajero*, the *Conchero* and the *Jarana*. One of the principal Mexican dances, which can be seen on numerous occasions, is the *Venado* (stag dance) of the Yaquis, Maya and Tarahumaras of northern Mexico.

During your stay in Cancún, you can get a good overview of all these dances by going to see the Ballet Folklórico de Cancún, which performs every Saturday night at the Centro de Convenciones. The show, which includes dinner, recaps the major movements and various trends in traditional Mexican music, over the years and in each state.

Film

The Beginnings

Like most Latin American countries, Mexico discovered film at the beginning of the 20th century, in the middle of Porfirio Díaz's dictatorship. Film makers, busy following the dictator's official activities, didn't see the Revolution coming. All Mexican cinematic productions showed a cultivated, civilized, progressive country, in keeping with the upper classes' wishes.

The Revolution, however, led to the birth of the

political documentary, the first in the world, according to some critics, to tackle contemporary problems. The film *Memorias de un Mexicano* (1959), by Carmen Toscano, is a compilation of films made by Salvador Toscano, a pioneer of Mexican cinema, during the final years of the Díaz dictatorship.

At the same time, fictional foreign films were exerting a strong influence on the public's tastes. From 1916 to 1930, fictional Mexican films imitated foreign models, and had melodramatic plots. Perhaps the only exception is *La Banda del automóvil gris* (a silent film about a gang of criminals from Mexico City, 1919). From that point on, melodrama played a predominant role in Mexican cinema.

The year 1930 marked the advent of the "talkie." Antonio Moreno's *Santa* is the prototype of the prostitute melodrama with a naive narrative, a genre that would subsequently become very popular. The year 1938 saw the birth of the *ranchera* comedy, films with simplistic scenarios centred around a certain kind of hero, the *Charro*, a Mexican cowboy riding about in search of adventure.

The Golden Age

In the 1940s, when the United States suspended its Hispanic production in order to concentrate on anti-Nazi propaganda, Mexico became the world's leading producer of Spanish-language films. This was the "golden age" of Mexican cinema,

marked by an impressive number of productions and the apogee of melodrama, nationalism and religious sentiment.

Mexican film echoed the official line regarding national unity, reclaiming the pre-Hispanic past and redefining the role of natives in society. *Cabaretera* (harlot) movies, derived from the prostitute-as-heroine tradition, led to a revival of the moral melodrama and dominated the screen. This trend endured until the early 1960s.

Hollywood know-how got the better of these modest productions, and the Mexican film industry collapsed in the early 1960s. Only a few directors, no doubt influenced by Italian neorealism, shot films about the "real" Mexico.

Contemporary Mexican Cinema

In 1964, the Centro Universitario de Estudias Cinematograficas de México, the Mexican university centre for studies in film, was founded, followed by the Instituto Nacional de Cinematografia, in 1970, in order to help out the film studios. Thanks to these two institutions, many quality films were put out in the early 1970s. However, the privatization of production companies led to the closing of hundreds of movie theatres. To make matters worse, thousands of films were destroyed in a fire at the Cinemateca Nacional, the national film

Movies filmed in the Yucatán

Against All Odds
(USA, 1985)
By Taylor Hackford, with Rachel Ward and Jeff Bridges

Zorro Rides Again
(USA, 1937)
By John English, with John Carroll

Rastro de Muerte
(Mexico, 1981)
A political thriller by Arturo Ripstein, with Pedro Armen Dariz, Jr.

La Momia Azteca
(Mexico, 1957)
Followed by **Attack of the Mayan Mummy** and **Face of the Screaming Werewolf** (USA, 1964), by Rafael López Portillo

Marie Galante
(USA, 1934)
By Henry King, with Spencer Tracy

Mexican Films

A Few Directors

Roberto Sneider
Dos crimenes, 1995

Alfonso Arau
Como Agua para chocolate, 1992 (*Like Water for Chocolate*, from the novel by Laura Esquivel)

Jaime Humberto Hermosillo
El Compleaños del Perro, 1974; *The Passion According to Berenice*, 1976; *Shipwreck*, 1977; *María de mi Corazón (Mary my Dearest)*, 1979; *Doña Herlinda and Her Son*, 1984; *Intimacy in a Bathroom*, 1989 and *La Tarea (Homework)*, 1990.

Felipe Cazals
Aunt Elizabeth's Garden, 1971; *Canoa*, 1975; *Apando (The Isolation Cell)*, 1975 and *Las Poquianchis*, 1976.

Arturo Ripstein
Time to Die, 1965; *The Castle of Purity*, 1972; *El Lugar sin Límites*, 1977; *La Viuda Negra*, 1977 and *Trace of Death*, 1981.

Paul Leduc
Frida Kahlo, 1984 and *John Reed*, 1971.

Emilio Fernández
Janitzio, 1938

Luis Buñuel
Buñuel, who was born in Spain in 1900 and died in Mexico in 1983, liked to say that he had learned his trade in Mexico. Upon arriving here in 1946, he returned to his career as a film-maker, which he had abandoned in 1932. He shot 21 films in Mexico between 1946 and 1965, including: *The Forgotten Ones*, 1951; *Nazarín*, 1959; *The Young One*, 1960; *Viridiana* (Spanish-Mexican co-production), 1961; *The Exterminating Angel*, 1962 and *Saint Simeon of the Desert*, 1964.

A Few Actors and Actresses

María Félix

Cantinflas and **Tin Tan** (two great popular comics)

Pedro Infante

Dolores del Río

archives, in 1982. Since the early 1980s, furthermore, many Mexicans have given up going to the movies, preferring to watch *tele-novelas*. These television soap operas, whipped together at lightning speed, are extremely popular throughout Latin America.

Literature

Bishop Diego de Landa destroyed almost all the Mayan codices. Afterward, he redeemed himself slightly by recording his observations of the Mayan people in his *Relaciónes de las Cosas de Yucatán*. However, a number of Aztec documents have survived to this day thanks to other missionaries; among them, a Spanish monk named Bernardino de Sahagún (1500-1590). These works, heroic poems for the most part, have a strong lyrical quality. Other extant Náhuatl writings, translated into Spanish, were the work of poet-king Netzahualcóyotl (1402-1472), King Huegotzingo and Aztec Prince Temilotzin. The Náhuatl literature was translated by Eduard

Georg Seler (1849-1922), among others.

Mayan literature, for its part, is represented by *Rabianl-Achi*, a play explaining the customs and lifestyle of the Maya. One of the few remaining copies of the *Popol Vuh* (book of counsel) translated by Fray Francisco Ximénez in the early 18th century, is a source of information on the customs and traditions of the Kichés, a Mayan ethnic group.

Mexican literature written in Spanish originated, of course, with the Spanish conquest, whose leading chroniclers were Bernal Díaz de Castilo (1492-1580), a companion of Hernán Cortés; Bartolomé de las Casas (1474-1566); Jerónimo de Mendieta (1525-1604) and Antonio de Solis (1610-1686).

The colonial era was dominated by the omnipresent Spanish influence, preventing the evolution of a uniquely Mexican literature. Certain writers nonetheless succeeded in creating original works: Juan Ruiz de Alarcón y Mendoza (1581-1639) and Iñes de la Cruz (1648-1695), a nun considered to be one of the greatest poets of the Spanish language in the 17th century. Carlos de Sigüenza Y Góngora is a worthy representative of the new Spanish baroque. In the days of José Manuel Martínez de Navarrete (1768-1809), who drew his inspiration from French neo-classicism, Mexico was in search of a national identity.

John Lloyd Stephens

The American globetrotter John Lloyd Stephens undertook two expeditions in Central America and Mexico between 1839 and 1842, accompanied by the British painter and illustrator Frederick Catherwood. His explorations led him to the archaeological sites of Palenque, Chichén Itzá, Kabah, Labna and Uxmal. He published two highly successful travel narratives that prompted more in-depth research on the Mayas: *Incidents of Travel in Central America, Chiapas and Yucatán* (1841) and *Incidents of Travel in Yucatán* (1843).

When nationalist uprisings started raging in Mexico in 1810, almost all the country's literature converged around the topic of independence, forming one huge polemic. The realistic novel came next, focusing largely on politics. Toward the end of the 19th century, many Mexican writers were influenced by Spanish and French romanticism. A countercurrent emerged immediately afterward, led by Manuel Gutiérrez Najera (1859-1895), considered the father of modern Mexican literature.

In Mexico, the Revolution marked the advent of contemporary literature inspired by nationalist sentiments. Mariano Azuela (1873-1952) is the principal representative of this movement. One of his more noteworthy works is *The Underdogs* (published in Spanish in 1916), a lively, colourful account of the Revolution. In the 1920s, writers began focusing once again on Mexican history. Artemio de Valle Arizpe (1888-1961) is the main author to have analyzed the colonial period. Carlos Fuentes (1928), author of *Where the Air Is Clear, The Death of Artemio Cruz* and *The Old Gringo*, has attained celebrity status.

The most internationally renowned Mexican author is Octavio Paz (1914-1998), awarded the Nobel Prize for Literature in 1990. In addition to producing numerous essays, works of poetry and translations, Paz has also been a lecturer, a diplomat and a journalist. He is the author of *The Labyrinth of Solitude* (1950), among others. Along with Alfonso Reyes (1889-1959), he is considered Mexico's master essayist.

Today, a number of talented young authors belonging to the group *Espiga amotinada*, founded in 1980, are breathing new life into Mexican literature. These include Augusto Shelley, Juan Buñuelos and Oscar Olivas.

Outstanding authors from the Yucatán include poet and essayist Wilberto Cantón (1925-1979), who was awarded numerous prizes for his body of work; and playwright, professor and film critic Miguel Barbachanco Ponce (1930). Journalist, historian and narrator Héctor Águilar Camil (1946), who has written a great deal about the Mexican Revolution, won the national prize for journalism, the *Premio nacional de Periodismo*, in 1986.

Painting

Magnificent pre-Columbian frescoes adorned many Mayan temples in Mexico. Traces of the reds and famous Mayan blue that once covered the walls are still visible. Shortly after the Spanish conquest, European artists began teaching in Mexico City, in a school founded by the Franciscans.

Colonial art flourished in the 17th century, when numerous painters managed to incorporate European style into their own art. Works from this period grace churches, cloisters and museums in many towns.

The Mexican baroque was born in the late 18th century and proved re-

markably immune to any native influence. Mexican painters continued to be influenced by the European masters right up until the 20th century. It wasn't until the Revolution of 1910 that an original, uniquely Mexican movement took shape: muralism (the Minister of Education at the time, José Vasconselos, allowed painters to use the walls of schools and other public buildings, hence the name of the movement).

The birth of muralism was marked by an exhibition of secessionist artists, organized by Gerardo Murillo (1875-1964), who liked to be called Dr. Atl. Political caricaturist Guadalupe Posada (1851-1913) is considered the precursor of this trend, characterized by the use of pre-Columbian motifs and colours and the renunciation of Spanish elements. The paintings glorified the country's native heritage and the Revolution. A manifesto denouncing paintings in museums was published in 1923. Diego Rivera, David Alfaro Siqueiros and José Clemente Orozco were three of the leading painters of this period.

Religion and Holidays

Mexico's largely Catholic population is very devout as a whole. The churches, always full, ring with the sounds of the faithful lifting their voices in song. The year is punctuated by religious holidays. The Catholic Church, which established itself here in the early days of the Span-

A Few Painters

Diego Rivera (1886-1957) painted huge frescoes inspired by the Italian Renaissance, as well as Mayan and Aztec art, and which depicted the social and political realities of Mexico. He married painter Frida Kahlo (1910-1954). Kahlo, trapped in a wheelchair from the age of 18 onward, painted lucid images fraught with anguish. She has only recently attained a certain level of renown.

Painter **Rufino Tamayo** (1899-1991), of Zapotec origin, is considered the master of modern art, refusing to use his art for any political ends whatsoever. He drew inspiration from various modern trends, especially cubism, while borrowing elements from Mexican popular art.

ish conquest, was very powerful, controlling education and interfering in politics and everyday life.

In keeping with their mixed roots, Mexicans, when practising their religion, combine traditional Catholic rituals with the mystical beliefs of the natives. For example, they worship the dead (*Día de los Muertos*). Religious festivities, very important here, are colourful events that draw large crowds.

December 30 to January 6
Feast of the Three Kings (Magi) (*Fiesta de Los Tres Reyes Magos*)
This holiday is celebrated in Tizimin, a little town situated north of Valladolid, the second-largest city in the state of Yucatán. Here, the Magi are feted in many ways.

January 1
New Year's Day (*Año Nuevo*)
Major festivities all over the country and agricultural fairs in rural areas.

January 6
Epiphany (*Día de los Reyes*)
On this day, children receive gifts. At many social gatherings, a ring-shaped cake with a tiny doll hidden in it is served; the person who gets the piece of cake containing the doll has to host another gathering on February 2, Candlemas.

January 17
San Antonio Abad's Day
On this day, domesticated animals are honoured all over Mexico. Animals and livestock are decorated

and blessed in the local churches.

February 2
Candlemas (*Candelaria*)
Festivities, parades and bullfights. The streets are decorated with lanterns.

February 5
Constitution Day (*Día de la Constitución*)
Commemoration of the constitutions of 1857 and 1917, which contain the fundamental laws of present-day Mexico.

Variable
Pre-Lenten Carnival
Music, dancing and parades in many seaside resorts, including Cancún, Isla Mujeres and Cozumel.

February 24
Flag Day

March 21
Benito Juárez's Birthday
A holiday in honour of the beloved former president (1806-1872), born of Zapotec parents. He effected numerous reforms during his time in office, including the abolition of Church privileges, the

introduction of civil weddings and public schools, and industrialization.

March 20, 21 or 22
Vernal equinox
For about 15 minutes on this day, the sun shines down on the great pyramid at Chichén Itzá in such a manner as to create the spectacular illusion that a snake is crawling down the edge of the monument, all the way to the ground. This phenomenon also occurs during the autumnal equinox (September 20, 21 or 22).

March 27 to April 3
Holy Week (*Semana santa*)
Holy Week, which starts on Palm Sunday, is the most important religious celebration in Mexico and is marked by festivities all over the country.

First Sunday in April
Easter

April
Regata Sol a Sol
A regatta between Florida and Cozumel, with numerous festivities to mark the occasion.

May 3
Holy Cross Day (*Día de la Santa Cruz*)
On this day, construction workers put decorated crosses on top of the buildings they are erecting. Holy Cross Day is also celebrated with picnics and fireworks.

May 5
Battle of Puebla (*Cinco de Mayo*)
Commemoration of the Mexican army's victory

over Napoleon III's troops in Puebla in 1862.

May 15
San Isidoro Labrador
Festivals held in Panaba, near Valladolid, and in Calkini, southwest of Mérida.

May
Various festivities held on Isla Mujeres.

June
Fishing tournaments in Cozumel and Cancún.

June 24
St. John the Baptist's Day (*Día de la San Juan Bautista*)
Fairs, religious festivities and swimming.

August
Cancún Cup
Lancha (canoe) races in Cancún.

September 15-16
Independence Day (public holiday)
Mexico's Declaration of Independence (1810) is celebrated throughout the country. At 11pm, on September 15, *El Grito* (The Call), a re-enactment of Father Hidalgo's famous appeal to his compatriots to rise up, is presented on the central square of most towns. The president opens the traditional ceremonies on Constitution Square, in Mexico City. Nearly all institutions and places of business are closed on these two days.

Parades during daytime and fireworks at night.

September 20, 21 and 22
Autumnal equinox
(see March, vernal equinox)

September 27
Columbus Day (*Día de la Raza*) (public holiday)
Festivities commemorating the blending of the indigenous and European peoples of Mexico.

October 23 to November 2
Cancún festival

October 31
Hallowe'en
In the Yucatán, candles are placed on tombstones. The first of eight days devoted to remembering the dead.

November 1
President's State of the Nation address (*Informe Presidencial*)
(public holiday)
The Mexican president delivers this annual speech before Congress.

November 1 and 2
All Saints' Day (*Día de los Muertos*)
On these two days, the country celebrates death with festivities that combine Christian and native traditions. Skulls and skeletons made of sugar and miniature coffins are sold everywhere, and there are processions to the cemeteries, where the altars

and tombstones are elaborately decorated. This *fiesta* offers Mexicans a chance to evoke the memory of their dearly departed.

November 20
Anniversary of the Mexican Revolution (public holiday)
Commemoration of the beginning of the civil war, which lasted 10 years (from 1910 to 1920) and claimed the lives of millions of Mexicans.

December 1-8
Numerous festivities held on Isla Mujeres.

December 12
Festival of the Virgin de Guadalupe
This is Mexico's most sacred holiday, celebrating the country's patron saint. Pilgrims from all over the country converge on the cathedral in Mexico City, where a shroud mysteriously imprinted with the saint's image is displayed.

December 16-24
Posadas
Processions and festivities commemorating Joseph and Mary's trip to Bethlehem. Music fills the streets and *piñatas* are broken open.

December 25
Christmas (*Navidad*)
This family holiday is celebrated at home.

Table of Distances (km)
via the shortest route

	Cancún	Chichén Itzá	Mérida	Mexico City	Playa del Carmen	Tulum
Chichén Itzá	202					
Mérida	315	113				
Mexico City	1651	1445	1332			
Playa del Carmen	69	256	384	1582		
Tulum	132	193	306	1519	63	
Valladolid	158	44	157	1489	212	149

Example: The distance between Playa del Carmen and Cancún is 69km.

© ULYSSES

Practical Information

It is relatively easy to travel all over Mexico, whether you are alone or in an organized group, but to make the most of your trip it is best to be well prepared.

This Chapter is intended to help you plan your trip to Cancún and the Riviera Maya. It also includes general information and practical advice designed to familiarize you with local customs.

Entrance Formalities

Before leaving, make sure to bring all of the documents necessary to enter and leave the country. While these formalities are not especially demanding, without the requisite documentation it is impossible to travel in Mexico. Therefore, take special care of official documents.

Passport

To enter Mexico, you must have a valid passport. This is by far the most widely accepted piece of identification, and therefore the safest. If your passport expires within six months of your date of arrival in Mexico, check with your country's embassy or consulate as to the rules and restrictions applicable.

As a general rule, the expiration date of your passport should not fall less than six months after your arrival date. If you have a return ticket, however, your passport need only be valid for the duration of your stay. Otherwise, proof of sufficient funds may be required. For travellers from most Western countries (Canada, United States, Australia, New Zealand, Western European countries) a simple passport is enough; no visa is necessary. Other citizens are advised to contact the nearest consulate to see whether a visa is required to enter Mexico. Since requirements for entering the country can change quickly, it is wise to

double-check them before leaving.

Your passport is a precious document that should be kept in a safe place. Do not leave it in your luggage or hotel room, where it could easily be stolen. A safety-deposit box at the hotel is the best place to store important papers and objects during your stay.

Travellers are advised to keep a photocopy of the most important pages of their passport, as well as to record its number and date of issue. Keep these copies separate from the originals during your trip and also leave copies with friends or family at home. If ever your passport is lost or stolen, this will facilitate the replacement process (the same is true for citizenship cards and birth certificates). In the event that your passport is lost or stolen, contact the local police and your country's embassy or consulate (see addresses further below), in order to be reissued an equivalent document as soon as possible. You will have to fill out a new application form, provide proof of citizenship and new photographs, and pay the full fee for a replacement passport.

Minors Entering the Country

In Mexico, all individuals under 18 years of age are legally considered minors. Each traveller under the age of 18 is therefore required to present written proof of his or her status upon entering the country, namely, a letter of consent signed by his or her parents or legal guardians and notarized or certified by a representative of the court (a justice of the peace or a commissioner for oaths).

A minor accompanied by only one parent must carry a signed letter of consent from the other parent, which also must be notarized or certified by a representative of the court.

If the minor has only one legally recognized parent, he or she must have a paper attesting to that fact. Again, this document must be notarized or certified by

a justice of the peace of a commissioner for oaths.

Airline companies require adults who are meeting minors unaccompanied by their parents or an official guardian to provide their address and telephone number.

Tourist Cards

Upon your arrival in Mexico, after your proof of citizenship and customs declaration form have been checked, the customs officer will give you a blue tourist card (*tarjeta turística*). This card is free and authorizes its holder to visit the country for 60 days. Do not lose it, as **you must return it to Mexican immigration when you leave the country**. Take the same precautions as you did with your passport, by recording the tourist card number somewhere else—on your airline ticket, for example. In case of theft or loss of your tourist card, contact Mexican immigration at ☎*(998) 884-1404*.

Airport Departure Tax

Except for children under two years of age, all passengers taking international flights out of Mexico are required to pay a tax of about $18. The major airlines often include this tax in the ticket price; ask your travel agent.

Customs

On the way to Mexico, flight attendants will hand

out a custom's declaration to all air passengers, which must be completed before your arrival. If you have items to declare, your luggage will be searched. If not, you will have to activate a random "traffic light." A green light permits travellers to pass without searches; a red light means a search.

Of course, it is strictly forbidden to bring any drugs or firearms into the country. Any personal medication, especially psychotropic drugs, must have a prescription label. If you have any questions regarding customs regulations, call the customs office at Cancún airport, ☎*(998) 848-7200*.

Embassies and Consulates

Embassies and consulates can provide precious information to visitors who find themselves in a difficult situation (for example, loss of passport or in the event of an accident or death, they can provide names of doctors, lawyers, etc.). They deal only with urgent cases, however. It should be noted that costs arising from such services are not paid by these consular missions.

Abroad

Canada
45 O'Connor St., Suite 1500
Ottawa, ON K1P 1A4
☎*(613) 233-8988*
≈*(613) 235-9123*

Consulate:
2055 Rue Peel, bureau 1000
Montreal QC H3A 1V4
☎*(514) 288-2502/2707/4916*
⇆*(514) 288-8287*
www.consulmex.qc.ca

Consulate:
Commerce Court West, 199 Bay
St. Suite 4440
Toronto, ON M5L 1E9
☎*(416) 368-1847*
⇆*(416) 368-8141*

Consulate:
710-1177 West Hastings St.
Vancouver BC V6E 2K3
☎*(604) 684-1859*
⇆*(604) 684-2485*

Denmark
Strandvejen 64E,
2900 Hellerup, Copenhagen
☎*39 61 05 00*
⇆*39 61 05 12*

Germany
Klingelhööferstraßße 3
10785 Berlin
☎*030/26 93 23-0*
⇆*030/26 93 23-700*

Great Britain
42 Hertford St., London W1J 7JR
☎*(0)20 7499 85 86*

United States
2132 3rd Avenue
Seattle WA 98121
☎*(202) 728-1600*
⇆*(202)728-1766*

Consulate:
27 East 39th St.,
New York NY 10016
☎*(212) 217-6400*
⇆*(212) 217-6493*

Consulate:
2401 W. 6th St.
Los Angeles CA 90057
☎*(213) 351-6800*
⇆*(213) 389-9249*

Consulate:
300 North Michigan Ave., 2nd
floor Chicago, IL 60601
☎*(312) 855-1380*
⇆*(312) 855-9257*

In Mexico

Canada
Plaza Caracol II, 3er piso, local
330 Boulevard Kukulcán,
Km 8.5, Zona Hotelera, 77500
Cancún, Quintana Roo, Mexico
☎*(998) 883-3360*
⇆*(998) 883-3232*

Denmark
Calle Tres Picos 43, Apartado
Postal No-105-105, Col.
Chapultepec Morales, 11580
Mexico D.F.
☎*(55) 255 3405*
⇆*(55) 554 5797*

Germany
Punta Conoca no. 36, block 24
77500 Cancún, Quintana Roo,
Mexico
☎*(998) 884-1898 or 887-2127*
⇆*(998) 887-1283*

Great Britain
The Royal Sands Hotel,
Kukulkán Blvd., Km 17, Zona
Hotelera, 77500 Cancún,
Quintana Roo, Mexico
☎*(998) 881-0100*
⇆*(998) 848-8229*

Netherlands
Isleta Comerical Mexico-Lindo
Local no. 8, Aeropuerto Cancún,
77515 Cancún Quintana Roo,
Mexico
☎*(998) 886-0134*
⇆*(998) 886-0128*

Sweden
Calle Cenzontle 2 - Casa 3
Zona Hotelera, 77500 Cancún,
Quintana Roo, Mexico
☎*(998) 892-3347*

United States
Kukulkán Blvd., Plaza Caracol
Dos, Zona Hotelera, 77500
Cancún, Quintana Roo, Mexico
☎*(998) 883-0272*

Tourist Information

Abroad

The purpose of these offices is to help travellers prepare a trip to Mexico. Office staff can answer questions and provide brochures.

North America

Mexican Tourism Council
☎*800-446-3942*

Canada
1 Place Ville-Marie, Suite 1931
Montréal, Québec, H3B 2C3
☎*(514) 871-1052*
⇆*(514) 871-3825*
www.visitmexico.com

2 Bloor St. W, Suite 1502
Toronto, ON M4W 3E2
☎*(416) 925-2753*
⇆*(416) 925-6061*

999 W Hastings St, Suite 1110
Vancouver, BC V6C 2W2
☎*(604) 669-2845*
⇆*(604) 669-3498*

United States
21 East 63rd St.
Third floor, New York, NY 10021
New York N.Y. 10021
☎*(212) 821-0314*
⇆*(212) 821-0367*

2401 W Sixth St.
Los Angeles CA 90057
☎*(213) 351-2075*
⇆*(213) 351-2074*

Practical Information

300 N. Michigan, 4th Floor
Chicago, IL 60601
☎*(312) 606-9252*
≈*(312) 606-9012*

Germany
Taunusanlage 21
D-60325 Frankfurt/Main
☎*(69) 25 35 09*
≈*(69) 25 37 55*

Great Britain
Wakefield House
41 Trinity Square
London EC3N 4DJ
☎*020 7488 9392*
≈*020 7265 07 04*

Getting There

By Plane

Many agencies offer convenient holiday packages that include airfare and accommodation. Such packages are usually put together for the major tourist centres of the country, notably Cancún and Cozumel.

Another option is to buy airfare only and to reserve your own accommodations or find a place to stay once there. Accommodation options are plentiful, and this way travellers can visit more of the area, choosing lodgings from day to day. Outside of high seasons (Christmas holidays and Holy Week), it is usually not difficult to find a room, neither in out-of-the-way spots nor in the popular tourist centres. Reservations remain the surest approach nonetheless.

Mexicana
Av. Cobá no. 39, Cancún
☎*(998) 887-4444*

Aeromexico
Av. Cobá no. 80, Cancún
☎*(998) 884-1097*

Airports

The Yucatán Peninsula has two international airports, one in Cancún and one in Cozumel. There are smaller airports in Chichén Itzá, Playa del Carmen and Mérida. As well, daily domestic flights are offered to Acapulco, Mérida and Mexico City.

Cancún International Airport (☎*998-848-7200*) is about 20km southwest of the hotel zone. It is one of the most modern airports in Mexico owing to recent renovation work. In addition to an exchange bureau and a duty-free shop, it has a few stores, restaurants and bars where the prices, just as in any place with a high concentration of tourists, are higher than those in town.

Bus

There is a shuttle service between Cancún and the airport, called Transfert, that costs approximately $10. This service is often included in the price of holiday packages. The buses are spacious and surprisingly punctual. On the way to the airport, be careful as it is possible that the shuttle will arrive at your hotel early and leave for the airport without waiting. To avoid this catastrophe, be 30min ahead of schedule and wait for the shuttle outside.

Taxis

Note that taxis are only authorized to bring travellers to the airport from the hotel zone or the town, and, conversely, public buses may only take tourists from the airport to their hotels.

Car Rental

Many car rental agencies have counters at the airport. To avoid excessive costs, it is preferable to rent a car before departure and to shop around. Most established agencies may be reached from all over the Americas by toll-free numbers. When comparing prices, take account of taxes, free mileage and insurance. Following are the agencies located at the Cancún airport:

Monterrey Rent
☎*(998) 886-0239 or 884-7843*

Economovil
☎*(998) 887-6487 or 887-0142*

Avis
☎*(998) 886-0221 or 866-0222*

Budget
☎*(998) 886-0026 or 884-0204*

National Tilden
☎*800-361-5334*

Hertz
☎*(988) 887-6604 or 887-6634*

Cozumel International Airport (☎*987-872-3456*) is nearly 4 km northeast of San Miguel. It has a restaurant-bar and a few souvenir shops, tour operators on the upper floor, and car-rental agencies.

Getting Around

By Car

The Road Network

Until the 1950s, Mexico did not have a highway system that covered the whole of the country's tortuous topography. Since then, road work has constituted an essential element of the integration of isolated regions into the national economy.

Much of the new Mexican highway network is a product of the private sector. Modern, safe, four-lane toll highways now link the large cities of the country. While they are very expensive, these new roads represent immense progress compared to the older roads, which are often poorly maintained and crowded with trucks and buses.

Planning one's itinerary depends on the distances that separate the attractions one wishes to see. For example, did you know that the hotel zone in Cancún is 22km long and it can take up to 45 min to reach downtown? Roadwork is also common and can slow traffic considerably, which can be very unpleasant under the tropical sun.

For years now the government has been pouring millions of pesos into highway infrastructure in this region. Highways and main roads are therefore well paved and generally in good condition. The main arteries in the area of Cancún and the Riviera Maya are Highway 307, which runs along the coast from Punta Sam, north of Cancún, past Tulum to Chetumal, and Highway 180, which runs from Cancún to Mérida via Valladolid and Chichén Itzá. The 70km-long section of Highway 307 between Playa del Carmen and Tulum has been the object of extensive repair and widening work since January 1997.

Travelling on secondary roads remains a perilous endeavour. They are often covered in loose stones and overgrown with weeds. Some are paved, but the majority are strewn with holes of various sizes, and must therefore be navigated slowly and carefully. These roads meander through small villages where it is especially important to drive slowly as pedestrians and animals can appear without warning. Speed bumps, also called silent policemen, have been placed on these roads to slow drivers in towns and are often poorly indicated.

Driver's Licence

The driver's licence from your home country is valid in Mexico.

Driving and the Highway Code

Road signs are rare (speed limits, stops, and right of way are all poorly indicated). It is not uncommon for directions to be inscribed on a piece of cardboard hung from a tree, and drivers must often simply ask passersby for help.

Traffic is rarely busy on these roads, except in downtown Cancún and in the hotel zone. Elementary driving rules are often not respected—Mexicans drive fast and do not always check their blind spots when passing. Turn signals are also a rarity, as is the use of seatbelts.

Since most roads have neither lights nor adequate marking, it is strongly recommended to avoid night driving, when the risk of robbery also increases: Never pick up hitchhikers after dark, avoid pulling over on the shoulder, and lock your doors.

The speed limit is 110 km/h on four-lane highways and 90 km/h on two-lane roads.

Accidents

As some Mexican roads are poorly lit and marked, avoid driving at night off the main streets. Look out for speed bumps and potholes. Slow down at level crossings. Authorities do not take parking violations lightly. Always remember to lock your car doors.

In case of an accident or mechanical failure, pull onto the shoulder and raise the hood of the car. Assistance from other motorists should be quick in arriving. Main roads are patrolled by "green angels" (Los Angeles Verdes), government towtrucks driven by mechanics who speak English.

The Police

Police officers are posted along highways to monitor motorists. They have the power to stop anyone who commits an infraction of the highway safety code, or simply to check a driver's papers. In general, they try not to bother tourists, but it can happen that certain officers will try to extract pesos from foreign motorists. If you are sure that you have not committed any infraction, there is no reason to disburse any sum. Occasionally, tourists are stopped long enough to have their papers checked. As a rule police officers are obliging and helpful should you have trouble on the road.

Gasoline

Gasoline is sold by the litre, in two grades: Nova (blue pumps) is leaded gasoline with an octane rating of 81, and Magna Sin (green pumps) is unleaded. Magna Sin is easy to find. Look for a PEMEX sign (Petroleos Mexicanos, the state gas-station monopoly).

A gas station attendant usually receives a tip of a few pesos. There are no self-service stations. The price of gasoline seems high to Americans, but for Canadians it is more or less average, while it is low for Europeans. One last tip: fill up whenever you have the opportunity, as gas stations are rather rare.

Car Rentals

Renting a car in Mexico is not a simple affair. Expect rates to be high and choice to be limited. All of the large car rental agencies operate in Mexico, including many American and some Mexican companies. Renters must be at least 21 years old and possess a valid driver's license and a recognized credit card. Clients must sign two credit card slips, one for the rental and one to cover potential damages, which is common practice in Mexico. Toll-free telephone numbers of car-rental agencies are listed in the section "Getting There" (see p 32).

Expect to pay an average of $50 per day (unlimited mileage is not always included) for a small car, not including insurance and tax. Choose a car in good condition, preferably new. A few of the local agencies have lower rates, but their cars are often in poor condition and they offer limited service in case of breakdown.

At the time of the rental you must subscribe to a Mexican automobile insurance policy, as your own policy is not valid in Mexico. Deductibles are very high *(about $1,000)*. Before signing a rental contract, be sure that methods of payment are very clearly stated. When you sign, your credit card should cover the cost of the rental and the insurance deduct-

ible, should it be necessary.

It is far better to reserve a rental car from home: it costs less and the paperwork is simpler. To guarantee the rate that is offered ask that confirmation be faxed to you.

By Scooter

It is possible to rent scooters by the hour or by the day in many places. Isla Mujeres and Cozumel are especially suited to this mode of transportation. In Cancún, traffic is too busy and fast for scooters.

By Taxi

Taxis run 24hrs a day and, in general, have quite reasonable rates, despite the fact that they are higher in resort areas than in the towns of the interior. It is best to ask the price of a trip before boarding a cab, since most do not have meters. There are usually a few taxis waiting for customers outside of hotels. If there are not, ask a reception clerk to call one.

By Public Bus

Public buses, known as *camiónes* in Mexico, travel Cancún's hotel zone. You will never have to wait more than three minutes, unless there is traffic. The fare is about 5 pesos, regardless of the distance travelled. Official bus stops are indicated by blue signs, although a wave of the hand will also stop the bus.

In downtown Cancún, buses serve major intersections. Service is 24hrs.

These buses are not necessarily uncomfortable, except for the fact that the competition among the different companies is pretty heavy. Generally, buses barely slow down to allow passengers to board and take off again as quickly as possible. A tip: hold on tight! Elderly or frail people should definitely avoid this mode of transportation in Cancún.

Prepare the exact fare or tickets before boarding a bus, as drivers do not provide change. The driver must remit to passengers a receipt, which they may be asked to produce during the trip. Ask for it, if it is not offered.

In Cozumel, there is no public bus service.

By Boat

Ferry services for foot passengers and automobiles link many points in the Yucatán Peninsula.

From Puerto Juárez to Isla Mujeres: there is a ferry service just north of Cancún; eight departures daily in both directions, 20-minute crossing:
☎(998) 877-0618
www.isla-mujeres.net.

From Playa del Carmen to Cozumel: two companies make the crossing; nine departures daily in both directions, 45-minute crossing.

By Bus

The network of Mexican coach services is very developed, linking all of the villages. Fares are incredibly inexpensive (the trip between Cancún and Tulum, for example, costs about $5), and service is frequent and rapid. Buses are generally relatively new and air-conditioned. Since second-class tickets do not offer much of a discount, opt for first class. Be forewarned that even modern buses can have poorly equipped washrooms: for longer trips, bring your own toilet paper and washcloths. Also bring a sweater since bus companies do not skimp on the air-conditioning.

Buses leave Cancún practically every hour for Mérida, Playa del Carmen, Tulum and Chichén Itzá.

Hitchhiking

Risky business! It is uncommon and highly inadvisable, although possible, to hitchhike in Mexico. Hitchhikers can end up spending a very long time on the roadside waiting for motorists to stop.

Excursions and Guided Tours

Since Cancún is the most common departure point for excursions to Chichén Itzá and Tulum, bus companies and tour operators swarm the city. Sales counters are usually found in hotel lobbies. Here is one of the largest agencies:

All World Travel
☎**(998) 884-7172**
All World Travel organizes excursons to Isla Mujeres, Chichén Itzá, Tulum, Xcaret and Cozumel, horseback rides, underwater tours, etc. All World Travel can also bring tourists to Isla Contoy, Mérida and Akumal.

Mayaland Tours
☎**(998) 887-2450**
www.mayaland.com
Mayaland Tours is more specialized, catering to the needs of adventurous travellers who won't faint at the sight of a hairy, multi-legged insect. Personalized service and profound knowledge of each destination are guaranteed.

Insurance

Medical

Travel insurance should be purchased before setting off on a trip. The insurance policy should be as comprehensive as possible, because health care costs add up quickly. When purchasing the policy, make sure it covers medical expenses of all kinds, such as hospitalization, nursing services and doctor's fees (at fairly high rates, as these are expensive), as well as sports injuries and those related to pre-existing medical conditions. A repatriation clause, in case necessary care cannot be administered on site, is invaluable. In addition, you may have

Practical Information

to pay upon leaving the clinic, so you should check your policy to see what provisions it includes for such instances.

Take the time to read the fine print in any policy before signing it. Ask questions, and compare a number of competing plans. Keep in mind that the various people who are authorized to sell travel health insurance are not necessarily experts in the field, despite their best intentions. Communicate directly with insurance companies to clear up any questions about a policy.

During your stay in Mexico, you should always keep proof that you are insured on your person to avoid any confusion in case of an accident.

Cancellation

Cancellation insurance is usually offered by the travel agent when you buy your airplane ticket or holiday package. It permits reimbursement for the ticket or package in the case of cancellation of a trip due to serious illness or death.

Theft

Most Canadian home insurance plans protect the insured for theft, including incidents of theft that occur outside the country. To submit a claim, a police report must be obtained. Depending on your coverage, it is not always useful to take out additional insurance. Europeans

should check whether their policies cover them when they are abroad, as this is not automatically the case.

Health

Travel is not hazardous to your health! Mexico is a wonderful country to explore; however, travellers should be aware of and protect themselves from a number of health risks associated with the region, such as malaria, typhoid, diphtheria, tetanus, polio and hepatitis A. Travellers are advised to consult a doctor (or travellers' clinic) for advice on what precautions to take. Remember that it is much easier to prevent these illnesses than it is to cure them. It is thus worthwhile to take the recommended medications, vaccinations and precautions in order to avoid any health problems.

Food and climate can also cause problems. Pay attention to the freshness of food and the cleanliness of the preparation area. Fresh fruits and vegetables that have been washed but not peeled can also pose a health risk. Make sure that the vegetables you eat are well-cooked and peel your own fruit. Do not eat lettuce, unless it has been hydroponically grown (some vegetarian restaurants serve this type of lettuce; ask). Remember: cook it, peel it or forget it.

Good hygiene (wash your hands often) will help avoid undesirable situations. It is best not to walk

around barefoot as parasites and insects can cause a variety of problems, the least of which is athlete's foot.

Water

Drinking

The medical problems travellers are most likely to encounter are usually a result of poorly treated water containing bacteria that cause upset stomach, diarrhea or fever. To avoid this risk, drink only bottled water, which is available just about everywhere. When buying a bottle, whether in a restaurant or a store, always make sure that it is well sealed. Remember that in tropical countries, it is important to avoid dehydration by drinking at least 2 litres of water per day, and up to 6 litres of other non-alcoholic beverages. Don't wait until you're thirsty to drink, because by then your body has already started to get dehydrated.

Fruit and vegetables rinsed in tap water (those not peeled before eating) can cause the same problems. The same is true of ice cream, popsicles, sorbets and ice cubes, as they may be made with contaminated water. Unless you are sure of where such frozen items came from, it is best to avoid them altogether.

Swimming

Near the villages of Hato Mayor, Higüey, Nisibon and El Seibo, fresh water is often contaminated by an organism that causes schistosomiasis. This infection, which is caused by a parasite entering the body and attacking the liver and nervous system, is difficult to treat. Because of this and other harmful microorganisms, it is best to avoid swimming in bodies of fresh water unless you're sure of the water's purity. Seawater is less risky, but sand and mud baths should also be avoided for the same reasons. What's more, in several countries, beach sand (even on the water's edge) harbours larvae that can worm their way under the skin; it is therefore best to stretch out on a beach towel.

The Sun

Despite its benefits, the sun also causes numerous problems. It is hardly worth mentioning that the rising occurrence of skin cancer is due to overexposure to the sun's harmful rays. It is important to keep yourself well protected; always use sunscreen (with a minimum SPF of 15 for adults and 25 for children), which should be applied 20 to 30min before exposure. Many of the sunscreens on the market do not provide adequate protection so before setting off on your trip, ask your pharmacist which ones are truly effective against the UVA and UVB rays.

Remember to use sunscreen whenever you go outdoors, not just when lying on the beach or lounging by the pool,

and even when the sky is overcast. Also take note that having a tan offers no protection against the sun's harmful rays—you'll still need to apply cream regularly. Even with adequate protection, avoid prolonged exposure, especially during the first few days of your trip, as overexposure can cause sunstroke, symptoms of which include dizziness, vomiting and fever.

A parasol, a hat and a good pair of sunglasses are indispensable accessories to help you avoid harmful exposure while still enjoying a day at the beach. However, remember that the sand and water reflect the sun's rays, which can still reach you even in the shade!

It's best to wear light clothing and avoid synthetic fabrics—cotton and linen are ideal. Taking several cold showers per day (if possible) is a great way to keep the heat at bay, and don't go rushing around during peak afternoon hours. But above all, remember to drink water, water and more water!

Diarrhea

If you come down with diarrhea, soothe your stomach by avoiding solids and drinking plenty of water. When you start eating again, do so gradually, avoiding dairy products, coffee, tea, carbonated beverages and alcohol. It is better to stick with easily digested foods that are rich in carbohydrates, such as rice, potatoes and

pastas. As dehydration can be dangerous, drinking sufficient quantities of liquid is crucial. You can make a rehydration solution by mixing one litre of pure water with one teaspoon of salt and eight teaspoons of sugar.

Pharmacies sell various preparations for the treatment of diarrhea, with different effects. Pepto Bismol and Imodium will stop the diarrhea, which slows the loss of fluids, but they should be avoided if you have a fever as they will prevent the necessary elimination of bacteria.

Oral rehydration products, such as Gastrolyte, will replace the minerals and electrolytes which your body has lost as a result of the diarrhea. If symptoms become more serious (high fever, persistent diarrhea, or diarrhea with bleeding), see a doctor as antibiotics may be necessary.

Insects

A nuisance common to many countries, mosquitoes are no strangers to Mexico. Protect yourself with a good insect repellent. Repellents with DEET are the most effective. The concentration of DEET varies from one product to the next; the higher the concentration, the longer the protection.

In rare cases, the use of repellents with high concentrations (35% or more) of DEET has been associated with convulsions in young children; it is therefore important to apply these products sparingly, on exposed surfaces, and to wash it off once back inside. A concentration of 35% DEET will protect for four to six hours, while 95% will last from 10 to 12 hours. New formulas with DEET in lesser concentrations, but which last just as long, are available. There are also sunscreens with insect repellent on the market, allowing sun-worshippers to simultaneously protect themselves from the sun and mosquitoes.

Insects are generally more active at dusk, and those that carry malaria are especially to be feared at night, when they feed. Moreover, even in certain temperate latitudes, visitors must be wary of a diurnal insect that carries dengue fever, which is unfortunately becoming increasingly prevalent.

To further reduce the possibility of getting bitten, do not wear perfume or bright colours. Sundown is an especially active time for insects. When walking in wooded areas, cover your legs and ankles well. Insect coils can help provide a better night's sleep. Before bed, apply insect repellent to your skin and to the headboard and baseboard of your bed. If possible, get an air-conditioned room, or bring a mosquito net.

Lastly, since it is impossible to completely avoid contact with mosquitoes, bring along a cream to soothe the bites you will invariably get.

Snakes

Among a country's rich and diverse fauna, there are bound to be some species that are less congenial than others. Accordingly, Mexico is home to several kinds of snakes, some of which are poisonous. There is no need to get too alarmed, as you are unlikely to cross paths with one during your visit. Nevertheless, it is important to keep your eyes open and watch where you step. In the forest, look around before you lean against something or sit down somewhere. When hiking, be careful as you part the foliage that sometimes hangs across the path, and check the shores as well as the surface of the water if you go swimming in a river. Some people think they are faster than a snake and tease it, or poke it to see if they can make it move; needless to say, this is not a good idea! The presence of snakes should not prevent you from exploring everything that Mexico has to offer. Like most wild animals, snakes avoid contact with humans as much as possible.

Jet Lag and Travel Sickness

The discomfort caused by major jet lag is unavoidable. There are tricks to help reduce its effects, but the best way to recover from jet lag is to give your body the time to let itself adapt. You can slowly adjust your daily schedule before your departure and once you have boarded the plane. Eat well and drink plenty of water. As soon as you arrive, it is strongly advised that you force yourself to abide by the local time. In other words, stay awake if it's the morning or go to bed if it's night. This will make it easier for your body to get accustomed to the change.

To minimize travel sickness, avoid strong jolts as much as possible and keep your eyes locked on the horizon (for example, sit in the middle of a boat or in the front of a car or bus). Eat light meals only and avoid overeating before and during the journey. Various accessories and medications can help reduce symptoms such as nausea. A piece of good advice: try to relax and keep your mind on something else.

Illnesses

This section is intended to give a brief introduction to some of the more common illnesses and thus should be used for information purposes only.

Malaria

Malaria (or paludism) is caused by a parasite in the blood called *Plasmodium sp*. This parasite is transmitted by anopheles mosquitoes, which bite from nightfall until dawn. The risk is minimal and anti-malaria drugs are not necessary for short stays in resort areas. It is nevertheless a good idea to take measures to prevent mosquito bites (see p 37).

The symptoms of malaria include high fever, chills, extreme fatigue and headaches as well as stomach and muscle aches. There are several forms of malaria, including one serious type caused by *P. falciparum*. The disease can take hold while you are still on holiday or up to 12 weeks following your return; in some cases the symptoms can appear months later.

Hepatitis A

This disease is generally transmitted by ingesting food or water that has been contaminated by fecal matter. The symptoms include fever, yellowing of the skin, loss of appetite and fatigue, and can appear between 15 and 50 days after infection. An effective vaccination by injection is available. Besides the recommended vaccine, good hygiene is important. Wash your hands before every meal, and ensure that the food and preparation area are clean.

Hepatits B

Hepatitis B, like hepatitis A, affects the liver, but is transmitted through direct contact with body fluids. The symptoms are flu-like and similar to those of hepatitis A. A vaccination exists but must be administered over an extended period of time, so be sure to check with your doctor several weeks in advance.

Dengue

Also called "breakbone fever," Dengue is transmit-

ted by mosquitoes. In its most benign form it can cause flu-like symptoms such as headaches, chills and sweating, aching muscles and nausea. In its hemorrhagic form, the most serious and rarest form, it can be fatal. There is no vaccine for the virus, so take the usual precautions to avoid mosquito bites.

Typhoid Fever

This illness is caused by ingesting food that has come in contact (direct or indirect) with an infected person's stool. Common symptoms include high fever, loss of appetite, headaches, constipation and occasionally diarrhea, as well as the appearance of red spots on the skin. These symptoms will appear one to three weeks after infection. The type of vaccination you receive (it exists in two forms, oral and by injection) will depend on your trip. Once again, it is always a good idea to visit a travellers' clinic a few weeks before your departure.

Diphtheria and Tetanus

These two illnesses, against which most people are vaccinated during their childhood, can have serious consequences. Before leaving, check that your vaccinations are valid; you may need a booster shot. Diphtheria is a bacterial infection that is transmitted by nose and throat secretions or by skin lesions on an infected person. Symptoms include sore throat,

high fever, general aches and pains and occasionally skin infections. Tetanus is caused by a bacteria that enters your body through an open wound that comes in contact with contaminated dust or rusty metal.

Polio

Poliomyelitis, or polio, as it is commonly known, is caused by a virus and is sometimes transmitted by contaminated food or water. Symptoms may include fever, nausea and vomiting, and the virus can even go so far as to affect the central nervous system and cause permanent paralysis. Those who get vaccinated as children are normally immunized for life.

First-Aid Kit

A small first-aid kit can prove very useful. Bring along sufficient amounts of any medications you take regularly as well as a valid prescription in case you lose your supply. It can be difficult to find certain medications in small towns in the Mexico. Other medications such as anti-malaria pills and Imodium (or an equivalent), can also be hard to find. Finally, do not forget self-adhesive bandages, disinfectant cream or ointment, analgesics (pain-killers), antihistamines (for allergies), an extra pair of sunglasses or contact lenses, as well as your prescription, contact lens solution and medicine for upset stomach. Though these items are all available in the Mexico, they might be difficult to find in remote villages.

Climate

Like most tropical countries, Mexico has two principal seasons, a rainy season and a dry season. In general, precipitation and temperatures increase from June to October, while from November to May it is cooler and dryer.

In the Yucatán, the proximity of the coasts has a definite influence on the temperature and on the humidity level. During the summer, regions bordering the Caribbean and the Gulf of Mexico stay cool because of the trade winds, whereas in the jungle of the interior the air is hot and heavy. Rain showers are common in April and May and between September and January, when temperatures hover at about 30°C. The risk of hurricane is high in September and October, and the sky is often cloudy. Winter is the most pleasant season in the area.

Packing

Luggage

For carry-on luggage choose a bag with shoulder straps and pockets, that closes properly and is big enough to hold a cosmetics bag, a book and a bottle of water. A side pocket is handy, especially at the airport when it comes time to deal with paperwork (passport, airplane ticket, etc.). This bag will also be practical for day trips.

Since you will undoubtedly return with suitcases full of pottery, jewellery, blankets and other marvels found during your trip, it is best to pack light. A good trick is to bring an empty flexible travel bag in which to pack your clothing and to save your hard cases for fragile souvenirs. The ideal hard suitcase has a combination lock, wheels and a strap. Choose high-quality cloth bags made of waterproof, tear-proof nylon.

Clothing

The first thing to do before piling clothes into suitcases is to envision what sorts of activities await, for example, visiting a church, an evening in a fancy restaurant, dancing, or climbing the temple of Chichén Itzá on hands and knees... Choose permanent-press, fast-drying clothes that match (in the neutral tones that are the mainstay of any traveller's wardrobe).

The type of clothing visitors should pack varies little from one season to the next. In general, loose, comfortable cotton and linen clothing is most practical. For walking in the city, it is better to wear shoes that cover the entire foot, since these provide the best protection against cuts that can become infected. For cool evenings, a long-sleeved shirt or sweater can be useful. Remember to wear rubber sandals on the beach. When visiting certain sights (churches for example), a skirt that hangs below the knees or a pair of pants should be worn, so don't

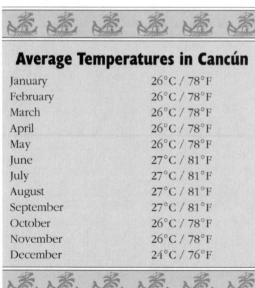

Average Temperatures in Cancún

January	26°C / 78°F
February	26°C / 78°F
March	26°C / 78°F
April	26°C / 78°F
May	26°C / 78°F
June	27°C / 81°F
July	27°C / 81°F
August	27°C / 81°F
September	27°C / 81°F
October	26°C / 78°F
November	26°C / 78°F
December	24°C / 76°F

Your Suitcase

- Camera and film (check the battery)
- Alarm clock
- Hat or cap
- Telescopic umbrella or nylon jacket
- Money belt
- Sunglasses
- Sunscreen
- Bathing suit
- Address book for sending postcards or E-mail
- Cosmetics in sample-size quantities
- Laundry detergent powder (biodegradable)
- Toothbrush and toothpaste (biodegradable)
- Medication and first-aid kit
- Rechargeable batteries

forget to include the appropriate article of clothing in your suitcase. If you intend to go on an excursion into the countryside, take along a pair of good walking shoes. Finally, don't forget to bring a sunhat and sunglasses.

Safety and Security

Mexico is not a dangerous country, but just as anywhere else, robbery is a risk. Remember that in the eyes of the majority of people here, whose income is relatively low, travellers possess quite a few luxuries (cameras, leather suitcases, video cameras, jewellery...) which represent a good deal of money. It is obviously appropriate to follow the normal rules for per-

sonal safety. Avoid counting money in the open, and refrain from wearing flasy jewellery. Keep electronic equipment in a nondescript bag slung across your chest. Conceal traveller's cheques, passport and some cash in a money belt that fits under your clothing; this way if your bags are ever stolen you will still have the papers and money necessary to get by. In the evening and at night avoid poorly lit streets. Get directions before venturing off to explore new areas. Remember, the less attention you attract, the less chance you have of being robbed.

If you bring valuables to the beach you will have to keep an eye on them, which will not be very relaxing. A better option is to leave these objects in

the safety-deposit box provided by your hotel.

Money and Banking

Currency

The country's currency is the nuevo peso or peso. There are several symbols for pesos in use. You will see MEX, NP, MXN, MXP and $P. There are 10, 20, 50, 100, 200 and 500 peso bills and 1, 5, 10, 20 and 50 peso coins, as well as 5, 10, 20 and 50 centavo pieces. Prices are often also listed in US dollars, especially in touristic areas, which can be confusing since both currencies are represented by the dollar sign.

It is a good idea to exchange the value of 20 to 30 US dollars before leaving for Mexico. The exchange offices at the airport will be closed if your flight arrives at night and you will be forced to wait until the next day to settle tips and taxi fares, or even to buy bottled water. The restaurant at your hotel might also be closed, and your arrival would then be a real nightmare.

Although US dollars are accepted in major hotels, it is advisable to use pesos during your trip. You will not risk having your money refused, and you will save money too, since most merchants that accept dollars offer poor exchange rates.

Practical Information

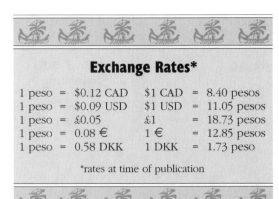

Exchange Rates*

1 peso	=	$0.12 CAD	$1 CAD	=	8.40 pesos
1 peso	=	$0.09 USD	$1 USD	=	11.05 pesos
1 peso	=	£0.05	£1	=	18.73 pesos
1 peso	=	0.08 €	1 €	=	12.85 pesos
1 peso	=	0.58 DKK	1 DKK	=	1.73 peso

*rates at time of publication

Banks

The two largest Mexican banks are Banamex and Bancomer. These are linked to the Cirrus and Plus networks, and their automatic teller machines even offer menus in English as well as Spanish. Some automatic teller machines offer money in pesos or US dollars. Banks are open Monday to Friday, from 9am to 5pm.

US Dollars

It is always best to travel with cash or traveller's cheques in US currency, since, in addition to being easy to exchange, it benefits from the best exchange rate.

Exchanging Money

For the best rate of exchange, make a cash withdrawal on your credit card; this will save you about 2%, which is generally more than the interest you'll have to pay when you get back. For the same reason, it is best to pay for purchases with your credit card whenever possible. If you make a deposit in anticipation of your trip, you can even avoid interest charges altogether. Most automatic teller machines accept Visa, MasterCard, Cirrus and Plus. This solution relieves you of having to buy traveller's cheques before your vacation, and of having to run around to Mexican banks to cash them during your trip. Also, automatic teller machines are open 24 hours a day. Losing your credit card, however, can be problematic. A variety of financial options (credit cards, traveller's cheques, Mexican cash) is the safest approach.

Exchange offices *(casas de cambio)* have longer hours of operation than banks, extending well into the evening, faster service and numerous locations all over the cities. Banks often have better exchange rates, however. There is usually no service charge. You can check the Internet for up-to-date exchange rates at

www.xe.net/currency. An electronic calculator that has a conversion function can also be helpful.

Mexican currency is subject to major fluctuations and has been devalued numerous times in recent years. The exchange rates for various foreign currencies are listed in the exchange-rate box.

Traveller's Cheques

It is always wise to keep most of your money in traveller's cheques, which, when in US dollars, are sometimes accepted in restaurants, hotels and shops. They are also easy to exchange in most banks and foreign exchange offices. Be sure to keep a copy of the serial numbers of the cheques in a separate place, so if ever they are lost, the company that issued them can replace them quickly and easily. Nevertheless, always keep some cash on hand.

Credit Cards

Most credit cards are accepted in a large number of businesses, especially Visa and MasterCard. American Express and Diner's Club are less commonly accepted. Smaller stores often do not accept credit cards, so be sure to carry some cash along with credit cards and traveller's cheques.

When registering at your hotel, you may be asked to sign a credit card receipt to cover potential expenses during your stay.

This is common practice in Mexico.

When using a credit card for purchases, check bills carefully and destroy copies yourself.

Automated Teller Machines (ATMs)

Several banks offer ATM service for cash withdrawals. Most are members of the Cirrus and Plus networks, which allow visitors to make direct withdrawals from their personal accounts. You can use your card as you do normally—you'll be given pesos with a receipt, and the equivalent amount will be debited from your account. All this will take no more time that it would at your own bank! That said, the network can sometimes experience communications problems that will prevent you from obtaining money. If your transaction is refused by the ATM at one bank, try another bank where you might have better luck. In any case, be careful not to find yourself empty-handed.

Mail and Telecommunications

Mail

It costs about 5 pesos to send a postcard or letter to Europe and North America. Post offices are generally open from 9am to 6pm, Monday to Friday,

and Saturday mornings. It is also possible to send mail from the reception desks of most hotels. Stamps are normally available wherever postcards are sold.

Telephone

Area Codes	
Campeche	**981**
Cancún	**998**
Chetumal	**983**
Cozumel	**987**
Isla Mujeres	**998**
Mérida	**999**
Mexico	**55**
Playa de Carmen	**984**
Valladolid	**985**

Calling Mexico from Abroad

From North America:
Dial 011 (prefix for the international operator) + 52 (the country code for Mexico) + the area code + local number.

From Other Countries:
Dial the international prefix for your country + 52 (the country code for Mexico) + the area code + the local number.

Note that the toll-free numbers (**1-888** or **1-800**) mentioned in this guide are only accessible in North America.

Calling Abroad from Mexico

As a general rule, it is more economical to call collect; the best option for Canadian, American and

British citizens wishing to call someone in their native country is through a direct collect-call or calling card service (eg. Canada Direct). It is recommended that you not make calls abroad from hotels as rates are higher, even for collect and toll-free calls. Local calls from hotels can cost up to 3 pesos per call, while at phone booths they cost 50 centavos.

In addition, be wary of the service *Larga Distancia, To call the USA collect or with credit card Simply Dial 0* that is advertised throughout the area and at the airport. This business, which is also identified by a logo depicting a red maple leaf, sometimes confuses Canadian visitors who mistake it for Canada Direct. In reality it is a completely separate business, which charges exorbitant rates for every call. Calls to North America with this service cost no less than 23 pesos per minute and calls to Europe cost 27 pesos per minute, when the caller pays cash. Credit card payment is even more expensive.

For local calls, get yourself a Ladatel debit card. These cards are accepted in Ladatel public phones, which are everywhere. You can buy them for 50 pesos in airports and shopping centres.

In the lobby of large, deluxe hotels, you will find quiet telephone booths, some of which will even close, for more privacy.

Basic Telephone Vocabulary

Telephone	*Téléfono*
Long distance	*Larga distancia*
Collect call	*Una llamada por cobrar*
Is there a service charge?	*¿Cobra un cargo de servicio?*
Hello	*Hola*

Direct Access Numbers

Canada Direct
☎*01-800-123-0200*
(Tel-Mex)
☎*91-800-010-1991*
(Avantel)

AT&T (US)
☎*95-800-288-2872*

Sprint (US)
☎*95-800-877-8000*

MCI (US)
☎*95-800-674-7000*

BT (GB)
☎*800-89-0222*

Calling Direct

To call North America:
Dial 00-1 + the area code + the local number.

For other international calls: Dial 00 + country code + area code + local number.
For long-distance calls within Mexico, dial 0 + local number.

Country Codes

Canada	*1*
Denmark	*45*
Germany	*49*
Great Britain	*44*
Holland	*31*
Sweden	*46*
U.S.A.	*1*

Important Telephone Numbers

Operator assistance
8 (local calls)

Operator assistance
01 (calls within Mexico)

Operator assistance
020 (long distance)

English-speaking operator
52 (international calls)

Fax

Faxes may be sent from post offices.

Internet

There are companies that provide Internet access all over the cities.

Accommodations

Many types of accommodation are available to tourists in this region, from modest *palapas* to international-calibre luxury hotels. Usually, hotel reception employees speak at least a modicum of English. It is customary to leave $1 per bag for the porter and $1-$2 per day for the room-cleaning service, which may be left at the end of your stay or daily, well in view on the dresser. A tip upon arrival will guarantee excellent service.

Given that departure formalities are usually time-consuming, budget a few extra minutes for a delay at the reception desk. If you are planning to check out after 1pm, check with the reception desk staff. Most hotels accept extensions of one or two hours for check-out times if they have been forewarned. Once the bill is settled you will be given a pass *(pase de salida)* that you must remit to the bellhop upon departure.

Most larger hotels accept credit cards, while smaller hotels rarely do.

Prices and Symbols

The various services offered by each establishment are indicated with a small symbol. In no case is this an exhaustive list of what the establishment offers, but rather the services we consider to be the most important. Please note that the presence of a symbol does not mean that all the rooms have this service; you sometimes have to pay extra to get, for example, a whirlpool tub. And likewise, if the symbol is not attached to an establishment, it is probably because the establishment cannot offer you this service. However, please note that unless otherwise indicated, all hotels in this guide offer private bathrooms. For a key to the symbols used, please see the first few pages of the guide.

The rates mentioned in this guide are for a standard room for two people during the high season. A tax of 15% is added to these prices.

$	less than $50
$$	$50 to $80
$$$	$81 to $130
$$$$	$131 to $180
$$$$$	more than $180

Hotels

There are three categories of hotels. Near downtown areas are low-budget hotels offering minimal comfort. Rooms usually include a washroom and a ceiling fan. The second category includes moderately priced hotels that generally offer simply decorated, air-conditioned rooms. These are found in resort areas and in larger towns or cities. Finally, superior quality hotels have been established in Cancún's hotel zone and in Playa del Carmen, Cozumel and Isla Mujeres. These surpass all others in luxury and comort. Among the hotels of this category, there are many large international chains, notably Jack Tar Villge, Camino Real, Hyatt Regency and the Sheraton.

Most establishments have their own water purification systems, indicated by a sticker on the bathroom mirror; if you do not see this sticker, inquire at the reception desk. Otherwise, hotels often provide free bottled water, placed in the washroom.

Most hotels offer satellite television, giving guests remote controls upon arrival, which must be returned. Beach-towel rental is also strictly monitored and there are expensive fees for guests who do not return towels at the end of each day.

Finally, some hotels offer all-inclusive packages, including two or three meals a day, as well as domestic drinks, taxes, and service (see further below).

Apartment Hotels

Apartment hotels are full-service hotels with rooms that include equipped kitchenettes. For longer stays in Mexico this is an economical option. Apartment hotels are especially practical for families traveling with children, who can eat at their convenience without having to suffer through their parents' long restaurant meals.

Time-Shares

Sales of time-share apartments in Mexico are soaring. In fact, Mexico ranks second in the world after the United States for the total number of time-share residences. This system, involving the sale of hotel stays for a set number of weeks per year extending over several years, has been the subject of much discussion.

Vacationers are often harrassed by salespeople who pop up at every street corner, especially in Cancún. Those who grant them an audience are generally offered appealing gifts to participate in an information session (meals, helicopter tours, free accommodation, cash). These offers are always "without obligation," but not without pressure... . If you are able to listen to an hours-long sales pitch without being drawn in, take advantage of these offers to visit fabulous resorts. Remember that if it sounds too good to be true, it probably is.

Haciendas

Haciendas are grand colonial homes that once belonged to the founding land-owners of Mexico. These are vast, magnificently decorated residences with interior courtyards. Some have been converted into hotels.

Cabañas

Cabañas can be found pretty much throughout the Riviera Maya corridor and consist of rooms in little detached buildings that are generally inexpensive and sometimes include a kitchenette.

Palapas

These circular buildings with thatch roofs are traditional Mayan homes. There are smaller ones, with only room for a hammock, and larger ones, with double beds and closets.

Bed and Breakfasts

The comfort of the bed and breakfasts found here varies greatly from one to the next and usually does not include a private bathroom.

Youth Hostels

Youth hostels, offering dormitories of single beds and cafeterias or common kitchens, are available in the region.

Campgrounds

Campgrounds are rare in Cancún and Cozumel. The best area for camping is the Cancún-Tulum corridor where little seaside hotel owners will let you put up a tent or hang a hammock for $5. These deals are negotiated rather informally, although there is an organized campground in Playa del Carmen that can accommodate recreational vehicles.

All-Inclusive Packages in Cancún

In recent years, a formula of all-inclusive holiday packages has become popular in Cancún: for a fixed rate, for stays of one or two weeks, the hotel provides three meals per day and local (non-imported) drinks. This formula seems to be a good deal for the client, but it does have several disadvantages. Imagine having 21 meals in one week at the same restaurant. Usually the "all-inclusive" hotels offer two or three restaurants, but actually guests eat most meals in a cafeteria from a buffet table that does not vary much from day to day.

Since restaurants are relatively inexpensive in Mexico, the all-inclusive package doesn't provide substantial enough saving compared to the pleasure of the area's range of restaurants, of choosing where to eat every day according to your mood, and of the joy of discovery. Is the luxury of whimsy not one of the main reasons people travel? In fact, most guests at all-inclusive hotels go out at least a few times and spend part of their savings anyway.

For some, another major inconvenience of an all-inclusive package is that most guests tend to spend all day at the hotel, and staff organize activities for them that are often disruptive and noisy, such as pool aerobics, volleyball tournaments, or dance competitions with blaring American music. Most of the time these activities have nothing at all to do with the Mexico many travellers come to discover.

Restaurants and Food

There is a multitude of excellent restaurants in this region, some specializing in Mexican cuisine and others in international cuisines, notably Italian and French. There are also a few vegetarian restaurants. Outside of the resort towns, though, restaurants serve only local cuisine.

Use your judgement when choosing a restaurant—if it is packed, it is probably for a good reason. Marvellous discoveries are waiting to be made outside your hotel. This guide includes a large selection of the best spots.

Meals take longer in Mexico, since the service is often slower and because it is customary to spend more time at the table. You will have to ask for the bill (*la cuenta, por favor!*), and you will without doubt have to wait a bit to get your change. This custom is thought of as polite, so there is no sense being impatient.

Prices

Prices described below refer to a meal for one person, including an appetizer, an entrée, and dessert.

$	less than $10
$$	$10 to $20
$$$	$21 to $30
$$$$	more than $30

Tipping

The term *propina incluida* signifies that the gratuity is included in the price. It is usually not included, and, depending on the quality of service, diners should budget for 10% to 15% of the total. Contrary to the practice in Europe, the tip is not included in the total, but rather must be calculated and remitted to the waiter by the diner.

Mexican Cuisine

Tortillas, tacos, empanadas, enchiladas, so many terms can be confusing to those encountering Mexican cuisine for the first time. Since prejudices die hard (dishes are too spicy, for example), too often visitors faced with new, unfamiliar flavours opt for "international" cuisine. Although some local dishes can prove particularly spicy, Mexican cuisine offers an infinite variety of dishes, from the mildest to the hottest. As a guide through the delicious meanderings of Mexican cuisine, we have assembled a gastronomic glossary below.

Mexican dishes are often served with rice *(arroz)* and black or red beans *(frijoles),* and a basket of hot tortillas is placed on your table. Of course, the hot sauce *(salsa)* is never very far and there are many kinds. Traditionally, salsa is prepared by mashing tomatoes, onions, coriander and different spices together with a mortar.

Breakfast is *desayuno* in Spanish, *almuerzo* means lunch and *cena* dinner. The *comida corrida* is served in the late afternoon, around 5pm or 6pm, and it consists of a daily menu, which is usually reasonably priced. Mexicans do not tend to eat a lot in the evening, so don't be surprised if you go to a village restaurant after 6pm and it's closed.

Practical Information

Basic Restaurant Vocabulary

An order of...	*una orden de...*
Beverage	*bebida*
Breakfast	*desayuno*
Cup	*taza*
Dessert	*postre*
Dinner	*cena*
Dish	*plato*
Fork	*tenedor*
Glass	*vaso*
Knife	*cuchillo*
Lunch	*comida*
Meal	*comida*
Menu	*menú*
Napkin	*servilleta*
Restaurant	*restaurante*
Snack or appetizer	*botana* or *antojito*
Spoon	*cuchara*
Table	*mesa*

May I see the menu?	*¿Puedo ver el menú?*
The bill (check) please	*La cuenta, por favor*
Where are the washrooms?	*¿Dónde están los sanitarios?*
I would like...	*Quisiera...*
I don't eat meat	*Yo no como carne*
I am vegetarian	*Yo soy vegetariano*

Recipes

Guacamole (Avocado dip)
serves 6

Ingredients:

2 large avocadoes
1 small onion, finely chopped
1 to 2 sliced hot peppers
1 large tomato, peeled and chopped
fresh or dried coriander
lime juice
salt

Guacamole should not be prepared in a blender because its texture is not supposed to be homogeneous. In a bowl, mash the avocadoes with a fork and sprinkle them with lime juice. Carefully mix the avocado, onion, peppers, tomato and coriander. Add a pinch of salt and serve immediately with tacos.

Cruda (Mexican sauce)
Makes about a cup and a half (350 ml)

Ingredients:

1 medium tomato, not peeled
1 onion, finely diced
2 tbsp. coarsely chopped coriander
3 finely chopped hot peppers
1/2 tsp. bitter orange juice
75 ml cold water

Cruda is a chunky, refreshing sauce for tortillas and is often served with eggs for breakfast, and with roasted meat and tacos in the evening. Chop the tomato and mix it with the other ingredients. This sauce can be prepared up to 3hrs ahead of time, but it is best eaten right away so that it doesn't lose its crunchy texture.

Ceviche
Raw shrimp, tuna or sea pike, "cooked" only in lime juice. In Mexico, onions, tomatoes, hot peppers and coriander are added.

Chicharrón
Fried pork rind, usually served with an apéritif.

Chile
Fresh or dried peppers (there are more than 100 varieties) that are prepared in a thousand different ways: stuffed, or as stuffing, boiled, fried, etc.

Empanadas
Thin corn pancakes shaped like turnovers, stuffed with meat, poultry or fish.

Enchiladas
Rolled and baked tortillas (see further below), enchiladas are generally stuffed

The unique architecture of Chichén Itzá is enhanced by a series of poignant statues and sculptures.

A combination of Mayan and Toltec cultures, El Castillo, the pyramid of Kukulkán, dominates Chichén Itzá from its high temple.

with chicken, covered with a spicy sauce, sliced onions and cream, and sometimes sprinkled with cheese.

Fajitas

Strips of marinated chicken grilled with onions. Fajitas are usually served with tomato sauce, cream and vegetables, and can be wrapped in a tortilla.

Gazpacho

A delicious and refreshing cold soup made with tomatoes, peppers, celery, onions, olive oil, cucumbers, lemon juice and garlic. Gazpacho is sometimes served with croutons.

Guacamole

Salted and peppered purée of avocado mixed with diced tomatoes, onions, fresh peppers and a bit of lime juice. Even when this dish is not on the menu, do not hesitate to ask for *guacamole con totopos* (with corn chips), a very common dish that makes a refreshing appetizer or snack.

Huevos Rancheros

Two or three fried eggs served on a corn tortilla and covered with a spicy tomato sauce. Huevos rancheros are sometimes served with potatoes on the side. This is a good dish for those with big appetites who want to start the day off with a hearty breakfast.

Mole

This term designates a category of creamy sauces composed of mixtures of spices, nuts, chocolate, tomatoes, tortillas, peppers, onions, and other foodstuffs varying by re-

gion. The most famous of these are mole Poblano and mole negro Oaxaqueno, both made with a base of chocolate and spices. These sauces accompany poultry and meat.

Nopales

Cactus leaves (without the spines, of course!) fried, boiled or served in a soup or salad. The juice of these is also offered at breakfast.

Pozole

A corn and pork stew with radishes, onions, coriander and lime juice. There are two varieties, red and green. The red is hotter.

Quesadillas

A sort of crepe stuffed with cheese and cream.

Sopa de Lima

A hot soup made with chicken, lemon or lime, and mixed with pieces of corn tortillas.

Tacos

A rolled corn tortilla often stuffed with chicken, but also frequently with other preparations. Stalls on the street make tacos with marinated, grilled meat which is served on a tortilla with your choice of salsa and vegetables.

Tamales

Beef, poultry or fish, combined with vegetables and spices, which vary depending on the region, tamales are wrapped in banana-tree leaves and steamed.

Topos or Totopos

These are a rough equivalent to North American potato chips. They are round or triangular pieces of fried corn tortillas.

Tortillas

These are the bread of latin America. As opposed to Spanish tortillas (made with eggs and potatoes), Mexican tortillas are flat pancakes with a corn-flour base, cooked on an unoiled griddle. Generally they accompany other dishes. Traditionally made by hand, today tortillas are mass produced in food-processing factories. Tortillas are also increasingly being made using white flour.

Tacos, quesadillas and burritos can be made with corn or white flour tortillas (especially tacos and quesadillas). The corn tortillas can be hard or soft, depending on your taste.

Mexican Drinks

Beer

Several companies brew beer in Mexico, among them the famous Corona, Dos Equis *(XX)* and Superior. All three are good, but the most popular is Corona. Many hotels and restaurants also carry imported beers.

Wine

Local wines are inexpensive and generally good. Try Calafia, L.A. Cetto or Los Reyes.

Tequila

The Mexican national drink is squeezed from the bulbous base of the agave, a plant indigenous to Mexico that looks like a pineapple. The juice collected is then slowly fermented producing a dry, white alcohol. The recipe for tequila was invented in the state of Jalisco, probably in the 18th century. As any Mexican will tell you, all tequilas are not created equal: the taste of tequila varies from more pungent white varieties, to golden *añejos* with a mellower flavour, close to brandy. The best brands are Orendain, Hornitos, Herradura Reposado and Tres Generaciones.

Margarita and Sangrita

The Mexican margarita is probably stronger than the one with which most travellers are familiar. It is made of tequila, Cointreau, lime, lemon and salt. Try a *sangrita*, grenadine with juice extracted from bitter oranges as a chaser to little sips of tequila.

Kahlúa

Kahlúa is a coffee liqueur originally distilled in Mexico and now produced in Europe as well.

Xtabentún

Many regions have a local liqueur. In the Yucatán it is *Xtabentún* (pronounced shta-ben-toun), a subtle, honey-based, anise-flavoured liqueur.

Responsible Travel

The adventure of travelling will probably be an enriching experience for you. But will it be the same for

your hosts? The question of whether or not tourism is good for a host country is controversial. On one hand, tourism brings many advantages, such as the economic development of a region, the promotion of a culture and inter-cultural exchange; on the other hand, tourism can have negative impacts: increase in crime, deepening of inequalities, destruction of the environment, etc. But one thing is for sure: your journey will have an impact on your destination.

This is rather obvious when we speak of the environment. You should be as careful not to pollute the environment of your host country as you are at home. We hear it often enough: we all live on the same planet! But when it comes to social, cultural and even economic aspects, it can be more difficult to evaluate the impact of our travels. Be aware of the reality around you, and ask yourself what the repercussions will be before acting. Remember that you may make an impression that is much different than the one you wish to give.

Regardless of the type of travel we choose, it is up to each and every one of us to develop a social conscience and to assume responsibility for our actions in a foreign country. Common sense, respect, altruism, and a hint of modesty are useful tools that will go a long way.

Travelling with Children

Travelling with children, however young they may be, can be a pleasant experience. A few precautions and ample preparation are the keys to a fun trip.

Aboard the Airplane

A good reclining stroller will allow you to bring an infant or small child everywhere you go and will also be great for naps, if needed. In the airport, it will be easy to carry with you, especially since you are allowed to bring the stroller up to the plane's gates.

Travellers with children can board the plane first, avoiding long line-ups. If your child is under the age of two, remember to ask for seats at the front of the plane when reserving your tickets since they offer more room and are more comfortable for long flights, especially if you've got a toddler on your lap. Some airlines even offer bassinettes.

If you are travelling with an infant, be sure to prepare the necessary food for the flight, as well as an extra meal in case of a delay. Remember to bring enough diapers and moist towels, and a few toys might not be a bad idea!

For older kids who might get bored once the thrill of taking off has faded, books and activities such as drawing material and games will probably do the trick.

When taking off and landing, changes in air pressure may cause some discomfort. In this case, some say that the nipple of a bottle or a pacifier can soothe infants, while a piece of chewing gum will have the same effect for older children.

In Hotels

Many hotels are well equipped for children, and there is usually no extra fee for travelling with an infant. Many hotels and bed and breakfasts have cribs; ask for one when reserving your room. You may have to pay extra for children, however, but the supplement is generally low.

Car Rentals

Most car rental agencies rent car seats for children. They are usually not very expensive.

The Sun

Needless to say, a child's skin requires strong protection against the sun; in fact, it is actually preferable not to expose toddlers to its harsh rays. Before going to the beach, remember to apply sunscreen (SPF 25 for children, 35 for infants). If you think your child will spend a long time under the sun, you should consider purchasing a sunscreen with SPF 60.

Children of all ages should wear a hat that provides good coverage for the head throughout the day.

Swimming

Children usually get quite excited about playing in the waves and can do so for hours on end. However, parents must be very careful and watch them constantly; accidents can happen in a matter of seconds. Ideally, an adult should accompany children into the water, especially the younger ones, and stand farther out in the water so that the kids can play between the beach and the supervising adult. This way, he or she can quickly intervene in case of an emergency.

For infants and toddlers, some diapers are especially designed for swimming, such as *Little Swimmers* by Huggies. These are quite useful when having fun in the water!

Shopping

What to Bring Home

It is always fun to bring interesting local products home from a vacation. Tequila, *Xtabentún*, and Mexican vanilla are all excellent choices. Mexican crafts are colourful and original. Every region has a hand-painted pottery industry, hand-woven and hand-embroidered fabrics, ceramics, fine leather goods, and various silverwork and silver jewellery. The silver content of

an item is indicated by the stamp "925," which signifies that the metal is 92.5% pure. *Huipiles* (dresses), *guayaberas* (shirts), hammocks and braided baskets are also good gift ideas. Lovely *piñatas* (papier-mâché stars or animals filled with candy for children to break open at Christmas) are another option. Terracotta nativity figurines (*nacimientos*) are also very popular.

Huge seashells can be found on the wilder beaches between Cancún and Tulum (no need to get swindled in Cancún's fancy shops). Do not forget to carefully clean shells before packing them; a fishmonger can do this for you.

The export of antique art objects, which are considered national treasures, is illegal. When purchasing reproductions, be sure that their status is well indicated to avoid headaches at customs.

Duty-Free Shops

Duty-free shops are found in airports and basically sell foreign products, such as perfume, cigarettes and liquor. Purchases must be made in US dollars. Prices in general are not especially advantageous since merchants take advantage of the tax break to increase profits.

In Mexico it is common to turn down the first price offered by a merchant and bargain over desired merchandise. A distinction is drawn, however, between fancy shops and poor artisans who sell their wares on the sidewalk at rock-bottom prices. In the latter case, bargaining is basically equivalent to an insult. Bargaining only has currency in stores outside of shopping malls. Shops are open from 9am or 10am to 1pm or 2pm, and from 4pm or 5m to 9pm or 10pm, seven days a week. In large shopping malls, where colonies of tourists gather, stores rarely close for lunch.

Be careful not to make purchases in excess of the maximum permitted by your country's customs authorities. Also think of the weight of your suitcases. Some shops can ship items that are too cumbersome for you to carry in your luggage.

Street Vendors

The tenacity of Mexican street vendors is legendary. If you display the least bit of interest in vendors' wares, expect them to latch onto you. The best way to avoid being bothered is to demonstrate total indifference to their merchandise and, when approached, to answer firmly but politely, "*no, gracias.*"

Miscellaneous

Taxes

Mexico has a value-added sales tax of 15% (10% between Cancún-Chetumal, it is the IVA, or

impuesto de valor agregado), payable by tourists and residents alike, and applicable to most items. The IVA is often "hidden" in restaurant bills, the price of store merchandise and organized trips. Other taxes are levied on telephone calls, in restaurants and in hotels.

Tour Guides

Near tourist centres, many people who speak some English introduce themselves as tour guides. Some of these people are barely competent, so be sceptical. The tourist information office is a good place to find out about competent guides, or to check the credentials of somebody who has offered you guide service. These guides sometimes demand large sums in remuneration for their services, so, before embarking on a tour with one, be clear that you have agreed on exactly what services will be rendered for exactly what payment, and only pay at the very end of the tour. You may not need a guide, however, as this book allows you to travel and tour independently.

Alcohol

The legal drinking age in Mexico is 18 years. The sale of alcohol is illegal after 3am, on Sunday and on holidays.

Smokers

Restrictions on smoking are increasingly common. Smoking on buses is prohibited, although this rule is not respected to the letter, and people are very tolerant. Smoking in all other public areas is permitted.

Electricity

Local electricity operates at 110 volts AC, as in North America. Plugs have two flat pins, so Europeans will need both a converter and a wall socket adapter.

Women Travellers

Women travelling alone in the Yucatán should not have any problems. In general, locals are friendly and not too aggressive. Although men treat women with respect and harassment is relatively rare, Mexicans will undoubtedly flirt with female travellers—politely, though. Dress is at women's discretion in Cancún, except in restaurants and churches. In smaller villages, foreign women stand out, especially when their dress is more revealing (short skirts, for example). Of course, a minimum amount of caution is required; for example, women should avoid walking alone through poorly lit areas at night.

Time Zones

Mexico is divided into three time zones. The country switches to daylight-saving time between the first Sunday in April and the last Sunday in October (clocks are put ahead one hour). The Yucatán is one hour behind Eastern Standard Time and six hours behind Greenwich Mean Time.

Newspapers and Magazines

Among the most prevalent publications in the Yucatán are a number of small magazines in which information is disseminated through advertisements. Their content, laid out in journalistic style, is nothing more than publicity. Updates consist of replacing cover photographs. These magazines are essentially useful for their maps.

The most popular of these magazines is definitely *Cancún Tips*, which covers in brief all of the topics in a traditional travel guide. Tourist information offices distribute this magazine as though it were an official government publication. *Cancún Tips*, available for free in Spanish and in English, is easy to consult. A more substantial version, with more in-depth articles, is distributed in hotel rooms (along with the Bible and the phone book).

For more substance and information on current events, *Por Esto* is a very interesting daily paper, published in Spanish, that is available everywhere. It covers in detail subjects related to the main economic base of the region: tourism (union crisis in a hotel, opening of a major new attraction, etc.). Slightly more highbrow, *Cronica de Cancún* publishes an interesting culture insert on Saturdays, entitled *"cada siete,"* which includes information on local celebrities and artists.

Finally, *Novedades de Quintana Roo*, a large-format magazine, provides in-depth coverage of political and national issues.

A veritable paradise for divers and watersports enthusiasts in general, the coasts of the Yucatán Peninsula provide the necessary geography for other activities as well, for the most part on the very grounds of hotels: golf, cycling on bicycle paths, bird-watching, hiking in national parks, tennis...

This region, with its large recreation centres (Xel-Há and Xcaret) and world-famous diving islands (Isla Mujeres and Cozumel), has much to offer.

This chapter lists the most popular outdoor activities, providing an overview of the sporting options in the area. In chapters devoted to specific regions, the sections "Parks and Beaches" and "Outdoor Activities" include additional, more detailed and precise information on outdoor activities.

Parks

The natural assets of this region have been protected by the establishment of numerous national parks. Isla Contoy, north of Isla Mujeres, is a haven for marine birds. An observation tower and an interpretive centre have been constructed on the island for easier observation and deeper understanding of these avian species.

The national park of Tulum conceals fabulous Mayan sites within its 672ha. The area is covered in mangrove swamps and coastal dunes, and its turquoise waters are inviting for swimming and scuba diving.

The Reserva de la Biósfera Sian Ka'an is situated a few kilometres south of Tulum and close to 100km of shoreline. It comprises a multitude of bays, lagoons and coral reefs that are part of the second-largest barrier reef in the world, and is inhabited by many aquatic species. Twenty-three ancient Mayan sites have been found in this reserve. Animal species such as the puma, the ocelot, the spider monkey and the toucan live here. A day trip into the reserve is possible with Amigos de Sian Ka'an *(www.amigosde siankaan.org)*, a private, non-profit organization.

Río Lagartos, on the north coast of the Yucatán, is a very special ecological reserve because it is the principal Mexican nesting ground of herons and large colonies of pink flamingoes.

Outdoor Activities

Swimming

The east coast of the Yucatán (including Cancún, Tulum, and Cozumel) has some of the calmest waters in Mexico, although ground swells are not completely unheard of here. These calm waters cover the palette of blues and greens, and their white sands stay cool under foot. The beaches are all public, offering unlimited access. Their limpid waters, dotted with coral reefs, shelter abundant marine wildlife.

Since the coast of the state of Quintana Roo is actually one long beach, it is possible to walk for long periods in perfect solitude. In Cancún, expect a completely different picture: the city is literally overrun during the high season.

In general, the beaches on the northern shore of Cancún are quieter than those on the east coast, and their calmer waters (protected from the wind)

are ideal for swimming. The more exposed east coast is battered by constant waves and wind, although it is still possible to find stunning cliffs and bays that are safe for swimming.

When the waves are very strong, regardless of where you are, avoid swimming altogether or do so very cautiously. Remember that few establishments provide lifeguard service. A flag system on the beaches indicates the degree of risk for would-be swimmers, sort of in the fashion of traffic lights. A red or black flag indicates danger; a yellow flag is cautionary; a blue or green flag signals that the situation is normal; ideal swimming conditions are represented by white flags.

Although the practice seems to be tolerated in Cancún and Playa del Carmen, most of the time it is strictly forbidden to sunbathe nude or topless and doing so will certainly cause quite a stir among residents and hotel employees, not to mention a few tourists.

Scuba Diving

Underwater adventurers are catered to by many diving centres, mainly found in Cancún, Playa del Carmen and Cozumel, and reefs are numerous in this region.

Certified divers can explore the secrets of the

Yucatec coastline to their heart's content. Others can still experience breathing underwater, but must be accompanied by a qualified guide, who will supervise their descent. There is little danger; however, be sure that the supervision is adequate. Some instructors take more than one diver down at a time, which goes against the rules.

Equipment can easily be rented from the centres along the coasts, but it can be expensive. If you have your own equipment you'll save money by bringing it along, especially if you are planning several days of diving.

Cozumel is world famous for the crystalline clarity of its waters, the richness of its marine life and its excellent facilities. Greater than half of the island's visitors come to it for one reason, and one reason only: diving. Isla Mujeres is equally highly rated. Cancún's many dive shops organize guided excursions to the best diving spots around the city.

Scuba diving makes it possible to discover fascinating sights like coral reefs, schools of multicoloured fish and amazing underwater plants. Don't forget that this ecosystem is fragile, though, and deserves special attention. All divers must respect a few basic **safety guidelines** in order to protect these natural sites: do not touch anything; do not take pieces of coral; do not feed the fish; be careful not to disturb anything with

A Fragile Ecosystem

Coral reefs are formed by minuscule organisms called coelenterate polyps, which are very sensitive to water pollution. The high level of nitrates in polluted water accelerates the growth of seaweed, which in turn takes over the coral, stops it from growing and literally smothers it. Sea urchins (whose long spikes can cause severe injuries) live on the coral and play a major role in controlling the amount of seaweed that grows on the coral by eating what the fish cannot. An epidemic threatened the survival of many reefs in 1983, when the waters became so polluted that sea urchins were affected and seaweed flourished in the Caribbean waters. Scientific studies have since proved the importance of urchins to the ecological balance, and the species has thus been restored on certain reefs. However, these little urchins cannot solve the problem on their own. Pollution control is essential if the coral reefs, upon which 400,000 organisms depend, are to survive.

your fins, and, of course, do not litter. If you want a souvenir of your underwater experience, take along a disposable underwater camera.

Snorkelling

It doesn't take much to snorkel: a mask, a snorkel and some fins. Anyone can enjoy this activity, which is a great way to develop an appreciation for the richness of the underwater world. Not far from several beaches, you can go snorkelling around coral reefs inhabited by various underwater species. Remember that the basic rules for protecting the underwater environment (see scuba diving section)

must also be respected when snorkelling.

Windsurfing, Jet-skiing and Waterskiing

These activities require calmer waters than the rough seas that bathe the coast of Cancún and surround Cozumel. The calm waters of the lagoon of Nichupté in Cancún, or of Bahía Mujeres, on the north coast, are therefore recommended.

If you have never tried these activities, there are a few safety measures to be aware of: choose a beach where the water is calm, watch out for swimmers and divers, don't head too far from shore (if you get

into trouble don't hesitate to wave your arms to signal your distress); and wear shoes so that you don't cut your feet on the rocks.

Cruises

Excursions aboard sailboats and yachts offer another enchanting way to freely explore the sea's sparkling waves. Some centres organize trips, while others rent sailboats to experienced sailors. You will find a few addresses throughout the guide.

Non-divers can appreciate the marvellous scenery of the deep sea without getting wet, thanks to observation submarines and glass-bottom boats

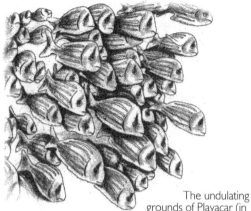

that allow for discovery of marine fauna and coral reefs.

Deep-Sea Fishing

It is possible to participate in day-long or half-day sport-fishing tournaments that depart from Cancún, Cozumel, Isla Mujeres and Playa del Carmen as long as you reserve a few days in advance with an outfitter. Mackerel, swordfish, tuna and red snapper are abundant in the area. Prices are between $300 and $900 per boat, per day.

Golf

The state of Quintana Roo is home to a few golf courses. Among these, Pok-Ta-Pok in Cancún was designed by world-famous landscape architect Robert Trent Jones Jr.

The undulating grounds of Playacar (in Playa del Carmen), designed by Robert von Hagge and considered one of the best courses in the country, are also worth a few tee-offs. Other courses can be found in Cancún at the Cancún Hilton, the Melia Cancún and the Resort Course of Puerto Aventuras. The Cancún Palace Hotel offers an original 36-hole mini-putt.

Bird-Watching

The national parks as well as the outskirts of the Yucatán's large archaeological sites are preferred locations for the observation of winged wildlife. A great variety of birds may be admired in the tropical forest of Sian Ka'an, on Isla Contoy (where 97 species are protected), as well as at Xaman-Há, an ornithological reserve in Playacar that shelters about 30 bird species, including toucans and parrots.

Cycling

In Cancún it is practically impossible to cycle anywhere other than on the 14km bicycle path along the west side of the hotel zone from Punta Cancún to downtown. This path, which runs alongside a busy two-lane road, is also used by in-line skaters and joggers, and is poorly lit at night. Do not overestimate your stamina—the sun beats down hard on this region and the roads are far from easy terrain. The best time for cycling is the very early morning, before temperatures peak. Avoid riding at nightfall since many roads are unlit.

Horseback Riding

There are several rental stables, Rancho Buenavista in Cozumel and Rancho Loma Bonita in Cancún among them. It is also possible to ride at Xcaret.

Tennis

Some hotels have tennis courts at guests' disposal. Many of these are lit for evening play.

Cancún

Before the Mexican government decided to transform a strip of sand inhabited by about a hundred Mayan fishers into a major tourist resort, Cancún was a peaceful, isolated paradise.

As they went about their usual business, the local fishers surely had little idea that scores of bureaucrats were studying all sorts of computer-compiled data indicating, beyond the shadow of a doubt, that Cancún had the potential to attract more tourists season after season than anywhere else in Mexico.

Gulf of Mexico
YUCATÁN
Chichén Itzá
QUINTANA ROO
Tulum
Cancún
Isla Mujeres
Playa del Carmen
San Miguel de Cozumel
Cozumel
Caribbean Sea

In a little over 25 years, Cancún mushroomed into a town of 400,000 inhabitants, with about 130 hotels able to accommodate a total of 3-million tourists year-round in some 25,000 rooms, as well as hundreds of restaurants and shops.

It all began in the 1960s, when Mexico became aware of its own tourist potential. In 1967, Cancún was officially chosen as the site on which to develop the infrastructure for a mega-project, thanks to its long, white-sand beach,

subtropical climate, turquoise Caribbean waters and proximity to the United States.

Construction was begun on roads, aqueducts and hotels in 1974, but the place remained relatively unknown until the mid-1980s, when a whirlwind of activity hit the area: hotels sprouted up and Cancún became a tourist resort par excellence.

Cancún has been designed to please its major clientele, American tourists, who account for 80% of all foreign visitors

to the city. It's just like home for them here, with the same big restaurant and hotel chains, the same supermarkets, the same music in the nightclubs. Everything is tailor-made to suit their tastes. Furthermore, English often prevails over Spanish in conversation. This divests the place of much of its exotic charm, but obviously appeals to many people: Cancún is one of the most popular Mexican destinations for foreign tourists.

Cancún is made up of Ciudad Cancún (Cancún City) and the Zona Hotelera (Hotel

Zone). It is one of the only cities in the world where residents and tourists are so clearly separated. The 22.5km-long Hotel Zone is covered with gigantic, international-class hotels. These stand side by side between the sea and a wide road.

Most residents of Cancún City work in the local hotels, bars and restaurants, and most were born elsewhere.

Cancún is a convenient gateway for travellers wishing to explore the Mayan archaeological sites of Chichén Itza and Tulum, and to immerse themselves in the traditional Yucatec lifestyle.

Finding Your Way Around

The Hotel Zone, for its part, is simply a strip of land, and thus seems like an easy place to find your way around. However, it is altogether possible to confuse the Laguna Nichupté with the Caribbean, making it hard to know whether to turn left or right! As you will probably be getting around by bus, ask the driver for directions in case of doubt.

In downtown Cancún, street names and numbers are generally indicated but

it is preferable to bring a map along on all outings, even though the downtown area is quite small. Picking out a few landmarks is a good trick.

The city is divided into *supermanzanas*, which are like districts. The addresses are thus followed by the letters SM and the appropriate number. Each SM has its own postal code.

There are four main avenues in downtown Cancún: Cobá and Uxmal run east-west, while Tulum and Yaxchilán run north-south. The latter two are the most commercially developed, with scores of shops, restaurants, hotels and exchange offices.

The best place to catch a bus (Ruta 1 or 2) to the hotel strip is near the traffic circle at the corner of Cobá and Tulum.

Cancún International Airport

Cancún International Airport (☎886-0028) is located about 20 km southwest of downtown. Thanks to recent renovations, it is now one of the most modern airports in Mexico. In addition to a currency exchange office and a duty-free shop, it houses several stores, restaurants and bars, whose prices, as in any airport, are slightly higher than in town.

Several car-rental agencies have counters at the airport. To get the best rates, reserve a car from

home after comparing prices. Ask the agency to fax you a confirmation of the rate and your reservation. Most big companies have toll-free (☎800) numbers that can be used anywhere in North America. When comparing rates, make sure to factor in the taxes, the number of free kilometres offered and any insurance fees. Here are the names and numbers of the agencies with branches at the airport:

Avis
☎(998) 886-886-0221
☎800-272-3652

Budget
☎(998) 886-0026
☎800-268-8970

Hertz
☎(998) 884-1326
☎800-263-0678

National/Tilden
☎(998) 886-0152
☎800-727-7368

Dollar
☎(998) 886-2348
☎800-800-4000

Getting to Cancún

If you rent a car at the airport, which is located 20km south of the city, it will take you only about 15min to get downtown. If you are going to the Hotel Zone, take Paseo Kukulcán, which you will see right after you get on Avenida Tulum. Within a few minutes, you will be at the bottom end of the Hotel Zone, which is shaped like the number 7.

There is a shuttle service between the airport and

downtown Cancún (about $8). The price of the return trip is included in some vacation packages. The buses are spacious and surprisingly punctual. Be careful on the day of your departure, as the shuttle driver might get to the hotel early and leave immediately for the airport without waiting for you. To avoid this catastrophe, be ready 30min before the shuttle is scheduled to arrive and wait for it outside.

It should be noted that taxis are only allowed to take travellers to the airport, while public buses can only carry tourists from the airport to their hotel.

If you are driving to Tulum (or farther south) from the Hotel Zone, you will save yourself a lot of time by avoiding the downtown area. Drive to the southern tip of the Hotel Zone, toward Punta Nizuc, then continue to Highway 307, where you will see a sign showing the way.

To get to Valladolid, Chichén Itzá or Mérida, take Avenida Uxmal (Highway 180) from downtown Cancún.

A toll highway is located south of the airport.

If you want to go to Isla Mujeres, you will have to take the ferry at Puerto Juárez, 3km north of Cancún. To get there by bus, go to the terminal at the intersection of Avenidas Tulum and Uxmal. Buses (Ruta 8) depart frequently and it's

only a 3km trip. Another much more expensive but more convenient option is to take a water taxi which leaves from Playa Linda or from Playa Tortugas, in the northern part of the Hotel Zone.

A ferry (the *Mexicano*) runs between Cancún and Isla Mujeres, departing from Playa Linda (at the *embarcadero* of Cancún's hotel zone), during peak times. The price ($15) is twice as expensive as the ferry from Puer to Juárez, however, if you're staying in the hotel zone you'll probably find it is worth the extra cost.. Departures are at 9:30am, 10:45am, 11:45am and 2:15pm; return trips are at 12:30pm, 3:30pm, 5:30pm and 6:30pm.

Other taxi boats or ferries leave Playa Caracol (located between the Fiesta Americana and Coral Beach hotels, Asterix Water ☎886-4270 or 886-4847), Playa Langosta or Playa Tortugas, beaches in Cancún's Hotel Zone. Isla Mujeres is situated 11km from the Hotel Zone and the crossing takes about 45min.

Many agencies organize cruises to Isla Mujeres, and some have transformed this short crossing into an elaborate excursion including meals and open bar, snorkelling and bands. Of course these expeditions are more expensive than simple ferry crossings, but they can be very pleasant. Before boarding be sure that the boat is going to land at the island, as some cruises just go around it.

Arrive at least a half-hour early to get a good seat.

The following company organizes cruises to Isla Mujeres from Cancún:

The Shuttle
☎*(998) 883-3583 or 883-1963*

By Car

Unless you have a serious aversion to public transportation, renting a car to travel back and forth between your hotel and downtown Cancún is a needless expense and is sure to cause you all sorts of headaches. There is frequent bus service, the fares are cheap and the downtown area is not that big. You will waste a lot of time looking for parking—and trying to find your way! Furthermore, the car-rental rates are fairly high in Cancún. If you do rent a car for an excursion, you will undoubtedly have to drive through the city. Bear in mind that the speed limit is 40km/h. There is a Pemex service station on Highway 307, between Cancún and the airport. Make sure to fill up your tank, as gas stations are hard to find in this region.

The major car-rental agencies have branches at the airport (see p 32) and downtown, as well as in many hotels.

By Taxi

The local taxis have no meters, so the fare depends on the distance covered, the cost of gas and your bargaining skills. The staff at the front desk of your hotel can tell you what the going rates are. The farther your hotel is from downtown, of course, the more you will have to pay. Always determine the fare with the driver before getting in the taxi. There is a taxi drivers' union (☎880-4056), where you can obtain information or file a complaint.

By Coach

Bus station
24hrs
Corner of Av.s Tulum and Uxmal
☎*(998) 884-1378*
☎*886-8610 (tickets)*
The bus station is open 24hrs a day and offers service to a whole slew of destinations, from the capital, Mexico City, to Chetumal, on the Belize border. The fares for first-class and second-class buses are almost identical.

ADO Bus Terminal Cancún
☎*(998) 884-4352 or*
884-4804

By Bus

Within Cancún City and the Hotel Zone, the bus fare is 5 pesos *(about US $0.50)*. The buses tear up and down Paseo Kukulcán, which runs through the Hotel Zone. If you are not at one of their official stops, you can sometimes flag one down one with a wave of your hand, provided they are not full. Most buses run between 6am and 10pm. Buses on Ruta 1 and Ruta 2 travel

between the downtown and the Hotel Zone, while those on Ruta 8 go to Puerto Juárez, where passengers can catch the ferry to Isla Mujeres.

Practical Information

The area code in Cancún is *998*

Tourist Office

Quintana Roo tourist office
everyday 9am to 9pm
Av. Tulum no. 26, between the Multibanco Comerex and city hall
☎*881-9000*
The staff here can provide some helpful information. They are sure to give you the latest edition of the complimentary publication *Cancún Tips*, which is full of advertisements but nonetheless contains some pertinent information, as well as some very useful maps of the city.

They also have a rate sheet for Cancún hotels.

Post Office

Post office
Av. Sunyaxchén, near Av. Yaxchilán
☎*884-1418*
It is open from 9am to 3pm on weekdays and from 9am to 1pm on weekends. Most hotels in the Hotel Zone sell stamps

and can mail your letters or postcards.

Telephone

You need a Ladatel phone card to use the public telephones, which are all over the place but don't always work very well. If you are tempted to use the phone in your room, bear in mind that there is an exorbitant charge for each call. Hotels even collect a 60% surcharge for overseas calls! Pick up a Ladatel card as soon as you arrive, in case you need to make a call. Cards are sold at many shopping centres, as well as certain exchange offices.

Yellow Pages of Mexico
☎*800-021-2345*
Standard number for all the country except Mexico City, Guadalajara and Monterrey

Banks and Exchange Offices

You can cash traveller's cheques at the front desk of your hotel, at a bank or at any of the numerous exchange offices *(casas de cambio)* downtown and in the Hotel Zone. Exchange offices usually offer better rates than banks and stay open later, until 9pm. Banks are open on weekdays from 9am to 5pm. Here are two you might try:

Banamex
Av. Tulum no. 19, next to city hall
☎*884-5411*

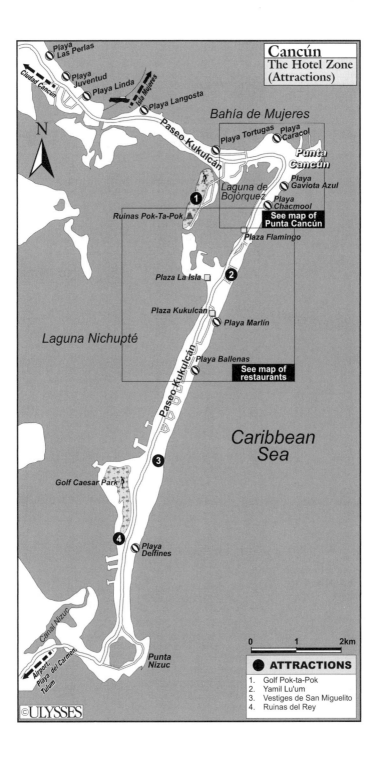

Bancomer
Av. Tulum 20
☎884-4400

There is an exchange office at the airport, but it is not always open and better rates are available downtown.

You will find automated teller machines (ATMs) all over the city as well as in the Hotel Zone.

Safety

Police Station
Av. Andrés Quintana Roo
☎884-1913 or 884-2342
The police station is located some distance from downtown. In case of emergency, call the police at ☎060.

Health Emergencies

For assistance in English:

Hospital Americano
Calle Viento 15
☎884-6425

Total Assist
Claveles n° 5, angle Av. Tulum
☎884-8083

Exploring

The island of Cancún has been occupied by Mayas since the beginning of the Common Era, long before it became the great seaside resort it is today. The city of Cancún as such was built in the 1960s and is more functional than beautiful. Its only real charm is its inhabitants. On the

other hand, many ancient Mayan constructions have been excavated in the area, mainly between Punta Cancún and Punta Nizuc, along the shore in the Hotel Zone. Cancún's main tourist attractions are its long beach washed by the Caribbean, its renowned golf courses and its luxury hotels.

The Hotel Zone (Zona Hotelera)

Cancún's ancient Mayan remains, major shopping centres and Centro de Convenciones (convention centre) are all located in the Hotel Zone (Zona Hotelera), where the hotels and other buildings are lined up in the shape of a 7. If you decide to tour the Hotel Zone on foot, bear in mind that the distances are considerable; bring along some change so that you can hop on a bus when you feel like it. You can also stop in at any of the hotels along the way and take a little rest in one of its bars or restaurants.

If you set out from downtown Cancún, your first stop will be the **Golf Pok-Ta-Pok** *(Paseo Kukulcán, between Km 6 and 7)*, where two small Mayan structures have been integrated into the course. You have to ask for permission to visit the site at the club entrance, and walk for about 15min. Another, less interesting structure, **Ni Ku**, is integrated into the architecture of the Camino Real hotel, on the Punta Cancún beach, in the angle of the 7. On the Punta

Cancún, you will see the **Centro de Convenciones** *(Paseo Kukulcán, Km 9, ☎881-0400)*, a modern building where many cultural events and all sorts of other gatherings are held; it contains two restaurants, an ATM, shops and service businesses.

On the ground floor of the Centro de Convenciones, there is a museum devoted to Mayan history and the archaeology of Quintana Roo: **The Museo de Cancún** ★★ *(30 pesos; Mon-Fri 9am to 8pm, Sat and Sun 10am to 5pm; Paseo Kukulcán, Km 9.5; ☎883-3671)*, the national institute of anthropology and history. It displays over 1,000 interesting Mayan relics, such as decorated terra cotta vases, jade jewellery and masks, as well as a bust of the king for whom the city "Ruinas del Rey" was named.

The two structures of **Yamil Lu'um** *(Paseo Kukulcán, Km 12, on the grounds of the Sheraton hotel)*, believed to date back to the 13th or 14th century, stand on the highest point in the Hotel Zone. The small, square structure no doubt served as an observation post. These remains are easy to reach. As the site is completely exposed to the sun, visitors are advised to wear a hat and sunglasses.

Continuing southward, you will see traces of **San Miguelito** *(Paseo Kukulcán, Km 16.5)*, a tiny structure made up of stone columns.

Right across the Paseo Kukulcán, in front of the

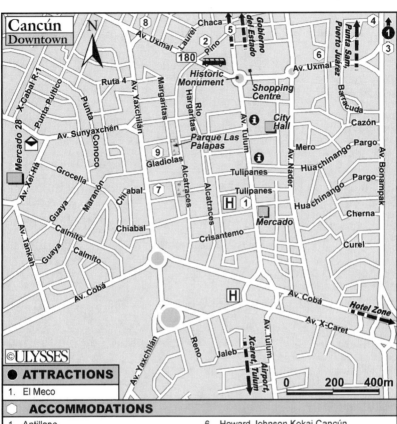

Cancún
Downtown

N

● **ATTRACTIONS**

| 1. El Meco |

○ **ACCOMMODATIONS**

1. Antillano	6. Howard Johnson Kokai Cancún
2. Best Western Plaza Caribe	7. María de Lourdes
3. Blue Bay Club and Marina	8. Mexico Hostel
4. El Patio	9. Posada Lucy
5. Holiday Inn Centro Cancún	

©ULYSSES

El Pueblito hotel, lie the **Ruinas Del Rey** *(around $3; free admission Sun; every day 8am to 5pm)*, the most extensive Mayan site in Cancún. Made up essentially of two large squares surrounded by palaces, temples, pyramids and other structures dating from AD 1300 to 1400, this site was fully excavated and opened to tourists in the mid-1970s, but had already been visited by a number of archaeologists during the 19th century. Its name, "El Rey," comes from a sepulture found on the site which is now on display at the Museo de Cancún.

Around Cancún

★
El Meco

The El Meco archaeological site lies between Puerto Juárez and Punta Sam, on the left side of Highway 307, north of Cancún. Built between AD 1200 and AD 1500, this large city probably began as a fishing village. It includes a main temple, known as El Castillo, a number of stone buildings and various sculptures, including snakes' heads.

The main pyramid is the highest structure in the region.

★
Isla Contoy

See Isla Mujeres, p 98.

**Barco Asterix
Ecoadventures**
Marina Carlos 'n Charlie's
**☎886-4270
⇌886-4755**

Cruises

Finally, as Cancún is a major seaside resort, one of the most pleasant things to do here is to take a cruise. Most boats take passengers to Isla Mujeres, located just to the north. These cruises generally include live music, dancing, games and a meal served with plenty of drinks. Some boats don't actually stop at Isla Mujeres but simply go around it, so make sure to check before boarding. Most excursions start at Playa Tortugas, on Paseo Kukulcán. The following companies offer a variety of outings:

From 6pm to 11pm, the *Caribbean Carnival* (*☎884-3760*) offers a tropical cruise and show for 400 passengers, complete with a limbo competition, music, dancing and a buffet. Departures from Playa Tortugas.

Have you always dreamed of taking an evening cruise aboard a boat with a night-club ambiance, complete with a casino, a buffet and karaoke? If so, the *Pirate's Night Adventure* (*☎883-3262*) will be right up your alley. The boat sets out from the Royal Mayan Marina, *Playa Langosta.*

Captain Hook's Galleon (*☎883-3736 or 849-4451*) offers water activities and a paella buffet during the day. There is no charge for children under 12 accompanied by their parents. At night, the boat is transformed into a seafood restaurant, and then a nightclub until 1:30am. Departures from Playa Linda.

From Monday to Saturday, you can enjoy a quiet dinner cruise on the Laguna Nichupté aboard the *Columbus* (*☎883-1488 or 883-3283*), a replica of Christopher Columbus's three-masted ship. The ship sets out from the Royal Mayan Marina, Blvd. Kukulcán, Km 16.5.

Aqua World Cancún Queen (*☎885-2288*) is a paddle-wheeler that offers cruises accompanied by games, tropical drinks, fine food and mood music.

Beaches

As you already know, Cancún's Hotel Zone is shaped like a 7. In the north part, which is more sheltered from the wind, the beaches are much calmer than those to the south, which face onto the Caribbean. Keep an eye on the coloured flags on the beaches, which indicate whether or not it is safe to go swimming.

Playa Las Perlas

The beach closest to downtown Cancún, Playa Las Perlas lies at the north-west end of the Hotel Zone. Like the neighbouring beaches as far as Punta Cancún, it is sheltered from the wind, but its waters are not as clear as those of Playa Tortugas and Playa Langosta, farther east.

Playa Juventud

This beach lies in front of the Villas Juveniles (see p 71) youth hostel, hence its name. Naturally, the crowd here is fairly young, with a taste for water sports and late-night partying. Playa Juventud has the advantage of being located just 2km from downtown Cancún.

Playa Linda

Located at Km 4, between Playa Juventud and Playa Langosta, this beach lies at the border of the Hotel Zone and Ciudad Cancún, where the Nichupté bridge links the island beaches to the mainland. The pier at Playa Linda harbours many cruise ships as well as ferries to Isla Mujeres.

Playa Langosta

One of the prettiest beaches in Cancún, Playa Langosta (Km 5) has a small, rocky area that quickly turns into a lovely strip of white sand. Located near the Casa Maya hotel, it is literally covered with palapas.

Playa Tortugas

Many boats are anchored at the marina at Playa Tortugas. Some regularly shuttle back and forth between this beach and Isla Mujeres. Playa Tortugas remains fairly peaceful, despite the region's unbridled development. It offers one of the loveliest views of the Bahía de Mujeres (Bay of Women).

Playa Caracol

This beach forms the bend of the Hotel Zone. Located near the most luxurious hotels and the convention centre, peaceful Playa Caracol, the beach of choice among Cancún's older crowd, skirts gently round the Camino Real hotel and Punta Cancún, then links up with Playa Chacmool.

Playa Chacmool

Playa Chacmool is located near the commercial activity in the Hotel Zone. The restaurants and various services have helped make this a popular spot

with city dwellers, who still flock here with their families on weekends. A statue of Chacmool stands on the dune overlooking the beach, watching over the swimmers.

Playa Delphines

This lovely beach, located between Km 18 and Km 20, is one of the largest in the zone. Most of the people who come here are guests of the big hotels nearby. On the other side of the road is the Hilton's golf course and some vestiges of the Mayan city Ruinas del Rey.

Laguna Nichupté

The Hotel Zone stretches around the vast Laguna Nichupté, where tourists have a ball water-skiing and sailing. The area is home to numerous boat-rental and tour agencies. More and more hotels and businesses are located on the laguna, including the new shopping mall La Isla.

Punta Nizuc

Located near the southern end of the Hotel Zone, near Club Med, Punta Nizuc is popular for its coral reefs, which are less impressive than those off Cozumel and Chetumal but nonetheless interesting. Furthermore, the mangroves lend the spot a jungle feel.

Outdoor Activities

Water Sports

Cancún is one of the best-equipped cities in the world for water sports. Everything revolves around the water here, and all the gear necessary for snorkelling and scuba diving is available at most big hotels in the Hotel Zone. There are also scores of rental outfits, as well as full-service marinas, on the Laguna Nichupté, for example.

Introductory scuba-diving courses are available, but make sure to check the instructor's qualifications before putting your trust in him or her.

The following places rent out equipment for diving, sailing, jet-skiing, water-skiing and sometimes even sportfishing. They also offer a variety of excursions.

Aqua World
Paseo Kukulcán, Km 15.2
☎*848-8300*
This marina is one of the biggest in the area. You will be given a new snorkel for your outing, for obvious hygienic reasons.

Aqua Tours Adventures
7am to 9pm
Paseo Kukulcán, Km 6.5
☎*883-0400*
This outfit offers daily deep-sea fishing excursions and gourmet cruises.

Cancún

Aqua Fun
Paseo Kukulcán, Km 16.5
☎*885-2930*
Head to Aqua Fun for sailing lessons and canoe and pedal-boat rentals. The locker-room is free.

Aquaworld's Space Jungle Tours
8am to 8pm
at the Marina Barracuda, Paseo Kukulcán, Km 14.1
☎*848-8300*
Jungle Tours organizes daily jet-skiing expeditions through the mangroves to the reef at Punta Nizuc, at the southern tip of the Hotel Zone, near Club Med.

Marina Punta del Este
Paseo Kukulcán, Km 10.3
☎*883-1210*
For an outing on calm waters, climb aboard one of the little motor boats at this marina, for a ride alongside the tropical jungle to take in the natural sights.

Underwater Sightseeing

Two glass-bottomed boats sail the waters off the shores of Cancún, offering passengers a chance to check out the coral reef:

Subsee Explorer
$40
☎*848-9200*

Nautibus (Playa Linda)
$35 for 1.5hrs
☎*883-3720*

Golf

Pok-Ta-Pok golf course
Cancún golf club
Paseo Kukulcán, Km 7.5
☎*883-1277 or 883-1230*
In the Laguna Nichupté, a peninsula has been skilfully landscaped by Robert Trent Jones Jr. to evoke a Mayan city. The result is this internationally renowned, 18-hole golf course. Right next to it, moreover, are the vestiges of a real Mayan temple. In addition to this outstanding course, there are two tennis courts, a swimming pool and a restaurant. Visitors can take lessons and rent all the necessary equipment at the club. Reservations are required at least one day in advance.

Hilton Cancún
Paseo Kukulcán, Km 17
☎*881-8000 or 881-8016*

Meliá Cancún
Paseo Kukulcán, Km 15
☎*881-1100*

Both these hotels have an 18-hole golf course. Though less spectacular than the Pok-Ta-Pok course, they both offer a magnificent view, the former of the Laguna Nichupté, the latter of the ocean. You do not have to be a hotel guest to play on either course.

Cancún Palace hotel
Paseo Kukulcán, Km 14.5
☎*885-0533 ext. 6655*
Cancún has something to offer fans of miniature golf

as well! You can mini-putt here from 11am to midnight on a course inspired by Mayan pyramids.

Deep-Sea Fishing

The waters around Cancún are teeming with over 500 species of fish. A deep-sea fishing trip costs between $350 and $550, depending on how long you stay out. Aqua Tours and Aqua World, which have offices around the Laguna Nichupté, offer a variety of expeditions. The fishing season runs from March to July.

In-line Skating

This sport still hasn't really caught on in Cancún. It should be stressed that the sidewalks in the Hotel Zone are ill-suited to in-line skating, due to the deep diagonal lines that the municipal authorities insist on carving into them. There is, however, a place where skaters can glide about at ease: the bike path that runs along the Hotel Zone to downtown Cancún.

Rent-a-Roll
Paseo Kukulcán, opposite the La Boom nightclub
It has recently become possible to rent skates in Cancún, thanks to this outfit which also rents mopeds.

Jogging

There is not really any pleasant place in Cancún to jog, unless you run barefoot by the sea. Throughout the Hotel Zone, there is heavy, potentially dangerous traffic on Paseo Kukulcán, and the downtown streets are in pitiful condition. Die-hard joggers can try the bike path early in the morning.

Cycling

The bike path that runs alongside the Hotel Zone is constantly expanding. Though it is partially protected from the sun by a few trees, the best time to use it is still very early in the morning or in the late afternoon. The path is not lit at night.

Go-Karting

Karting International Cancún
every day 10am to 11pm
Km 7.5
☎*882-1246 or 882-1275*
This is a 1000m go-kart track along the highway linking Cancún City to the airport. Its little race cars can travel at speeds of 25, 80 and even 130km/h. There is bus service from Avenida Tulum, in Cancún, to the race track.

Accommodations

Cancún City is linked to the Hotel Zone by a small bridge near Playa Linda. When referring to Cancún, therefore, it is necessary to distinguish between the city itself, on the mainland, and the Hotel Zone (*Zona Hotelera*), a strip of sand about 20km long and shaped like a figure "7," which skirts round the Laguna Nichupté. From the far end of the Hotel Zone, the bus-ride to the city can take up to 45min.

Cancún boasts a number of very luxurious hotels, some ranking among the loveliest in the world. Generally speaking, a hotel in town will be less expensive than one of equal quality in the Hotel Zone. When choosing a place to stay, you have to decide if you are going to spend most of your time on the beach or would rather check out the restaurants and nightclubs downtown. As many downtown hotels provide their guests with free transportation to the beach, staying in town can be an economical and attractive option for some.

The Hotel Zone, for its part, tries to be self-sufficient by creating a somewhat unreal urban environment with its bars, restaurants and shopping centres. Many hotels in the zone also offer all-inclusive packages during the high season.

Cancún City

There are a few camping spots around Cancún, but only the Villas Juveniles youth hostel allows campers to pitch their tent within the city limits. You'll find a campground (which accommodates RVs) near the airport and another north of Cancún, on the road to Puerto Sam.

Mecoloco–Trailer Park
$
Carretera Puerto Juárez, Km 3
☎*843-0324*
Located some 150m from the beach, the Mecoloco campground welcomes RVs of all sizes as well as tents. It is laid out next to the Mayan city that became the Le Meco archaeological site. The place offers every service for both tents and RVs.

Mexico Hostel
$
⊗
Calle Palmeras no. 30
(near Av. Uxmal)
☎*887-0191*
Located about five blocks from the bus station, Mexico Hostel offers budget travellers and those travelling in groups all the services needed for a pleasant stay. The youth hostel offers the cheapest accommodations in town (*$10 per person*), and is definitely the most conveniently located accommodation in its category for travellers passing through. The hostel is divided into dorms, each of which has six beds. Guests have access to a well-equipped communal kitchen to prepare their own meals, as well as on-site Internet

Cancún

access. The hostel also features private lockers and a strongroom for luggage. Lastly, on the third floor is a lounge with chaises longue and hammocks.

Posada Lucy
$
⊗, ℜ, ≡
8 Gladiolas, SM22
☎884-3888
This establishment's 33 little rooms, with their salmon-pink walls, are quite and sheltered from the noise of the street. They offer a nice view of the ocean. Some of the rooms in the adjacent building can be rented by the month.

El Patio
$$
≡, ⊗
Av. Bonampak no. 51, corner of Calle Cereza
☎884-3500
⇄884-3540
The Le Patio hotel occupies a hacienda-style building with an interior courtyard dotted with plants and flowers. The hotel's decor is original yet elegant, the service top-notch and the rooms impeccable. Although devoid of a swimming pool or a bar, the establishment's elegance and refinement set a peaceful and contemplative mood. A small dining hall, a games room and a library round out this oasis of tranquility.

Antillano
$$
≡, ≈, ⊗
Av. Tulum at Claveles
☎884-1532 or 884-1132
⇄884-1878
One of the oldest downtown hotels, the Antillano

has 48 pretty, comfortable rooms with wooden furniture and ceramic-tile floors. This attractively decorated and well-kept hotel also houses a bar and a boutique.

Best Western Plaza Caribe
$$
≡, ≈, ℜ
Av. Tulum, at Av. Uxmal 36
☎884-1377 or 884-1685
⇄884-6352
www.bestwestern.com
The Best Western has 140 rooms in the heart of all the downtown action and nightlife, as well as a small but very pretty L-shaped pool. The Tulum cinema, the bus station and the Comercial Mexicana market are all near by.

Howard Johnson Kokai Cancún
$$
≡, ≈, ⊛, ℜ, ⊗
Av. Uxmal 26, SM2A
☎884-3218
⇄848-4335
www.hotelkokai.com
The 48 rooms here are relatively small but comfortable and well-equipped. The hotel also has a restaurant that specializes in Mexican cuisine. Guests are offered free transportation to the beaches in the Hotel Zone.

María de Lourdes
$$
≡, ≈, ℜ
Av. Yaxchilán 80
☎884-4744
⇄884-1242
www.hotelmariadelourdes.com
María de Lourdes is a charming, 50-room hotel located in the heart of the

downtown action. The pool is small but quite pretty. A souvenir shop, laundromat and travel agency are all located on the premises.

Holiday Inn Centro Cancún
$$$$
≡, ≈, ⊗, ⊘, ℜ
Av. Nader 1
☎887-4455
⇄884-7954
In the heart of downtown Cancún, the Holiday Inn offers guests free transportation to the beach of the Avalon hotel. The hotel has a pretty, palm-tree shaded inner courtyard with a pool and a bar-restaurant, and its colonial atmosphere is very pleasant. In addition to a small grocery store, a pharmacy, a beauty salon and a travel agency, the hotel offers a variety of services for businesspeople.

Blue Bay Club and Marina
$$$$$ all incl.
≡, ⊗, ≈, ⊘, ℜ
Carretera Punta Sam, Km 1.5
☎881-7900
This hotel, on the road leading to Punta Sam, about 13km north of Cancún City, is affiliated with the Blue Bay Village, located in the Hotel Zone. This five-storey hotel has 202 rooms with a colonial decor. During the day, guests can enjoy all sorts of water sports, and at night Latin music fills the air at the nightclub. It is very easy to get to and from Cancún from here.

Hotel Zone

Villas Juveniles
$
⊗, ℜ
Paseo Kukulcán, Km 3
☎*849-4360*
Visitors on a tight budget can find refuge at this youth hostel, which has 300 beds in separate men's and women's dormitories. On Playa Juventud beach (see p 66), guests can play basketball and volleyball. It is also possible to camp here.

Aristos Cancún Plaza Hotel
$$
≡, ⊗, ≈, ℜ
Paseo Kukulcán, Km 20.5
☎*885-3333 or 800-359-4827* ⇄*885-0236*
www.aristoshotels.com
This establishment, which faces onto Playa Chacmool, is located right near the Centro de Convenciones and the shopping centres in this part of the Hotel Zone. It has 300 attractively decorated rooms on four floors; some offer a lovely view of the sea. Hotel amenities include two tennis courts; a swimming pool surrounded by palm trees and equipped with a slide; a gift shop and a small pharmacy, as well as a variety of services, such as car- and motorcycle-rentals.

Barcelo Club Las Perlas
$$
≡, ≈, ℜ, ⊗
Paseo Kukulcán, Km 2.5
☎*848-9100 or 848-9111*
www.clublasperlas.com
Club Las Perlas is located right near downtown

Cancún, at the beginning of the hotel strip, and is flanked on two sides by the Playa Las Perlas. The hotel has 194 rooms, each with a balcony; two tennis courts and two swimming pools with slides.

Carisa Y Palma
$$$
≡, ≈, ⌂, ⊘, ⊗
Paseo Kukulcán, Km 10
☎*883-0211*
⇄*883-0932*
www.carisaypalma.com
This property, built in the 1970s, has 90 rooms in two adjacent buildings. It is located near the Mini Tienda flea market and the Centro de Convenciones. Very well maintained, it has hardly aged at all. The rooms are charming, and ensuring everyone's comfort is clearly a top priority. Guests here can use the beach of the neighbouring hotels a few metres over, since the shore in front of the Carisa Y Palma is covered with big rocks.

Costa Real Hotel and Suites
$$$
≡, ≈, ℜ, ⊗, ⊘
Paseo Kukulcán, Km 4.5
☎*881-1300 or 883-3966*
⇄*883-3945*
Not all of the 316 rooms here have a sea view, but the hotel's outstanding location makes up for this minor drawback. Built near a landing stage, where boats pick up passengers throughout the day for excursions to Isla Mujeres, the Costa Real is a lovely hotel comprising seven pink buildings of varying shapes and heights. Babysitting and laundry services are available for a small extra fee. All sorts of so-

cial, artistic and water activities are organized for hotel guests.

Girasol
$$$
≈, K, ℜ, ⊗
Paseo Kukulcán, Km 9.5
☎*883-2066*
⇄*883-2246*
The Girasol, located right next to the Carisa Y Palma, was recently renovated. The restaurant at this "condo-hotel," located right next to the pool, offers several Yucatec specialties, and also serves as a bar. The rooms, spread over eight floors, all have private balconies.

Suites Brisas
$$$
≡, ≈, ℜ, K, ⊗
Paseo Kukulcán, Km 19.5
☎*885-0302*
⇄*885-2720*
www.suitesbrisas.com
This hotel numbers 105 suites, each with a living-room/dining-room area and one bedroom. Though hardly extraordinary, they are nonetheless comfortable. The bathrooms have a shower but no bathtub. Hotel amenities include a restaurant, a swimming pool with a wading pool and a small grocery store.

Tucancún Beach Resort and Villas
$$$
≡, ≈, K, ℜ, ⊘, ⊗
Paseo Kukulcán, Km 13
☎*885-0814 or 885-1816*
⇄*885-1850*
www.tucancunbeach.com
The design of this six-storey earth-coloured building with white balconies is mildly reminiscent of a Mexican *pueblo* (little village). The rooms, with

Cancún

their rattan furniture and peach-coloured walls, all have private balconies and kitchenettes. Near the round swimming pool, hammocks and *palapas* add to the typically Mexican ambiance of this 315-room hotel.

Holiday Inn Express Cancún
$$$ bkfst incl.
≡, ≈, ⊗, ℜ
Paseo Pok-Ta-Pok
☎*883-2200*
⇄*883-2532*
Located near the Pok-Ta-Pok golf course, the Holiday Inn Express Cancún differs from the other hotels in that it faces onto the Laguna Nichupté. It has 119 rooms, on two floors, each with a private balcony. The building as a whole has a colonial look about it. The hotel has no restaurant, but there is a snack bar near the pool. A travel agency can also be found on the premises, and laundry service is available.

Ambiance Villas
$$$
⊗, ≈, ℜ, ≡
Paseo Kukulcán, Km 8,5
☎*883-1100*
⇄*883-1101*
www.ambiancevillas.com
Set near the lovely beach of Caracol, Ambiance Villas has 150 accommodation units with standard rooms, or one-to-four bedroom suites. The beach is amongst the widest of the hotels around.

Plaza Las Glorias
$$$
≡, ≈, ℜ, K, ⊗
Paseo Kukulcán, Km 3.5
☎*883-0811*
⇄*883-0901*
Located near pretty Playa Caracol, the Plaza Las Glorias has two modern buildings set face to face, and is located near downtown Cancún. Some of the 140 simply decorated rooms have a kitchenette. This little hotel has a travel and car-rental agency, a small market and equipment for all sorts of water sports, making it a convenient place to stay.

Miramar Misión Cancún Park Plaza
$$$
≡, ≈, ℜ, ⊗
Paseo Kukulcán, Km 9.5
☎*883-1755*
⇄*883-1136*
All the 226 rooms at this hotel have private balconies with a view of either the sea or the lagoon. Though their decor is a bit outdated, they are fairly spacious and comfortable in a simple way. Two square pools, set side by side, face the lovely Playa Chacmool. Other amenities include five restaurants and bars (among them the Batacha, which features tropical music), a beauty salon with massage services, a shop and various other facilities.

Dos Playas
$$$
≡, ≈, ℜ, ⊗
Paseo Kukulcán, Km 6.5
☎*849-4920*
⇄*849-4921*
www.dosplayas.com
Located next to Fat Tuesday Marina, Dos Playas has three small buildings with a total of 108 rooms. Though the place looks a bit gloomy from the outside, the entrance is charming. The atmosphere is pleasant, particularly near the beach, where lots of catamarans and sailboats liven up the landscape. The hotel is equipped with two tennis courts and a pretty round pool. Some of the studios have closed rooms.

Solymar
$$$
≡, ≈, ℜ, ⊗
Paseo Kukulcán, Km 18.7
☎*885-1811*
⇄*885-1689*
www.solymarcancun.com
Near the El Rey Mayan remains on Delfines beach, the Sol Y Mar is a 180-room, pyramidal building, decorated in traditional Mexican style. Numerous sports can be enjoyed here: scuba diving, snorkelling, waterskiing, fishing, cycling and tennis. Depending on your finances, you can also play golf at the Hilton's 18-hole course, located on the other side of Paseo Kukulcán.

Westin Regina Resort Cancún
$$$
≡, ≈, ℜ, ⊛, ⌂, ☉, ℜ, ⊗
Paseo Kukulcán, Km 20
☎*848-7400*
⇄*885-0666*
The 293 rooms here are attractively decorated and have a little area near the window where you can relax. The square-shaped pool is not very big, but the hotel has a private marina where guests can enjoy non-motorized activities at no extra charge.

Cancún
Hotel Zone
(Accommodations)

Playa Las Perlas

Playa Juventud

Playa Linda

Ciudad Cancún

Playa Langosta

Bahía de Mujeres

Paseo Kukulcán

Playa Tortugas

Playa Caracol

Punta Cancún

Playa Gaviota Azul

Laguna de Bojórquez

Playa Chacmool

See map of Punta Cancún

Ruinas Pok-Ta-Pok

Plaza Flamingo

Plaza La Isla

Caribbean Sea

Plaza Kukulcán

Playa Marlín

Laguna Nichupté

Paseo Kukulcán

See map of restaurants

Playa Ballenas

Golf Caesar Park

Playa Delfines

Canal Nizuc

Airport, Playa del Carmen, Tulum

Punta Nizuc

©ULYSSES

| 0 | 1 | 2km |

ACCOMMODATIONS

1. Barcelo Club Las Perlas
2. Beach Palace
3. Blue Bay Getaway and Spa
4. Calinda Beach Spa Cancún
5. Cancún Palace
6. Caribbean Village
7. Casa Turquesa
8. Club Carrousel Cancún
9. Club Las Velas
10. Club Med
11. Costa Real Hotel and Suites
12. Crowne Paradise Club
13. El Pueblito Beach Cancún
14. Fiesta Americana Condesa Cancún
15. Hilton Cancún Beach and Golf Resort
16. Holiday Inn Express Cancún
17. Jack Tar Village
18. Le Méridien Cancún Resort & Spa
19. Marriott Casa Magna Cancún
20. Meliá Cancún Grand Resort
21. Meliá Turquesa
22. Mex Condominiums Cancún Plaza
23. Oasís Cancún
24. Oasís Playa
25. Plaza Las Glorias
26. Ritz-Carlton Cancún
27. Royal Solaris Caribe Hotel & Marina
28. Sheraton Cancún
29. Solymar
30. Suites Brisas
31. Sun Palace
32. Tucancún Beach Resort & Villas
33. Villas Juveniles
34. Westin Regina Resort Cancún

Mex Condominiums Cancún Plaza
$$$$

⊗, ≈, ℜ, ≡

Paseo Kukulcán, Km 20.5

☎*885-1110*

⇌*885-1175*

Permanent residents and visiting tourists share the more than 200 rooms spread through the many buildings of the Mex Condominiums Cancún Plaza. It is easy to get lost in this labrinth, where the architecture is pleasing but not complicated. The hotel has a bar and restaurant.

Jack Tar Village
$$$$

≡, ≈, ℜ, ⊗, ✪

Retorno del Rey, Lote 37 2nd

☎*885-1366*

⇌*885-1363*

There is no shortage of water activities at the Jack Tar Village, which has its own little marina. Located next to the imposing Ritz-Carlton and the Plaza Kukulcán, this hotel has eight floors of rooms (175 in all), each with a view of the ocean or the Laguna Nichupté. Amenities include four restaurants, a lounge, four bars and a spa as well as an unusual swimming pool shaped like an "8."

Krystal Cancún
$$$$

≡, ≈, ⊛, ⌂, ⊘, ℜ, ⊗

Paseo Kukulcán, Km 9.5

☎*883-1133 or 848-9800*

☎*800-231-9860*

⇌*883-1790 or 883-1922*

www.krystalcancun.com

The various brochures singing Cancún's praises often show a picture of some big, stone columns set in a semicircle. These are what you'll find surrounding the pool at the Krystal Cancún, creating a very dramatic effect. The hotel itself is a rectangular building containing 325 rooms distributed over eight floors and decorated with rattan furniture. There are no balconies, but the rooms have big windows overlooking the sea or the lagoon. Four restaurants, four bars and two tennis courts surround the pool. The beach, however, is not very big.

Oasis Cancún
$$$$

≡, ≈, ⊘, ℜ, ⊗

Paseo Kukulcán, Km 17

☎*885-0867*

⇌*885-1210*

www.oasishotels.com

This is one of the biggest hotels in Cancún with 1024 rooms housed in four pyramids, each of which is either four or five stories high. Located near the El Rey and San Miguelito Maya sites, this huge complex covers more than 14ha. The renovated rooms all have stone-tile floors and a balcony. The enormous swimming pool is surrounded by palm trees and equipped with three bars. Other amenities include several restaurants and bars, a large nightclub, two tennis courts, a nine-hole golf course and a fully equipped gym.

Sierra Cancún
$$$$ all incl.

≡, ≈, ℜ, ⊗, ⌂

Paseo Kukulcán, Km 10

☎*883-2444 or 883-3655*

⇌*883-3486*

This 260-room hotel boasts quite an unusual site. The Laguna Nichupté breaks the string of hotels at this point, so the Sierra is surrounded by water, with Playa Chacmool and its heavy surf on one side and the calm lagoon on the other. The hotel has tennis courts, several shops and its own little marina.

Royal Sunset Club
$$$$ all incl.

≡, ≈, ⊛, ℝ, ℜ, K, ⊗

Paseo Kukulcán, Km 10

☎*881-4500*

⇌*881-4694*

Not far from the Plaza Caracol, nestled in the bend of the Hotel Zone, is the Royal Sunset Cancún, which has 204 modern rooms, most with kitchenettes. The rooms are decorated in pastel colours and have large windows looking out onto the lagoon or the ocean. There are about twenty *palapas* on the beach to protect guests from the harsh rays of the sun.

Meliá Turquesa
$$$$

≡, ≈, ℝ, ℜ, ⊗

Paseo Kukulcán, Km 12

☎*881-2500*

⇌*881-2622*

www.meliaturquesa.solmelia.com

This pyramidal, white building, is located near Planet Hollywood and the Plaza Flamingo. All of its 450 rooms have a private terrace decked with plants. The hotel has a café, two restaurants, three bars, two tennis courts and a large pool. Evenings are often enhanced by live music.

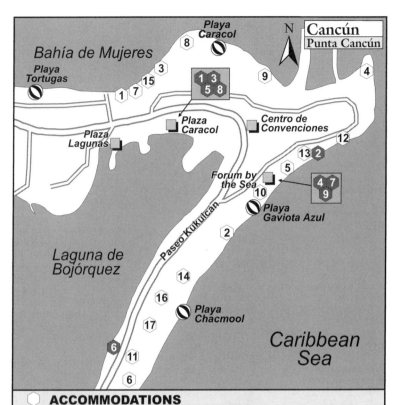

ACCOMMODATIONS

1. Ambiance Villas
2. Aristos Cancún Plaza Hotel
3. Calinda Viva
4. Camino Real Cancún
5. Carisa Y Palma
6. Continental Plaza Cancún
7. Dos Playas
8. Fiesta Americana Cancún
9. Fiesta Americana Gran Coral Beach
10. Girasol
11. Hyatt Cancún Caribe Villas & Resort
12. Hyatt Regency Cancún
13. Krystal Cancún
14. Miramar Misión
15. Presidente Inter-Continental Cancún
16. Royal Sunset Club
17. Sierra Cancún

RESTAURANTS

1. Bellini
2. Bogart's
3. Casa Rolandi
4. Hard Rock Café
5. La Fisheria
6. Lorenzillo's
7. Rainforest Cafe
8. Savio's
9. Suchi Itto

0   500   1000m

Casa Maya
$$$$
≡, ≈, *K*, ⊛, ℜ, ⊗, ℝ
Paseo Kukulcán, Km 5.5
☎*883-0555*
⇌*883-1822*
www.casamaya.com
At the Playa Langosta (see p 66), the modern and well-equipped rooms look out onto the Caribbean Sea. Here you'll find Internet access, a supermarket, a tennis court, an outdoor playground for children, a restaurant and two snack bars. A 3m-high replica of the temple at Chichén Itzá greets guests at the hotel entrance.

Calinda Beach Spa Cancún
$$$$ all incl.
≡, ≈, ℜ, ☉, ⊗
Paseo Kukulcán, Km 4.6
☎*849-4510*
⇌*849-4506*
Cylindrical in shape, The Calinda Beach Spa Cancún bears no small resemblance to the Hilton, located at Km 17. There is another building adjacent to the pyramid, bringing the total number of rooms to 470, each with a view of the ocean or the Laguna Nichupté. This hotel spares no expense on activities and entertainment, offering its guests a marina, two tennis courts lined with palm trees, live music every night and festivities as often as possible. The Calinda Beach also has two restaurants and three bars.

Calinda Viva
$$$$
≡, ≈, ℜ, ⊗
Paseo Kukulcán, Km 8.5
☎*883-0800 or 883-0019*
⇌*883-2087*
The Calinda Viva is opposite the Plaza Caracol. It has 210 rooms and two large suites, all with a view of the sea, which is fairly calm in this area. There are a number of adjoining rooms. Both travel and car-rental agency are located on the premises, and a babysitting service and children's activities are available for a small additional charge.

Oasis Playa
$$$$
≡, ≈, ℝ, ℜ, ☉, ⊗
Paseo Kukulcán, Km 19.5
☎*891-5000*
⇌*885-1076*
www.oasishotels.com
The Oasis Playa has 388 modern, functional rooms with a view of the sea or the Laguna Nichupté. The building is shaped like a pyramid and laid out around a large *L*-shaped pool fringed with palm trees. The hotel has three restaurants and four bars.

Club Carrousel Cancún
$$$$ all incl.
≡, ≈, ℝ, *K*, ⊛, ☉, ℜ, ⊗
Paseo Kukulcán, D-6, km 3.5
☎*883-0513*
⇌*883-2312*
Just a few kilometres from downtown Cancún, the Carrousel Cancún faces onto Playa Linda, not far from the landing stage. This hotel has 158 rooms distributed among just three floors. Shaped like a *C*, it wraps around a tennis court and a big pool. Its large, peaceful beach lies nestled in the curve of the Bahía de Mujeres. The hotel organizes a variety of water activities every day and presents shows in the evening.

🚢 Casa Turquesa
$$$$
≡, ≈, ℝ, ⊛, ℜ, ☉, ⊗
Paseo Kukulcán, Km 13.5
☎*885-2924 or 885-2925*
⇌*885-2922*
www.casaturquesa.com
Reminiscent of the luxurious haciendas of the previous century, the Casa Turquesa is a small pink and white hotel with 33 lavishly appointed suites, each with a king-size bed, a whirlpool bath and a private balcony. In front of the hotel, at the foot of a long flight of stairs and almost right in the sea, is a large pool surrounded by tents and palm trees. The Casa Turquesa is a member of the Small Luxury Hotels of the World association. The service is first-rate.

Presidente Inter-Continental Cancún
$$$$
≡, ≈, ⊛, ☉, ℜ, ⊗
Paseo Kukulcán, Km 7.5
☎*848-8700*
⇌*883-0414*
www.cancun.inter continental.com
This hotel has 300 huge rooms that combine Mexican decor with modern comfort. One of the oldest hotels in Cancún, the Presidente was renovated and redecorated in 1988. Guests can enjoy all sorts of watersports here. The hotel also has a beauty salon, two swimming pools, several shops, two restaurants, a bar and a tennis court.

🛥 Fiesta Americana Cancún

$$$$

≡, ≈, ℜ, ⊗

Paseo Kukulcán, Km 9

☎*881-1400*

⇄*881-1409*

Along with the Camino Real and the Presidente, the Fiesta Americana was one of the original hotels in Cancún. With its four attractively laid-out, peach-coloured buildings, it resembles a Mexican village, an effect heightened by the inner court, where a restaurant with a thatched roof is surrounded by a big, round pool and scores of palm trees.

🛥 Ritz-Carlton Cancún

$$$$

≡, ≈, ⊛, △, ☺, ℜ, ☼, ⊗

Paseo Kukulcán, Retorno del Rey 36

☎*881-0808*

⇄*881-0815*

www.ritzcarlton.com

Like all hotels in this chain, the Ritz-Carlton Cancún is very elegant. It is located just a short distance from the Plaza Kukulcán, slightly elevated from the Paseo Kukulcán. A glimpse of the reveals all you need to know about this hotel. Richly decorated with a marble floor it offers a foretaste of the 365 rooms, which are both beautiful and very comfortable. Everything discretely evokes the architecture and ambiance of a lavish Mexican home. The Ritz-Carlton boasts one of the finest restaurants in Cancún, the **Club Grill** (see p 86), as well as an Italian restaurant, a Mexican-American restaurant and a restaurant near the pool. There is also a spa, a beauty salon, three tennis courts and a number of shops.

Caribbean Village

$$$$$ all incl.

ℜ, ⊛, ≈, ☺, ≡

Paseo Kukulcán, Lote 18

☎*885-0112*

⇄*885-0999*

Two steps away from the Plaza Kukulcán, the aptly named Caribbean Village is an all-inclusive resort which offers everything so that visitors never have to leave the hotel. When seen from the sky, this hotel complex forms a Y. Myriad activities are offered to the clientele, who are mostly young Americans seeking fun under the hot Mexican sun. All kinds of sports activities are organized around the pool, and there is a wide range of water-sports opportunities. Lavish buffets are offered for breakfast, lunch and dinner. Four restaurants (Mexican, Continental, Brazilian and Italian), a snack-bar, four bars and a nightclub are reserved exclusively for guests of the hotel. There are also a car-rental service and travel agency on site.

🛥 El Pueblito Beach Cancún

$$$$

≡, ≈, ℜ, ⊗

Paseo Kukulcán, Km 17.5

☎*881-8800*

⇄*885-0731*

www.pueblitohotels.com

As indicated by its name, El Pueblito is a little village made up of five pink and white buildings set on a gently sloping hillside. On one side, the water from a fountain flows from the top of the property down to the swimming pool, and on the other, five small pools of varying depths follow one after the other down a hill toward a round restaurant with a thatched roof. The 250 comfortable rooms all have a Mexican decor and a private balcony.

Blue Bay Getaway and Spa Cancún

$$$$$

Adults only

≡, ≈, ℜ, ☺, ☼, ⊗

Paseo Kukulcán, Km 3.5

☎*848-7900*

⇄*848-7994*

www.bluebayresorts.com

This property has 383 rooms divided among several two- and three-storey buildings facing onto the sea or the garden. The decor of the rooms is simple but decent. The hotel has five restaurants, six bars and a small souvenir shop. Other services include scuba and Spanish lessons. Evening entertainment includes gambling, Mexican dance shows and competitions.

Beach Palace

$$$$$

≡, ≈, ⊛, ☺, ℜ, ☼, ⊗

Paseo Kukulcán, Km 11.5

☎*891-4110*

www.palaceresorts.com

This hotel has 205 rooms decorated in traditional Mexican style. The bar, covered with a thatched roof, rises from the middle of the pool. Amenities include three restaurants, a bar, laundry service, a tennis court and a small gift and craft shop. The Yamil Lu'um remains are nearby.

Cancún

Club Las Velas
$$$$$
≡, ≈, ℜ, ⊗
Paseo Kukulcán, Km 3.5
☎*891-4080*
≓*849-4575*
Attractively located on the Laguna de Nichupté, Club Las Velas looks like a small colonial town. As you stroll by the little houses scattered here and there, you will feel as if you are in a village, an impression heightened by the fountains, squares and flower-filled gardens. Each of the 285 rooms has a bar, a television and a telephone. The hotel also has two swimming pools, two restaurants and two bars and organizes a number of activities, including windsurfing, volleyball, tennis and scuba diving.

Continental Plaza Cancún
$$$$$ all incl.
≡, ≈, ℜ, ⊗
Paseo Kukulcán, Km 10
☎*881-5500*
≓*881-5697*
You will find few hotels in Cancún that offer as many services and activities as the Continental Plaza Cancún, which has 638 rooms, each with a balcony overlooking the sea or the lagoon. The hotel, a grouping of two- and three-storey buildings, has five restaurants, two bars, two shops, a tennis court, a travel agency and a car-rental agency.

Crowne Paradise Club
$$$$$
≡, ≈, ℜ, ⊗, ☺, △
Paseo Kukulcán, Km 18.5
☎*848-9000*
≓*885-1707*
When seen from above, this hotel is shaped much like the Hotel Zone itself,

in the form of a number 7. All of the 616 rooms have an ocean view and private balconies. Amenities include four restaurants, four swimming pools, one of which is covered, a beauty salon and four bars with live music in the evening. The hotel also offers children's activities.

Camino Real Cancún
$$$$$
≡, ≈, ℝ, ℜ, ☺, △, ✿, ⊗
Paseo Kukulcán, Km 8.5
☎*848-7000*
≓*883-1730*
www.caminoreal.com
The Camino Real at Punta Cancún was one of the first hotels built in Cancún. It boasts the best site possible, in the bend of the Hotel Zone, with a view of the ocean on both sides. It is also located right near the area's commercial and nighttime activity. It has 381 rooms with Mexican decor, four restaurants, three bars, a beauty salon, a pool surrounded by stone towers and three tennis courts. A shop and a car-rental agency/tour operator can also be found on the premises.

Club Med
$$$$$ all incl.
Adults only
≡, ≈, ℜ, ☺
Punta Nizuc
☎*881-8200*
≓*881-8280*
www.clubmed.com
Club Med is somewhat isolated from the other hotels in the zone. First, it is located at the southern tip of the string of hotels, and second, it is a good distance from Paseo

Kukulcán. It is made up of small, two- and three-storey buildings decorated, like the 426 rooms they contain, in traditional Mexican style. Like all Club Meds, this is a fantastic place to enjoy a variety of sports, including scuba diving, waterskiing, tennis and golf. There are also two restaurants and a nightclub with a terrace facing onto the beach, where the atmosphere really livens up come evening, thanks in part to the famous G.O.'s. Club Med is designed to meet the needs of couples as well as single travellers. It takes about 45min to get downtown by bus and about 30min to reach the Hotel Zone.

Fiesta Americana Condesa Cancún
$$$$$
≡, ≈, ⊛, ☺, ℜ, ⊗
Paseo Kukulcán, Km 16.5
☎*881-4200*
≓*885-2005*
One of the newest hotels in the Fiesta Americana chain is the Condesa Cancún, which resembles a beehive. It has two pueblo-style buildings containing a total of 502 rooms and suites. Upon entering, you will be struck by the luxurious lobby, with its marble floor and imposing paintings. The meandering curves of the vast swimming pool are bordered by *palapas*. The hotel has three restaurants, three bars and three covered tennis courts. The beach isn't very big, but there's plenty of room to lie in the sun.

Hyatt Regency Cancún
$$$$$
≡, ⊗, ≈, ℝ, ⊘, ℜ, △
Paseo Kukulcán, Km 8.5
☎ *883-1234*
⇄ *883-1349*
www.cancun.regency.hyatt.com

Located in the middle of the Hotel Zone, between the Camino Real and the Krystal, the Hyatt is a 14-storey building topped by a glass atrium. Its 130 renovated rooms all have wall-to-wall carpeting, rattan furniture and a balcony with a view of the sea. The hotel also has three restaurants, three bars, two swimming pools, a tennis court, a travel agency, a beauty salon and a number of shops.

🚢 Le Méridien Cancún Resort & Spa
$$$$$
ℜ, ⊛, ≈, ⊘, ✿
Retorno del Rey, Km 14
☎ *881-2220*
⇄ *881-2201*
www.lemeridien.com

This new hotel in Cancún's Hotel Zone belongs to the internationally renowned French hotel chain of the same name. Le Méridien stands out among the plethora of hotels in Cancún that cater to the most demanding clients. The smiling staff are always there to serve you, and their courtesy is so exemplary that they could be used as a model in international hotel management. The spacious rooms have a lovely view of the ocean and are decorated in the most discrete elegance possible. The Méridien features a top-notch restaurant, Aïoli (see p 84), as well as an amazing pool with three

different levels, each of which is set at a different temperature.

Hyatt Cancún Caribe Villas & Resort
$$$$$
≡, ⊘, ℜ, ≡, ⊗
Paseo Kukulcán, Km 10.5
☎ *848-7800*
⇄ *883-2715*
www.cancuncaribe.resort.hyatt. com

Two stone jaguars greet guests at the entrance of the Hyatt, a curved building with 226 rooms, each with a magnificent view, a private balcony and a huge bathroom. The elegant lobby is decorated with a judicious blend of pink marble, palm trees, works of art and replicas of pre-Hispanic stone sculptures. There are several shops on the premises, as well as the Cocay Cafe restaurant, which serves theme buffets, the Creole restaurant Blue Bayou, three tennis courts, three pools, a travel agency and a beauty salon.

Sheraton Cancún
$$$$$
≡, ≈, ℝ, ⊛, △, ⊘, ℜ, ⊗
Paseo Kukulcán, Km 12.5
☎ *891-4400*
⇄ *883-1450*

The Sheraton is situated near the Plaza Kukulcán and right next to the Yamil Lu'um remains. The resort features two buildings with 471 rooms in total. Amenities include a miniature-golf course, a garden with hammocks, a basketball court, four tennis courts and a large swimming pool shaped like a number 8. The hotel takes up nearly a kilometre of beach-front property.

🚢 Hilton Cancún Beach and Golf Resort
$$$$$
≡, ≈, ℝ, ⊘, ℜ, ⊗
Paseo Kukulcán, Km 17
☎ *881-8000*
⇄ *881-8080*
www.hiltoncancun.com

This resort slightly resembles the pyramid at Chichén Itzá. One of the loveliest and most expensive hotels in Cancún, it has 426 rooms, six restaurants, two outdoor whirlpool baths, a watersports centre and two tennis courts, which are lit at night. All the rooms offer ocean views, and include voice-mail service and a clock-radio. Guests also enjoy access to the Caesar Park golf club, on the other side of the Paseo Kukulcán, near to the remains of a Mayan temple.

Cancún Palace
$$$$$
≡, ≈, ℝ, △, ⊘, ℜ, ⊗
Paseo Kukulcán, Km 14.5
☎ *881-3600*
⇄ *881-3601*
www.cancunpalace.com

A combination hotel/timeshare condominium, the 560-room Cancún Palace offers numerous amenities, including car-rentals, a babysitting service, a souvenir shop, an exercise room, a sauna, four restaurants, three bars and two tennis courts. The beach is fairly small but well laid-out, and the view of the Caribbean is magnificent.

Cancún

Fiesta Americana Gran Coral Beach Cancún
$$$$

≡, ≈, ⊛, ☉, ℜ, ✿, ℝ, ⊗
Paseo Kukulcán, Km 9.5
☎881-3200
⇌881-3284
This establishment, located near the Centro de Convenciones and the Plaza Caracol shopping centre, has been ranked one of the 100 best hotels in the world by *Condé Nast Traveler* magazine. The lobby is adorned with big palm trees and opens onto the Bahía de Mujeres. The 602 suites, divided between two peach-coloured buildings, are attractively decorated in pastel hues and offer a view of the ocean. The hotel has five restaurants, five bars and three tennis courts. The large and very elegant swimming pool is surrounded by *palapas* and palm trees, and the numerous specialized shops and daily activities program (volleyball, windsurfing and exercise classes) guarantee a delightful stay.

Marriott Casa Magna Cancún
$$$$$

≡, ⊗, ≈, ℝ, ☉, ℜ, △
Paseo Kukulcán, Km 14.5
☎885-2000 or 881-2003
⇌881-2052
www.marriott.com
The Marriott, on Playa Ballenas, is a big, modern, six-storey, white and beige building. The Mediterranean look of this hotel is accentuated by vaults and domes. The 452 rooms and suites all have a private balcony and are decorated with tropical motifs in pastel colours. Waterfalls lend a delightful atmosphere to the swimming

pools, which are surrounded by four restaurants and bars. The hotel also has several tennis courts and offers a full program of activities for kids (diving, tennis, marina, etc.).

Meliá Cancún Grand Resort
$$$$$

≡, ≈, ℝ, ☉, ℜ, ✿, ⊗
Paseo Kukulcán, Km 16.5
☎881-1100
⇌881-1740
www.grandmeliacancun.com
The glass roof of the Meliá Cancún, the Spanish chain's first Mexican hotel, looks a bit like the Louvre pyramid. This big glass and concrete building has 794 medium-sized rooms, each with a large balcony. Its vast inner court is literally overrun with vegetation. Amenities include a golf course, one pool with a "swim-up" bar, and another whose sloping edge imitates the seashore, as well as a tennis court, five restaurants, four bars and a spa.

Royal Solaris Caribe Hotel & Marina
$$$$$

≡, ≈, ⊛, ☉, ℜ, ⊗
Paseo Kukulcán, Km 20.5
☎848-8401
⇌848-8402
www.clubsolaris.com
This large, 500-room hotel, consists of one main building surrounded by several annexes. Facing onto Playa Delfines, it stands right near the **Ruinas Del Rey** (see p 65). A daily water sports program and a nightclub with live Latin music make for a very lively atmosphere.

Sun Palace
$$$$$

≡, ≈, ⊛, △, ☉, ℜ, ⊗
Paseo Kukulcán, Km 20
☎891-4100
⇌891-4109
On the beach at the Sun Palace, the hotel managers bustle about making sure that nobody is bored! Guests can go kayaking, sailing, water-skiing or pedal-boating, and play volleyball, to name just a few of the possibilities. The yellow, seven-storey building contains 227 bright modern rooms, 19 suites and a small craft and gift shop. There are also several tennis courts on the premises, and a big whirlpool bath (large enough for 40 people) with a fountain in the middle.

Restaurants

Cancún City

Bakery-Pastry shop
$

Behind the shopping centre Lote 33, local 10 SM 2, Av. Tulum
☎880-7319
Good for a quick and simple bite to eat, this small bakery opens as early as 5am to serve fresh chocolate or almond croissants, baguettes or rolls. There are no seats, but a small park diagonally across the street makes a great spot to stop and eat.

RESTAURANTS

1.	100% Natural	5.	Pericos
2.	Bakery-Pastry shop	6.	Rolandi's Pizzeria
3.	La Habichuela	7.	Ty-Coz Baguettería
4.	La Parilla		

 **Ty-Coz Baguetteria**
$-$$
Right next to the Bakery
Right behind the shopping
centre, the Ty-Coz
Baguetteria recalls a
charming little French
bistro, and so does its
menu which offers all the
classics including ham-and-
cheese croissants or ba-
guettes, espresso and
capuccino. European signs
are plastered all over the
walls, and even the sign for
the bathroom says *toilette*
instead of *baños*. Friendly

service, and excellent
value for the money.

 **Los Almendros**
$-$$
11am to 10pm
Av. Bonampak corner Av. Sayil
☎887-1332 or 884-0942
This is a truly appealing
little restaurant that serves
Yucatec specialties like
sopa de lima and chicken
or pork cooked in banana
leaves (*pollo pibil* or
cochinita pibil). The *Paco
en Salsa de Alcaparras*
consists of thick slices of

turkey in a sauce made of
capers, olives, grapes and
tomatoes. The specialty of
the house is *Poc Chuc*,
pork marinated in the juice
of bitter oranges then
grilled and served with
black beans.

 **100% Natural**
$-$$$
Av. Sunyaxchén No.63
☎884-3617 or 884-0102
Here, as at this restaurant's
counterpart in the Hotel
Zone, freshness and a
smile are the order of the

Cancún

day. You'll find mountains of fresh fruits, a variety of delicious and nutritious juices and simple, mouth-watering vegetarian dishes, as well as chicken and seafood.

Pericos
$-$$$
Av. Yaxchilan
☎884-3152
This Mexican restaurant is easy to spot thanks to the old cart atop its thatched roof. The decor is wild and crazy with strange murals, life-sized papier-maché skeletons playing cards at a table with a bottle of tequila, saddles on the barstools, designer chairs, hats on the ceiling and old black-and-white photographs on the walls. Even the bathrooms are specially decorated with distorting mirrors—the ones in the ladies room will please those who would prefer a more slender, sylphlike silhouette, while those in the men's room will make you appear shorter or taller depending on how much you've had to drink.

Rolandi's Pizzeria
$$-$$$
Av. Cobá 12
☎884-4047
This pizzeria belongs to the same owner as the Casa Rolandi (see p 86). Though the pizzas cooked in the wood-burning oven get top billing here, steak and seafood dishes also figure on the menu. This restaurant, open since 1978, has a simple, fun and colourful decor. Delivery available.

La Habichuela
$$-$$$$
Calle Margarita, facing Las Palapas park, downtown
☎884-3158 or 887-1716
This restaurant specializes in the tropical cuisine of the Caribbean, with seafood dishes figuring prominently on the menu. A big mural, abundant greenery and numerous Mayan sculptures make for a lavish, relaxing ambiance. The specialty of the house is *cocobichuela*, shrimp and lobster in curry sauce, served in a half-coconut. In the evening, guests dine to the sounds of gentle jazz.

La Parilla
$$-$$$$
Av. Yaxchilán 51, near Av. Cobá
☎884-5398
Seafood, Yucatec specialties and steak share the extensive menu at Parilla. This Cancún institution, open since 1975, is popular with tourists and locals alike, a testimony to the authenticity of its cuisine. This is also *the* place to discover the various facets of tequila, the national drink, as the menu lists an extensive selection.

Hotel Zone

Bellini
$-$$
Plaza Caracol, 2nd floor
☎883-0459
Bellini is a small, modern café that serves simple dishes such as club sandwiches, pesto spaghetti and homemade cakes. This is just the place for those missing the flavours of home.

Sushi Itto
$-$$
Plaza Forum, by the sea
☎883-4602
For something a little lighter than quesadillas and tacos, try this Japanese restaurant, which prepares all the classics of this country: sushis, tempuras, teriyakis.

100% Natural
$-$$$
Av. Plaza Kukulcán, Km 8.3
☎883-1180 or 885-2904
Fresh, healthy food and a smile are guaranteed at 100% Natural, where mountains of fresh fruit, a variety of energy-boosting juices, simple but scrumptious vegetarian dishes, as well as chicken and seafood, are served. The restaurant also has a small terrasse good for watching passersby on Paseo Kukulcán.

Ok Maguey
$-$$$
Kukulcán Plaza, Km 13.5
☎885-0503
Ok Maguey has a lively and casual atmosphere made even livelier when the mariachis seranade patrons under dark, starry skies. The interior decor looks like a colonial village and the staff are dressed in traditional Mexican dress. The menu is typically Mexican and fairly consistent: *sopa de Lima*, guacamole, quesadillas and other Mexican specialties.

Pat O'Brien's
$-$$$
Flamingo Plaza, Km 11.5
☎883-0418
This is a seaside open-air bar-restaurant that serves decent meals that may not offer any culinary surprises,

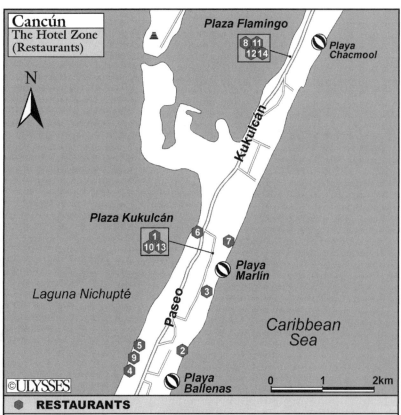

Cancún
The Hotel Zone
(Restaurants)

N

Plaza Flamingo

8 11
12 14

Playa
Chacmool

Kukulcán

Plaza Kukulcán

1
10 13

6

7

Playa
Marlín

Laguna Nichupté

3

Paseo

Caribbean
Sea

5
9
4

2

Playa
Ballenas

0   1   2km

©ULYSSES

RESTAURANTS

1. 100% Natural
2. Aïoli
3. Celebrity's
4. Dolce Vita
5. Faro's

6. La Destillería
7. La Mesa del Capitán
8. Los Rancheros
9. Mango Tango
10. Ok Maguey

11. Outback Steak House
12. Pat O'Brien's
13. Planet Hollywood
14. Sanborns

but are priced to stay within your budget. There is a breakfast buffet for $7, and a *table-d'hôte* breakfast for $10. The place livens up when the sun goes down and a waterfall is lit up by a huge, flickering flame. Things really get going after 9pm when a band starts to play and the dance floor fills up. From then on, the food plays second fiddle to the atmosphere. The bar serves great New Orleans–style Hurricanes.

La Mesa del Capitán
$$-$$$
Blvd. Kukulcán, Km 13.5
☎885-1755
La Mesa del Capitan is part of the Misión Miramar Hotel and is located two steps away from the Ok Maguey restaurant. However, it is more upscale than its neighbour. The menu offers Mexican and international cuisine: filet mignon, chicken supreme, filet of fish, lobster, etc. Inside, the mirrors on the walls have an enlarging

effect, while outside on the small terrasse, a pianist entertains those who prefer to dine au naturel.

Outback Steak House
$$-$$$
Plaza Flamingo
Blvd. Kukulcán, Km 11.5
☎883-3350
Meat-lovers might also want to keep this address, right next door to Pat O'Brien's (see p 82), in mind. This Aussie import is definitely a candidate for best steakhouse in

Cancún

Cancún. Fish and seafood are also on the menu and you can quench your thirst on Foster's Australian beer.

Rainforest Café
$$-$$$
Plaza Forum by the Sea, local B11

☎881-8130 or 881-8131

If you are looking for a family-style restaurant, the kids will definitely love the Rainforest Café. As its name suggests, the decor tries to recreate a tropical rainforest environment with colourful fish swimming in the giant aquarium, mechanically operated animals and rushing waterfalls. The menu lists pasta, sandwiches, chicken and salads. The souvenir shop which sells tons of merchandise with the restaurant's logo.

Sanborns
$$-$$$
Plaza Flamingo, Km 8.5

☎885-1069

The late-night diner in the Zona Hotellera, Sanborns does not serve the most creative dishes. It does, however, have its fans.

Santa Fe Beer Factory
$$-$$$
Plaza Forum by the Sea, Km 9.5

☎883-4469 or 883-4481

This restaurant shares a rear terrace with the Hard Rock Café (see p 85). This is just the spot to try one of the many home-brewed beers, look at the ocean and let the sea-breeze gently caress your face. If you are hungry, simple but salty Mexican dishes are available.

Yuppies Sports Café
$$-$$$
11am to 3am
Blvd. Kukulcán, Km 9

☎883-4300

Its name may be a little bit pompous, but this is a good place to chat with friends, have a bite to eat and watch your favourite team on the television.

La Fisheria
$$-$$$
Plaza Caracol, Km 8.5

☎883-1395

This seafood restaurant serves the famous *ceviche*, raw marinated fish in tomato sauce seasoned with onion and coriander. Main dish selections include trout amandine, octopus in *chipotle* sauce, grilled lobster and the catch of the day. The pizzas, cooked in a wood-burning oven, are also worth the trip.

🏝 Los Rancheros
$$-$$$
Plaza Flamingo, Km 11.5

☎885-2758

This restaurant, which also serves typical Mexican cuisine, has a festive atmosphere. Guests enjoy mariachi music and a folk ballet show every evening starting at 8pm.

Blue Bayou
$$-$$$
Hyatt Caribe hotel, Paseo Kukulcán, Km 10.5

☎883-0044

If you are looking for a relaxed, romantic atmosphere, the Blue Bayou will fit the bill perfectly. On the weekends you can enjoy live jazz music while dining. The menu is made up of traditional Creole and Cajun cuisine.

Dolce Vita
$$-$$$
Paseo Kukulcán, Km 14.5
Laguna Nichupté, across from the Marriott hotel

☎884-1384 or 885-0106

This fine Italian restaurant was a hit with downtown residents for over 10 years before it started attracting tourists. The terrace now looks out onto the lagoon, making it a very romantic spot for dinner. The menu features seafood and fresh pasta made right on the premises. The house specialty is a lobster and shrimp dish served on a bed of spinach pasta in a white wine sauce.

🏝 Aïoli
$$-$$$
7am to 11pm
Retorno del Rey, Km 14

☎881-2200 ext 2370
⇄881-2201

A chic restaurant in the Meridien hotel (see p 79), Aïoli is *the* place for a memorable culinary experience. The house speciality is obviously French cuisine with a Mediterranean twist. All the dishes are marvellously well-presented and prepared originally and elegantly with the freshest of ingredients. The simple but elegant decor is ideal for an intimate dinner or business lunch and is on a par with the flawless service.

Bogart's
$$-$$$$
Paseo Kukulcán, Km 9

☎883-1133

Bogart's is one of the most popular restaurants in town. The menu features classic international cuisine, and the decor is reminiscent of North Africa, or shall we say Morocco—after all, the restaurant is named after the star of the film Casablanca. Discrete, personalized service.

Faro's
$$-$$$$
Plaza Lagunas, Km 14.2
☎*885-1107*
Decorated entirely with colours and objects evocative of the sea, Faro's specializes in seafood. You will have a hard time choosing among dishes like shrimp with tequila, filets of fish *à la maya* and the generous Faro's fisherman's platter.

El Mexicano
$$-$$$$
noon to midnight
Centro Comercial La Mansión Costa Blanca, near the Plaza Caracol and the Centro de Convenciones, Km 11.5
☎*883-2220*
Musicians and dancers will entertain you while you dine at El Mexicano, a popular restaurant with tourists who like mariachi and folk-ballet shows. If you are looking for quiet, keep looking! There is lots of noise, lots of colour, lots of everything here! The culinary traditions of various parts of Mexico are represented on the menu, which is made up mainly of fish and seafood dishes and thick, juicy steaks. Caribbean shrimp (*camarones caribeños*), fresh from the local waters, are prepared in a variety of ways.

Hard Rock Café
$$-$$$$
Plaza Forum, Km 9
☎*881-8120*
Like Planet Hollywood (see further below), the Hard Rock is a world-wide institution. There is one in every big city on earth, including Cozumel. Burgers and sandwiches make up the bulk of the menu. The blaring rock music might not appeal to everyone.

La Destillería
$$-$$$$
Blvd. Kukulcán, Km 12.65
☎*885-1086*
Northwest of the Plaza Kukulcán, La Destillería, a replica of a Guadalajara tequila distillery, has a fiery orange facade. The chef uses only the freshest ingredients to concoct traditional Mexican dishes with regional influences from Campeche, Oaxaca, Puebla and, of course, the Yucatan. If you like tequila, there are over 150 kinds on the menu. There is a small terrace in back of the restaurant where you can enjoy your meal and a view of the ocean while being cooled by the seabreeze, which is the only form of ventilation. On Mondays and Wednesdays, the restaurant organizes information sessions about the process of making Mexico's national drink, followed by a tequila tasting and several Mexican dishes, all for only $5.

Planet Hollywood
$$-$$$$
Plaza Flamingo, Km 11.5
☎*885-3022*
Various stars of the big screen have opened restaurants like this one all over the world. This chain serves overpriced burgers, steaks and spare ribs, as well as Chinese and Italian food in a relaxed, even lax, atmosphere. At night (from 11pm on), the music plays full blast, and people work up a sweat on the dance floor.

Savio's
$$-$$$$
Plaza Caracol, Km 8.5
☎*883-2085*
Savio's is a two-storey restaurant located in a brightly lit building. The restaurant specializes in Northern Italian cuisine and serves such dishes as bruschetta, fettuccini primavera, Neopolitan lasagna and veal cutlets. And since the sea is right nearby, fish and seafood dishes make up a significant part of the menu.

Mango Tango
$$-$$$$
Paseo Kukulcán, Km 14.2
☎*885-0303*
Right near La Dolce Vita and the Ritz-Carlton, the Mango Tango has an extremely varied menu. Try the big Mango Tango salad (shrimp, avocado, chicken and mushrooms), the fettuccine with shrimp or the grilled fish served with slices of pineapple or banana. Reggae music and dancing are also on the menu until the wee hours.

Angus Butcher Steak House
$$$-$$$$
Blvd. Kukulcán, Km 9.5
☎*883-4301*
Great big, juicy steaks are served here. The softly playing jazz music gives this place a warm and mellow atmosphere.

Cancún

Casa Rolandi
$$$-$$$$
1pm to 11pm
Plaza Caracol, Km 8.5
☎*883-2557*

Credit for the delicious, authentic Italian cuisine at this restaurant goes to the owner and chef. All the pastas are fresh and made on the premises. The menu includes *antipasti* (appetizers), risotto, lasagna, lamb chops with thyme, pizza cooked in a wood-burning oven and every kind of pasta imaginable! The simplicity and tastefulness of the decor evoke the Mediterranean. Service is available in Spanish, English, Italian, German and French.

Hacienda El Mortero
$$$-$$$$
Paseo Kukulcán, Km 9
☎*883-1133*

This chic restaurant is an exact replica of an 18th-century *hacienda*, one of those luxurious homes owned by big landowners. This is a very popular spot, thanks to its Mexican specialties and mariachi music, so reservations are recommended.

Celebrity's
$$$-$$$$
Blvd. Kukulcán, Km 13.5
☎*885-2924*

Stars of all stripes frequent Celebrity's. The chef concocts a variety of international and local dishes, while the staff is extremely courteous. The chic and sober decor is perfect for a business lunch or an intimate dinner when the lights are dimmed and reflected in the radiant smiles of diners gazing at each other across the table.

Lorenzillo's
$$$-$$$$
noon to 11:30pm
Paseo Kukulcán, Km 10.5
☎*883-1254*

You have to go through an alley to get to this restaurant, whose thatch-covered dining room is decorated like a yacht club with life buoys, rudders and fishing nets. Lobster is the house speciality, and you can choose one fresh from the tank. Fish, meat and seafood dishes are also on the menu. This restaurant is very popular despite its high prices.

Ruth's Chris Steak House
$$$-$$$$
Plaza Kukulcán, Km 13.5
☎*885-0500*

This steakhouse is very popular with Americans for its big, juicy steaks, just like they make 'em back home. The decor is bland but the portions are enormous, and the meat is always fresh and served the way you like it. Pork ribs, marinated chicken and grilled shrimp are also offered.

Club Grill
$$$$
Paseo Kukulcán, Km 13.5
☎*885-0808*

One of the chicest and most expensive restaurants in Cancún is Club Grill, the restaurant of the Ritz-Carlton hotel. The cuisine is a sophisticated variation on the themes of French, Creole and Yucatec cuisine (try the seafood "Club-Grill"). The plush decor (beige and gold, deep chairs with armrests, round tables, fine tablecloths, elegant place settings, flowers on the tables, etc.) and professional service contribute to the restaurant's reputation.

Entertainment

Cultural Activities

Ballet Folklórico de Cancún
Tue and Sat 6:30pm
Paseo Kukulcán, Km 13
☎*883-0520*

This company puts on a show Tuesday and Saturday nights at 6:30pm at the Centro de Convenciones. A dozen or so dancers and as many singers perform traditional dances from the various Mexican states (the stag dance, the bottle dance, etc.). The show is preceded by a buffet-style Mexican meal.

Plaza de Toros
Wed 3:30pm
Av. Bonampak
☎*884-8372*

Imported from Spain, *corridas* are a tradition in Mexico. In Cancún, these bullfights are held every Wednesday at the Plaza de Toros. To entertain the audience beforehand, traditional Mexican songs and dances are performed, along with a *charrería*, a stunt which involves jumping from one galloping horse to another. The *corrida* is carried out in the purest Spanish style, with the *matador* decked out in a colourful costume.

Cinema

Several local movie theatres show popular American films; they include:

Tulum
Av. Tulum 10, SM2
☎*884-3451*

Cinemark La Isla Cancún
Paseo Kukulcán, Km 12,5
☎*883-5603 or 883-5604*

Cinepolis
Plaza Las Américas
☎*884-4055*

Bars and Nightclubs

Cancún City

Cancún's heart beats to the rhythm of the Latin, disco, dance and rock music played in its scores of crowded bars. Generally, the nightclubs are pretty empty until 11pm, but stay packed from midnight to dawn. The following is among the most popular.

Pericos
Av. Yaxchilán
☎*884-3152 or 887-4884*
☎*884-0415*
This restaurant (see p 82) is a good place to enjoy a little entertainment while dining. Patrons can have some wine and a good time listening to the musicians who take the stage in two theatres.

Hotel Zone

Azúcar
cover charge
11:30pm to 4am, closed Sun
Camino Real hotel
☎*848-7000*
One of the chicest and most pleasant places to spend the evening in Cancún is the Camino Real hotel, which often books excellent Cuban bands for an evening of boisterous salsa dancing. You can also simply have a seat, savour the music and the sophisticated decor, or take in the dazzling view of the sea. T-shirts and shorts are not appropriate attire here.

Bulldog
no cover charge Sun; ladies enter for free Tue and Thu
from 10pm on
next to the Krystal Hotel, Paseo Kukulcán
☎*848-9851*
At Bulldog, there is a different theme every night. Tuesday: wet T-shirt contest; Thursday: 1970s and 1980s music; Friday: male beauty contest. The place is aiming at a certain level of sophistication, and shorts and jeans are not allowed, though long bermuda shorts are tolerated.

Dady'O
cover charge
from 10pm on
Paseo Kukulcán, Km 9.5
at the Plaza Caracol
☎*883-3333*
Big stucco walls lend this nightclub a distinctive look. The spacious dance floor and laser-light show make it a very popular spot. The evening gets off to a mellow start with jazz around

9pm, then the beat picks up at just the right pace, with all types of music getting their due, the culmination being house music. This bar seems to attract a very young crowd. There is also a small restaurant (*$*) in case you get hungry.

Dady Rock
from 8pm on
Paseo Kukulcán, Km 9.5
☎*883-1626*
This nightclub is located right near its big brother, the Dady'O. It is both a restaurant and a bar where rock bands entertain a young crowd from 11pm onward.

La Boom
cover charge
Paseo Kukulcán, Km 3.5
☎*849-7587*
This nightclub has very elaborate sound and lighting effects, making it a popular dance club. There are different contests every night, and numerous video screens liven up the atmosphere.

Hard Rock Café
every day 11am to 2am
Plaza Forum, Paseo Kukulcán
☎*881-8120*
The huge dance floor of the Hard Rock Café attracts fans of classic rock. Live bands often perform around 11pm.

Planet Hollywood
11am to 1am
Plaza Flamingo, Paseo Kukulcán, Km 11.5
☎*883-0527*
This is a combination restaurant, bar and store, popular for its Hollywood atmosphere: patrons are swept up by the soundtracks of films like *Gone*

with the Wind, and cinematic hits from Hollywood's golden age are shown on four giant screens.

Señor Frog's

Paseo Kukulcán, Km 9.5
☎883-2188
A restaurant and nightclub rolled into one, Señor Frog's is a very lively place with loud music that attracts a young crowd. From 10pm on, dance music and reggae rule here.

Bar'n Roll

$-$$
Plaza Kukulcán
☎885-3133
With a name like this, you already have some idea of what kind of place this is and what to expect. Caricatures of famous people in the music world decorate this establishment. Salty, fattening food, like chicken wings and nachos, is served, as well as beer and an interesting selection of cocktails with amusing names such as Strawberry Dylan, Sex Morrison and Dunhill Lennon. The latest sporting events are broadcast on several televisions.

Los Agaves Tequilería

Ave. Playas no 79
This establishment offers 232 kinds of tequila, several kinds of mescal and various brand-name cigars. There is a small terrace that is not covered, but you can escape the heat by going upstairs where there are fans by the windows.

Shopping

Cancún is a real shopping city, with no fewer than 20 malls, not to mention all the little craft shops both downtown and in the Hotel Zone. One advantage of the latter is that the prices are negotiable.

Cancún City

Ki Huic

8am to 8pm
Av. Tulum 17
The Ki Huic flea market is where you'll find one of the largest craft shops and is highly recommended.

Mercado 28

SM8, at the corner of Av.s Zel-Ha and Tankah
This is an interesting group of stores and other businesses in the heart of downtown Cancún. Pretty handcrafted items can be purchased here at very reasonable prices.

The Hotel Zone

Plaza Kukulcán

Paseo Kukulcán, Km 13
☎885-0804
This large shopping mall is air-conditioned, spotlessly clean and features lots of shops. You can find just about anything here, including many high-priced

souvenir shops, a number of restaurants, a *Cancún Tips* tourist information counter, a pharmacy, a movie theatre, a bowling alley, and a video arcade.

Plaza Caracol

☎883-4760
Paseo Kukulcán, Km 8.5
Plaza Caracol is located right near the Centro de Convenciones on Punta Cancún. This mall is more inviting and livelier than Plaza Kukulcán and is also close to a number of good restaurants.

La Fiesta Paseo Kukulcán

Paseo Kukulcán, Km 9
☎883-2100
This is a big shopping centre where you can find lots of handicrafts, silver jewellery and leather goods. Despite what its ads say, the prices are quite high here.

La Isla Shopping Village

Blvd. Kukulcán, Km 12.5
☎883-5025
The hotel zone's very latest commercial development is worth visiting both for its new attractions and scores of shops and gourmet restaurants. La Isla offers a glimpse of the shopping centre of tomorrow. Fashion boutiques stand alongside sports stores or stylish-souvenir stands, while the mall's service area and modern layout give shoppers the impression they are roaming through an amusement park.

I sla Mujeres ★★★:

Island of Women. So close to Cancún and yet so different, this island evokes a sunny, enchanting paradise, where a large fishing village is fringed with white sand and turquoise waters.

Gulf of Mexico

YUCATÁN

Chichén Itzá

QUINTANA ROO

Tulum

Cancún

Isla Mujeres

Playa del Carmen

San Miguel de Cozumel

Cozumel

Caribbean Sea

L ocals have so far wisely preserved the island's human aspect, and Isla Mujeres remains a spring-fresh, privileged place with a quiet, laid-back pace of life.

T he island was named in 1517 by Francisco Hernández de Córdoba, who at the time was leading a Spanish expedition in search of labourers for the gold mines of Cuba. Four hundred years later, in 1917, the Mexican government erected a monument commemorating this arrival.

S everal historians recount that Córdoba was apparently inspired by the many statues representing the Mayan goddesses Ix-Chel, Ix-Hunic and Ix Hunierta that were found on the island. The island's temples are believed to have been built to honour Ix-Chel, the goddess of the Moon and

fertility. It seems that the Maya never actually inhabited the island, and that it served solely as a pilgrimage destination.

T hese idols, baring their breasts as was the custom for Mayan women, were dressed only from the waist down. This fact was strongly emphasized by all Spanish chroniclers and once again promulgated by historians, thus establishing the island as a place of worship for the goddesses of fertility, medicine and the moon.

B ut prior to the arrival of the Spanish, the island

was also a major source of salt for the rulers of Ecab, the capital of the province of the same name on the peninsula. As the harvesting of salt in the three salt marshes of Isla Mujeres was a seasonal activity, it is highly likely that the ancient Maya lived on the mainland. In fact, given the island's limited size, the agricultural produce harvested here could only sustain a few families.

I sla Mujeres was abandoned some time after the Conquest. In the 17th and 18th centuries, pirates who prowled the Caribbean Sea used the northern islands, including Isla Mujeres, as places of refuge and temporary home ports, in order to avoid pursuit by the Spanish navy.

During the mid-19th-century Caste War, Isla Mujeres became the refuge of Whites and *Mestizos* fleeing the vengeance of Maya insurgents. Pirate and slave-trader Fermín Mundaca was one of the island's most notorious residents. The tragic story of his love for a local woman, for whom he had a grand hacienda built here in the latter half of the 19th century, has become a legend worthy of a soap opera (see p 96).

From that time until the mid-20th century, fishing, subsistence farming and the exploitation of the Salinas, Salinitas and Salinas del Canotal salt marshes became the new colonists' main source of economic revenue.

During World War II, the Allies constructed a naval base here, which is used today by the Mexican government. In the early 1950s, the construction of the Mérida-Puerto Juárez road opened the door to tourism, changing the island's peaceful lifestyle forevermore. With the development of mass tourism, Isla Mujeres became the most accessible tourist destination on the Mexican coast. The salt marshes located south of town became garbage dumps, while the Salinas del Canotal yielded its last harvest in 1974. Most everyday products and foodstuffs were henceforth imported from the mainland.

Unlike the inhabitants of Cancún, who are considered "newcomers," islanders pride themselves on being the descendants of old families that have lived on Isla Mujeres for several generations. They are very proud of their culinary traditions and very colourful and ceremonial festivals, which punctuate the seasons.

The island is about 7.5km long and 800m across at its widest point. The enchanting charm of this locale is a combination of its many white-sand beaches, lagoons and coral reefs teeming with marine life. Its more than 15,000 inhabitants live in the centre and the north of the island. Most of the tourism-related services on the island are concentrated in the north.

In fact, the town of Isla Mujeres, spread out on the northern end of the island, has about 10,000 residents and 15 criss-crossing streets. Wrought-iron balconies and white-washed walls contribute to its altogether Mexican atmosphere; its several wooden houses evoke the island's Caribbean connection. Most of the restaurants, hotels and shops of the island are concentrated in this little city, which is best visited outside the tourist rush hour (mainly between noon and 3pm), when guides arrive along with throngs of visitors from Cancún.

The centre of the island is home to several lagoons and former salt marshes. Small towns (known as *colonias*) line the southern section of the Salinas Grande, while hotels and the Tortugranja (turtle farm) are located on the Sac Bajo, a finger of land that separates the sea from the vast Laguna Makax.

The many piers are generally located along the west coast. On the other side of the island, a scenic road follows the shore, here the sea is so rough that it is unsafe for water-sports. The rest of the island features numerous attractions, as described in the pages that follow.

It should be mentioned here that the Municipio or Isla Mujeres district extends to the mainland and comprises the northeastern point of the Yucatán peninsula. This territory encompasses scores of islands, including Isla Contoy, a managed wildlife reserve that receives a limited number of visitors daily. Only three agencies offer day trips to this bird sanctuary: one in Cancun and two in Isla Mujeres.

Finding Your Way Around

By Boat

Travellers can make the crossing from the mainland to Isla Mujeres from various places, such as the ferry landing (*embarcadero*) in the Hotel Zone, or that of Puerto Juárez or Punta Sam. On the island, the passenger ferry landing (*muelle fiscal, ☎998-877-0065*) is located in the town of Isla Mujeres, across from Calle Morelos. Parque Garrafón has its own ferry landing.

A slow but inexpensive option (15 pesos) that is much used by area resi-

dents, is the passenger ferry, which arrives almost every hour from Puerto Juárez *(☎998-877-0065)*. This port, a few kilometres north of Cancún, is accessible by bus *($1; Ruta 8 sur Avenidea Tulum)*, which goes to Punta Sam, by way of Puerto Juarez. You can also get there by taxi from downtown Cancún, or by car, heading north along Highway 180. If there are not enough passengers to fill the boat, the ferry may be delayed until the next scheduled departure time. The one-way fare costs around $4 and the trip takes between 30 and 40 min. The first departure is at 5am and the return is at 11:00pm *(return to Cancún every half hour between 6am to 8pm and 9pm, 10pm and 11pm)*

Faster, more comfortable boats *(☎998-877-0253 or 877-0618)* also leave from Puerto Juárez every half hour from 6am to 8:30pm and once at 11:30pm. The crossing, twice as fast as the ferry (20min), costs around 70 pesos (pay on the boat), for the round trip. Whichever boat you board, supply yourself with seasickness medication and eat lightly at least one hour before boarding, since the sea can be rough.

At Punta Sam *(Hwy. 180, 5km north of Cancún)* there is a car ferry that is slightly more comfortable than the Puerto Juárez shuttle. The fare is 15 pesos for foot passengers, 120 pesos for cars and 170 pesos for vans. The crossing takes 2hrs. It is recommended to arrive 1hr ahead of

departure time and to line up immediately with ticket in hand.

Departures from Punta Sam for Isla Mujeres:

8am, 11am, 2:45pm, 5:30pm and 20:15pm

Departures from Isla Mujeres for Punta Sam:

6:30am, 9:30am, 12:45am, 4:15pm, 7:15pm

Other taxi boats or ferries leave from Playa Caracol *(located between the Fiesta Americana and Coral Beach hotels ☎998-886-4270 or 886-4847)*, Playa Langosta, Playa Linda, Playa Tortugas, beaches in Cancún's Hotel Zone.

Many agencies organize such cruises to Isla Mujeres, and some have transformed this short crossing into an elaborate excursion including meals, open bar, live entertainment and snorkelling. Of course these expeditions are more expensive than simple ferry crossings, but they can be very pleasant. Before boarding be sure that the boat is actually going to stop at the island, as some cruises just go around it. Arrive at least half an hour early to get a good seat.

The following companies organize cruises to Isla Mujeres from Cancún:

Aqua Tours Adventures
☎*883-0400*

Carribean Carnaval
☎*884-3760*
⇋*887-2184*

Isla Mujeres

Addresses

Every commercial address on the island is known to all islanders, but no one uses door numbers to designate them. In fact, a query as to where this or that business is located is generally met with the following response: "Ah yes, it's just opposite the X hotel, between Avenida A and Avenida B."

On the Island

The city of Isla Mujeres occupies the northern tip of the island and comprises approximately 15 interconnecting streets, so it is almost impossible to get lost. The main street is Avenida Rueda Medina, which follows the west coast from one end of the island to the other, and leads south to Parque Nacional de El Garrafón, to the beaches, to the Mayan sanctuary dedicated to the goddess Ixchel and to the lighthouse on the point. It also leads to the very pretty Playa Norte, situated north of the village. The town square, surrounded by the Catholic church, the city hall and the police station, is between Avenidas Morelos and Bravo.

By Car

A car is more of a headache than a convenience on Isla Mujeres. The small size of the island does not justify the time and expense of the crossing. Nonetheless, if you cannot do without a car, the ferry landing is just facing Avenida Rueda Medina, which travels the entire island from north to south. The island's only gas station is on this street, north of the car pier, at the corner of Avenida Abasolo.

By Taxi

Taxi fares are set by the municipality and are posted near the pier. Nevertheless, be sure to agree on a price with the driver before entering a cab.

Taxis Syndicate
☎*877-0066*

By Moped or Golf Cart

These two means of transportation are definitely the most popular on Isla Mujeres. Rental agencies require a passport or driver's license as security. Note that mopeds and golf carts are generally insured for *daños a tercera persona*, that is to say for damages to a third party and not those incurred by the rented vehicle. It is therefore advisable to come to an understanding before renting. In case of an accident, you must negotiate with the lessor

and, should there be a dispute, the matter is referred to the Ministerio Público (the police).

Golf carts are not rented to children, but some tourists allow their children to drive them, which results in many accidents. People often forget they are driving on public thoroughfares and not on a golf course. Also watch out for taxi-drivers, some of whom drive quite recklessly. Helmets are not mandatory for moped-riders, but the roads being what they are, riders must be especially cautious. Finally, always check the gas tank, especially those of golf carts, as some are not adequately filled.

Gomar
Av. Francisco I. Madero, no. 65
☎*(998) 877-0604*

Pepe's Motorent
Av. Hidalgo no. 82B
☎*(998) 887-0019*

Moto Fiesta
Av. Rueda Medina (across from the passenger landing stage)

Ciros
Av. Guerrero and Matamoros
☎*(998) 877-0568*

Moto Kan-Kin
Av. Abasolo (between Av. Guerrero and Hidalgo)

Fiesta Rent
Av. Rueda Medina no. 3

María José Rent
Av. Francisco I. Madero no. 21
☎*(998) 877-0130*

Angel Rent
Av. Juárez no. 5
☎*(998) 844-9828*

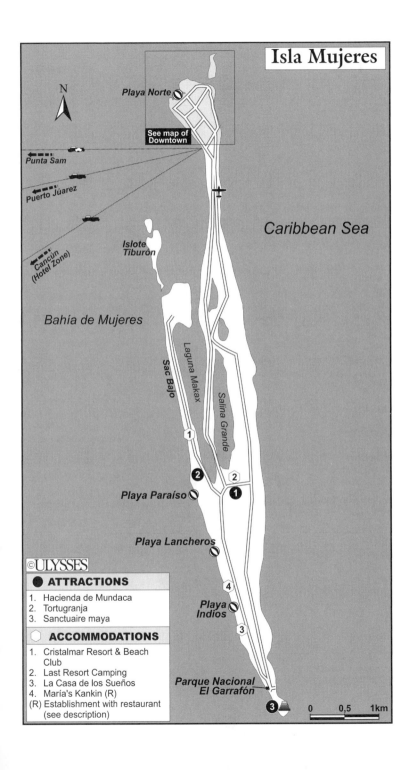

By Bicycle

A good mode of transportation for the island, a bicycle allows you to explore every corner of it at your own pace. Be careful of heatstroke and be sure to wear a hat.

If your hotel does not rent bicycles, many little shops in town do, especially near the port. Test the bicycle of your choice before renting it ("May I try it?" = "*¿Puedo probar?*") to be sure that it rides well. The rental fee is about 50 pesos per day.

Listed below are a few bicycle rental shops:

El Zoro Rent
Av. Rueda Medina, local 12; Av. Guerrero no. 7A

David Rent
Av. Rueda Medina (in front of the gas station)

Fiesta Rent
Av. Rueda Medina no. 3

By Bus

The buses heading towards Playa Lancheros leave from l'Avenida Rueda Medina, with departures every half hour between 6am and 10pm. It is possible to get off the bus at all stops during the journey. It costs 3 pesos one way.

Isla Contoy

Isla Contoy was formerly reached only Isla Mujeres, but visitors can now sail to the wildlife reserve directly from Cancún. The boat (*Barco Asterix:* ☎998-886-4847) from Cancún docks at Carlos & Charlie's marina in Cancún's Hotel Zone, and some agencies also offer their services with departures from Isla Mujeres. Note that only certain agencies have the necessary permit to visit the island. Other agencies offer a cruise around the island but cannot berth there.

Practical Information

The area code for Isla Mujeres is **998**.

Tourist Information

Mon-Fri 8am to 8pm
Av. Rueda Medina no. 130, north of the pier
☎/⇄*877-0307*

Post Office

Mon-Fri 9am to 4pm
corner of Av. Guerrero and Calle López Mateos
☎*877-0085*

Telecommunications

Fax
Mon to Fri 9am to 3pm, Sat 9am to 12:30pm
Av. Guerrero no.13
☎*877-0113*

Internet
Compucentro
every day 10am to 1pm
Av. Medero No.14
☎*877-0744*

Cybercafés

CyberBar and Café
Av. Hidalgo, between Av. Matamoros and Calle López Mateos

Isla Mujeres Internet Café
Av. Madero no. 10

Banks and Exchange Offices

Banco Bital
Mon-Fri 8:30am to 6pm
Sat 9am to 2pm
Av. Rueda Medina
(across from the ferry landing)
☎*877-0005*
There are two ATMs: one is at the entrance to the bank and the other is at Parque Garrafon. But don't count on them, as they are often empty on weekends. There are many exchange offices on the island, including:

Money Exchange
Av. Morelos, no. 9, Lote 4
☎*877-0104*

Health

Pharmacy

Farmacia La Mejor
Francisco I. Madero no. 17
☎*877-0116*

Hospital

Centro de Salud
Guerrerro, between Av. Madero and Morelos
☎*877-0117*

Emergencies

Hôpital Naval
Av. Admirante Rueda Medina
Colonia Salinas Grande
☎*877-0001 (emergencies only)*

Doctor

Doctor Antonio Salas
English-speaking general practitioner
Av. Hidalgo no.18
☎*877-0021*

Police (Security)

The Palacio Municipal
on the town square (houses the police station)
☎*877-0082*

Ambulance

The Isla Mujeres Red Cross
Cruz Roja Mexicana
Colonia Gloria
(in the middle of the island, near the Hacienda Mundaca)
☎*877-0280*
Doctor Greta M. Shorey, the director, is of British origin. Services offered include: emergency, family medicine, education, first-aid courses, health courses and the island's only ambulance.

The Red Cross depends on its own very limited budget. Donations of money, clothing, medicines or children's games are appreciated.

Miscellaneous

Laundry

Tim Pho
Av. Abasolo

Wash Express
Calle Abasdo no. 13

Marinas

Harbour Master/
Port Captain's Office
Av. Rueda Medina
☎*877-0095*

Marina Paraíso
at the entrance to the Laguna Makax
☎*877-0211*

Puerto Isla Mujeres
☎*800-400-3333*

Travel Agency

Mundaca Travel
Av. Hidalgo no. 15
☎*877-0025*
⇒*877-0076*
www.mundacatravel.com
Mundaca Travel is the only agency that books first-class bus tickets throughout Mexico. It also books airline tickets on international flights and offers guided tours of the island, the Riviera Maya and Chichén Itzá.

Bookshops and Exchanges

Cosmic Cosas
Matamoros no. 82 (facing the Hotel Caracol)
☎*986-03495*
Cosmic Cosas, run by young Americans Molly and Geneviève, is certainly the most heterogeneous shop on the island. Here, you can exchange, buy or sell new or used books in several languages. It's also a local art gallery (painting, sculpture and crafts) and the only place in town that rents digital cameras and develops photos in CD-ROM format. The shop also houses an animal shelter: *Amigos de los Animales.* This organization has taken on the mission of looking after stray animals. Donations of money or veterinary supplies are not only welcome, but very much appreciated.

Publications

Isla Mujeres's equivalent to Cancún's *Cancún Tips* is *Islander,* a monthly magazine that is distributed in the hotels and at the tourist information office. If you read a bit of Spanish you can keep up with current events with *Por Esto!,* a daily distributed throughout the state of Quintana Roo.

Exploring

Isla Mujeres

Isla Mujeres is greatly admired for the beauty of its beaches, its coral reefs and its landscape. Many tourists staying in Cancún come to these more authentic and more relaxing parts for a day or two of peace. It doesn't hurt that the island is home to some very good restaurants, hotels that offer good value for money and many craft shops.

Like all towns in Mexico, Isla Mujeres has its share of monuments commemorating historic events or honouring political figures. Among them are a bust of Benito Juárez, on display in front of the cemetery, and

Isla Mujeres

a monument to fishers, which stands at the corner of Avenidas López Mateos and Rueda Medina. Moreover, three lighthouses warn sailors of the dangerous waters off the island: one at either end of the island, and a *farito* at the mouth of the bay of Isla Mujeres.

In the City

At **Casa de la Cultura** *(Av. Guerrero,* ☎*877-0639)* the music reaches full swing twice a day when musicians, dancers, painters and other local artists express themselves in various media. English books are available on loan here.

The **Isla Mujeres cemetery**, *(located on Av. López Mateos, entrance opposite Av. Benito Juárez)*, is worth visiting for all those unfamiliar with the role, importance and extravagance of such places in Hispanic culture. There are mausoleums worthy of the wealthiest islanders juxtaposed against tombstones marking the passage of the humblest citizens.

The Southern Part of the Island

The century-old **Hacienda de Mundaca** *(15 pesos; every day 10am to 6pm)*, is located about 4km south of the city along Avenida Rueda Medina, near Playa Lancheros. According to legend, this house was built in the 19th century by slave-trader Fermín Antonio Mundaca to win the heart of a young island girl,

Triguena (the brunette). However, she left for Mérida and married someone else. Brokenhearted, Mundaca perished shortly thereafter. His tomb is in a cemetery on Calle López Mateos, in the city. One side of his tombstone reads, "*como eres, yo fui*" ("as you are, I was") and the other reads, "*como soy, tú serás*" ("as I am, you will be"). Mundaca's remains are actually in Mérida, where he lived out his last days.

The Hacienda de Mundaca is composed of two modest, not yet restored buildings surrounded by gardens and lanes and enclosed by a low wall. The entrance archway and a sundial remain in good condition. Several species of Yucatec fauna, including a jaguar, a *jabalí* (from the same family as the tapir), some spider monkeys, a black pheasant with a yellow crest and some boas live in rudimentary cages. To reach the Hacienda, follow the signs along Avenida Rueda Medina.

Tortugranja *(14 pesos; every day 9am to 5pm; Carretera Sac Bajo, Km 5,* ☎*877-0595)* is a turtle farm run by Eco Caribe, an environmental organization dedicated to breeding, studying and saving two species of marine turtles: the green turtle and the Loggerhead turtle, known by the scientific name *Carette Caretta*. The farm comprises several buildings, including a small museum and a shop; incubation and growing reservoirs as well as cages or

conservation stations have been set up on the shore. You can see turtles of varying ages. Every year the farm raises and protects thousands of baby turtles until they grow large enough to be released safely into the ocean.

The **Santuario Maya** *(free admission)*, located on the island's southern headland, is a small, Tulum-style building like those scattered along the east coast of the Yucatán peninsula. A well laid-out park gives centre stage to the monument, the lighthouse and the headland's impressive cliff. Built between the 12th and 14th centuries, the temple was very likely dedicated to Ix-Chel, the Mayan goddess of fertility, medicine and the moon.

Many think that the temple, in addition to being a pilgrimage destination, served as an astronomical observatory. For a smile and a small tip, the lighthouse keeper will let you climb to the top of the tower, from where you can take in a different perspective of the sea, Cancún and Isla Mujeres.

Parks and Beaches

Parks

The highly popular **Parque Nacional El Garrafón** *($10 or $45 package deal all incl., every day 9am to*

paradise for snorkelling enthusiasts, the waters lining the beach of Xcaret are filled with a thousand and one treasures to discover.

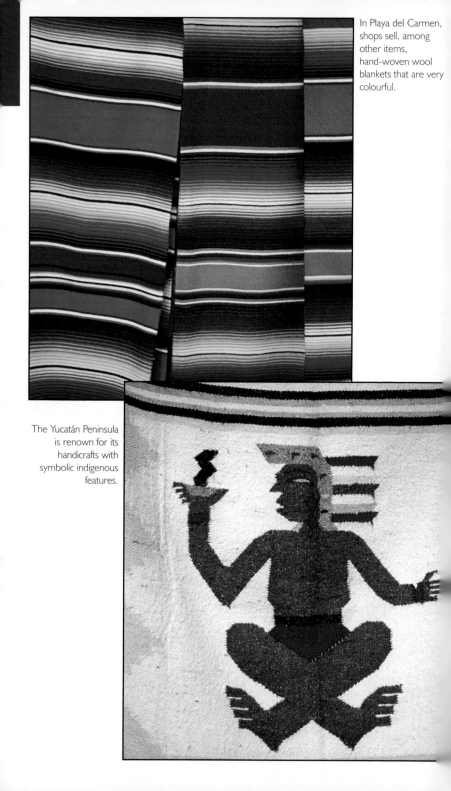

In Playa del Carmen, shops sell, among other items, hand-woven wool blankets that are very colourful.

The Yucatán Peninsula is renown for its handicrafts with symbolic indigenous features.

In Cancún, deck chairs and parasols await the loungers and sun-worshippers.

Paragliding over the beach of Cancún is a great way to take in beautiful sights and panoramas.

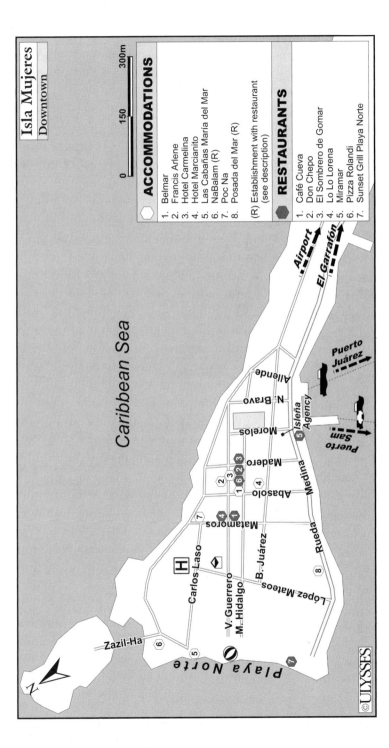

Isla Mujeres
Downtown

Caribbean Sea

ACCOMMODATIONS

1. Belmar
2. Francis Arlene
3. Hotel Carmelina
4. Hotel Marcianito
5. Las Cabañas María del Mar
6. NaBalam (R)
7. Poc Na
8. Posada del Mar (R)

(R) Establishment with restaurant
    (see description)

RESTAURANTS

1. Café Cueva
2. Don Chepo
3. El Sombrero de Gomar
4. Lo Lo Lorena
5. Miramar
6. Pizza Rolandi
7. Sunset Grill Playa Norte

© ULYSSES

5pm; about 6km south of the ferry landing, ☎*877-0082, www.garrafon.com)* was completely restored in 1998. Scuba diving, snorkelling or "snuba" diving (diving while breathing through a long tube linked to a scuba tank on the surface) can be practised here off the large reef that surrounds the island. In addition to offering various water-sports opportunities (all equipment can be rented on site), this beautiful national park features a trail that leads to the southern headland, as well as two restaurants and a large shop.

Note that the ***Garrafón Express*** makes the return trip *($24 for transportation and admission)* from Playa Linda, in Cancún's Hotel Zone.

Isla Contoy, located 24km north of Isla Mujeres, is bird sanctuary, and a big draw for birders. Among the numerous winged species that make their home in the mangrove swamps and lagoons on this tiny island, which is less than 7km long and 800m wide, are herons, pelicans and frigates. For those who are interested, the nesting season for frigate birds runs from April until July.

Isla Contoy is also a good snorkelling site. The island is rimmed with sandy beaches and coral reefs. Thus, the warm, crystal-clear waters that wash its beaches abound in colourful fish.

Captain Ricardo Gaitán
Av. Francisco I. Madero no. 16
☎*877-0434*
This agency has three boats: the *Estrella del Norte*, an 11m motor sailboat; the *Pelicano*, an 11.3m trimaran; and the *Afrodita*, a 10m twin-engine speedboat. The fee includes a tour guided by a marine biologist.

Note that it is possible to visit Isla Contoy from Cancún. The boat is docked at Carlos & Charlie's Marina, in the Hotel Zone of Cancún:

Barco Asterix
☎*886-4847*

Beaches

Playa Norte stretches along the north coast of the city. The sand at Playa Cocoteros, which is white and soft underfoot, along with the calm turquoise sea are magnificent. Because of its beauty, it is much prized by visitors.

Playa Paraíso spreads out just near the turtle farm. Although rather small, it is a pretty beach with ample shade and various shops and fast-food stands.

Playa Lancheros is near Hacienda Mundaca and its calm waters are perfect for swimming. Free local celebrations are sometimes organized here on Sundays.

Playa Indios, south of Playa Lancheros, offers basically the same services

and appeal as its neighbour but has the advantage of being less busy.

Outdoor Activities

Deep-Sea Fishing

Mundaca Divers
Av. Francisco I. Madero no. 10
☎*877-0607*
Mundaca Divers offers two- to four-person deep-sea fishing trips for $150 (4 to 5 hours) or $250 (7 hours). This includes fishing gear, bait, a snack and refreshments. The guides gut and prepare the fish upon your return.

Scuba Diving and Snorkelling

Divers on Isla Mujeres congregate at Parque Nacional de El Garrafón. It is recommended to go early in the morning to avoid the crowds.

Experienced, licensed divers will not want to miss the **caves of the sleeping sharks**, northeast of the island. The caves were discovered by an island fisher. For as yet unknown reasons, the sharks that inhabit these caves are plunged into a state of lethargy that renders them harmless. Many films have been shot at this spot, by Jacques Cousteau among others, and various theories have been proposed to explain this mysterious phenomenon.

Mundaca Divers
Av. Francisco I. Madero no. 10
☎*877-0607*
Mundaca Divers offers a variety of diving excursions to some 20 sites renowned for their abundant marine life. The Los Manchones, Banderas, Media Luna and Punta Sur dive sites, among others, are fairly shallow and perfect for beginners. Experienced divers can explore several shipwrecks that dot the shoals. The company also offers various PADI-certification courses.

Accommodations

The island has more than 40 hotels, with a total of over 600 rooms. There are small, quiet, affordable hotels, as well as those that are more luxurious and service-oriented. Neither is accommodation limited to the city, as tourism industry development has fostered the construction of an increasing numbers of hotels along the west coast of the island, near the lagoon along Sac Bajo.

Moreover, houses, apartments, villas or *cabañas* are available for rent. Information regarding long-term rentals is available on the Internet site: *www.isla-mujeres.net*

or through **The Lost Oasis**: *lostoasis@mjmnet.com*.

Last Resort Camping
$
ℜ
☎*888-0375*
This campsite is located on the southern part of the island, near the Hacienda Mundaca. Bicycle rental is available.

Poc Na
$
⊗, ℜ, *sb*
Av. Matamoros no. 91
☎/⇌*877-0090*
www.pocna.tripod.com
A good choice for globetrotters, this youth hostel features dorms, two common rooms for hammocks, double rooms and a large courtyard used as a campground. The in-house restaurant, offering simple fare, is open to the public 8am to 11pm and serves meals that cost between 25 and 35 pesos.

Hotel Marcianito
$
⊗
Av. Abasolo no. 10
☎*877-0111*
This small, 14-room hotel was renovated in 1999. The very clean rooms will satisfy budget travellers looking to spend some time on the island. It is a good idea to confirm reservations a few days in advance.

Hotel Carmelina
$
⊗
Av. Guerrero, at the corner of Av. Francisco I. Madero
☎*877-0006*
This 26-room hotel is located on a quiet street near the Casa de la Cultura. Simply decorated, the rooms are clean, ap-

pealing and have been renovated. Reservations recommended.

Belmar
$$
≡, ⊗, ℜ, , ⊛, ℝ
Av. Hidalgo no. 110
☎*877-0430*
⇌*877-0429*
This little hotel has only 11 rooms, but it is very pleasant. It is located in the heart of the city, above Pizza Rolandi, and can therefore be noisy at times. The rooms are comfortable and well appointed. The hotel also has a suite with a whirlpool bath, kitchenette and living room.

Posada del Mar
$$
≡, ⊗, ≈, ℜ
Av. Rueda Medina no. 15A
☎*877-0044*
⇌*877-0266*
www.posadadelmar.com
This establishment has 42 spacious and well decorated rooms with balconies and rattan furniture. The hotel is surrounded by a hibiscus and bougainvillea garden facing a beach on the Mujeres bay, which you can reach by crossing the street.

Maria's Kin Kan
$$
≡, ℜ, ℝ, *K*
Carretera Garrafón, km 4
☎*877-0015*
⇌*877-0395*
This hotel is a little oasis of tranquility next to the charming Casa de las Sueños. Though it is mostly known for its quality restaurant, the hotel has clean, well-equipped rooms of different sizes.

Francis Arlene
$$

≡, ⊗, ℝ
Calle Guerrero no. 7
☎*877-0310*
www.francisarlene.com
This friendly establishment has charming little rooms that are well-kept, well-equipped and economical. Run by the Magana family, this three-storey, 24-room hotel has become a favourite with couples in search of peace and comfort. Fitted out with tables and chairs, the balconies offer an unforgettable view of the sea at sunset. The Magana family, whose ancestors settled here in the mid-19th century, proves to be an inexhaustible source of information. Their help and judicious advice have enhanced the stay of many a guest.

Las Cabañas María del Mar
$$$ bkfst incl.

ℝ, ≡, ≈, ℜ, ⊗
Av. Carlos Lazo no. 1
Playa Norte
☎*877-0179*
www.cabanasdelmar.com
This establishment has 73 rooms that are decorated very attractively in typical Mexican fashion. You can take your hammock onto the balcony in the new, modern section of this establishment. Since the hotel is located diagonally across from Playa Norte, only one room has an ocean view. There is also a motorcycle- and golf-cart-rental counter on site.

La Casa de los Sueños
$$$ bkfst incl.

≡, ⊗, ≈, ❂, ⊘, ℜ
Carretera Garrafón
☎*877-0651*
⇌*877-0708*
www.casadelossuenosresort.com
One of the best establishments on the island by far, the inviting La Casa de los Sueños is a real little pearl of a bed and breakfast, located near the Parque Nacional El Garrafón. La Casa is owned by a friendly woman from Québec who rents pleasant and charmingly decorated rooms with ocean views. Part of the hotel is used to display paintings and other works by Mexican artists. After a day at the beach, read a book by the pool and listen to the chirping of the birds and the tinkling of the wind chimes, while the sea breeze gently caresses your face. La Casa de los Sueños is non smoking and for adults only.

Cristalmar Resort & Beach
$$$$

≡, ≈, ℜ, ℝ
Fracc. Laguna Mar Macax
☎*877-0390 or 877-0397*
⇌*887-0398*
www.cristalmarhotel.com
This hotel opens onto pretty Sac Bajo beach. Attractive, luxurious and clean, its 40 large rooms are ornamented with local crafts.

NaBalam
$$$$

≡, ≈, ℝ, ℜ, K
Calle Zazil-Ha no. 118
Playa Norte
☎*877-0279*
⇌*877-0446*
www.nabalam.com
A lovely little hotel situated on Playa Norte, Na-Balam

is divided into two sections: on one side, the balconies face the ocean, but the view is obstructed by luxuriant vegetation; on the other side, the rooms surround an interior courtyard. Rattan furniture and turquoise marble floors contribute to the pleasant ambiance of the rooms.

Restaurants

While there are fewer than 15,000 residents on the whole island, quality restaurants are abundant due to the high demand from tourists. As for dress codes, something thrown over a bathing suit and sandals will do.

Pinguino's
$

Av. Rueda Medina
☎*877-0212 or 877-0044*
Featuring one of the island's loveliest terraces, Pinguino's is located 300m north of the ferry landing and a few metres from the lighthouse on the northern headland. The Posada del Mar Hotel's bar-restaurant offers a unique and interesting view of the island's west coast and Cancún. Although the menu is somewhat limited (20 dishes), the fish *a la veracruzana* or the *filete a la plancha* is sure to leave you satisfied. To end your meal on a high note, be sure to try the cheesecake, which is quite simply exquisite.

Café Cueva
$

Av. Matamoros, between Hidalgo and Guerrero
This café offers pastries of all kinds, and its fresh-ground coffees are known as the best in town. Java junkies can try one of the iced coffees, including the iced mocha, iced cappuccino or iced latte.

Sunset Grill Playa Norte
$-$$

west side of Playa Norte (in front of Nautibeach Condos)
☎877-0785
This restaurant is special: the atmosphere is relaxing and the view of the sunset spectacular. Breakfast here is "all-you-can-eat," for the modest sum of 60 pesos. The menu offers typical island fare, save for the "outlandish" spinach salad. The owners—gregarious, free spirits—often serve customers personally and enhance the ambiance.

El Sombrero de Gomar
$-$$

corner of Av.s Hidalgo and Francisco I. Madero
The El Sombrero de Gomar restaurant offers authentic Mexican cuisine in a very Altiplano-like ambiance. The soups, salads, pasta dishes and burgers are to limited budgets what the shrimp, fish and lobster are to better-padded wallets.

Miramar
$-$$$

Rueda Medina
This restaurant is located near the pier, where boats from the Hotel Zone are docked next to fishing nets stretched out in the sun. Seafood, fish and tacos are on the menu.

Vegetarians

If you are vegetarian, don't worry about losing any weight during your trip to Mexico. However, if you are on a strict macrobiotic diet, you might have a harder time. If you do eat fish and seafood, you are in for some culinary delights!

Lo Lo Lorena
$-$$$

Av. Vicente Guerrero, corner of Matamoros
This restaurant, whose menu aptly bears the title "Flavours of the World," is sure to satisfy lovers of Asian, Arabic or European cuisine. The Belgian-born owner is a devotee of market cuisine, turning the day's best consignments into delectable Indonesian, Thai, Indian, Arabic or French dishes. The menu outlines possible selections: salads and vegetarian dishes, live lobster, fresh fish, giant shrimp and beef imported from Argentina. And for dessert, you can choose between *crème brulée*, chocolate mousse or flambéed bananas. The restaurant also offers a good selection of wines and teas to round off the feast. The all-wood, Belize-style building that houses Lo Lo Lorena offers diners a glimpse of what the town of Isla Mujeres was like in the

19th century. At night, the decor is muted by candlelight, enhancing the intimacy of the very personalized setting wisely created by the owner.

Don Chepo
$$

Av. Hidalgo, near Francisco I. Madero
The Don Chepo restaurant specializes in flambées, with everything from chicken to shrimp and lobster flambéed right before your eyes. Mexican flavours take on a Caribbean slant, but for a typically Yucatec meal, try the *arrachera* (*achiote* and *epazote* are Yucatec spices) or, for a touch of exoticism, the *camarones coco* (shrimp in coconut milk). Last but not least, fruit can also be flambéed for dessert.

María's Kin Kan
$$-$$$

Carretera Garrafón, Km 4
☎877-0015
≈877-0395
The fare served here is a variation on French cuisine, adapted for Yucatán specialties. María's Kin Kan is known as the only restaurant on the island that serves fresh rock lobster all year long. Fish and seafood are also on the menu, as well as delicious desserts. From the terrace there is a pretty view of the ocean.

Pizza Rolandi
$$-$$$

Av. Hidalgo, between Madero and Abasolo
☎877-0429
This restaurant has another location in Cancún and also serves delicious wood-oven-cooked pizza. In addition, beautiful mixed

Isla Mujeres

salads, seafood, pasta and calzones are available. The Italian owner is also the chef at Casa Rolandi in Cancún. Coffee lovers can savour excellent espresso and cappuccino here.

Zazil-Ha
$$-$$$
Calle Zazil, in the NaBalam hotel
☎877-0279
At Zazil-Ha, one of the NaBalam Hotel's three restaurants, diners will be hard-pressed to choose between the vegetarian and Mayan-style dishes. The restaurant, whose modern Yucatec cuisine is highly acclaimed, is set in a lush tropical garden and fits in well with this romantic environment. Zazil-Ha's garlic bread and exotic appetizers are hailed by local gourmets.

Entertainment

Come nightfall, Isla Mujeres offers enjoyable diversion in the few bars and restaurants scattered over the island. Most of these establishments have a "happy hour," or a two-for-one special, between 5pm and 7pm. Music is omnipresent on the island, and, after serenading supping restaurant patrons, many local musicians provide entertainment for dance-filled evenings.

Buho's
Las Cabaña's del Maria del Mar
Playa Norte
☎877-0179
Bubo's is a choice location for drinks on the patio before dinner. The music is not too loud and the ambiance is relaxing. Happy Hour is popular here, as are the swings around the bar.

Zazil-Ha
Hotel Balam Na
Playa Norte
☎877-0279 or 877-0058
⇌877-0446
For a pleasant, laid-back happy hour, head to the Zazil-Ha bar, where bands sometimes perform.

Festival

Isla Mujeres International Music Festival
In the month of July, the annual Isla Mujeres International Music Festival is held. During the few days of this event, groups of musicians and folk dancers come from all over the world to give outdoor performances.

Shopping

All of the organized tour guides lead their groups through shops that proffer them commissions. These are not entirely uninteresting spots, but Mexican and Guatemalan crafts are available for much better

prices elsewhere. Avenida Hidalgo is flanked by many small boutiques.

La Casa Isleña II
Av. Guerrero no. 3
☎877-0265
Forget about factory-made T-shirts: this boutique sells T-shirts that are hand-painted by a gifted artist.

Casa del Arte México
Av. Morelos, corner Guerrero
This shop is worth visiting for the stone sculptures created by a local artist. Hammocks, silver jewellery, batik clothing and leather goods are also on sale.

Van Cleef & Arpels
Av. Morelos, corner of Benito Juárez
Van Cleef & Arpels is among the world's most upscale jewellers. The quality of the gems and the originality of the pieces make it unique. They have been creating jewellery with diamonds, emeralds, sapphires, rubies, tanzanite and other gems for 20 years.

Las Máscaras
Av. López Mateos, between Hidalgo and Guerrero
Owned by a local artisan, this shop sells special, exquisitely made masks.

Cozumel

Cozumel ★★★
is the biggest island in Mexico. Surrounded by turquoise waters and a spectacular string of coral reef, it is a scuba-diver's paradise.

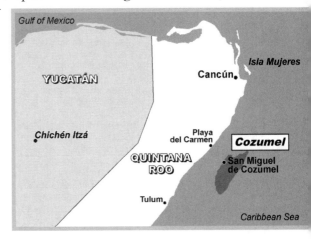

Since the release of the documentary by marine explorer Jacques Cousteau in 1961, Cozumel has become a choice location, visited by thousands of scuba divers every year. Hundreds of cruise ships also make stop-overs here. The surrounding waters abound in countless aquatic species, colourful reefs and the remains of sunken Spanish galleons. In fact, more than 20% of visitors to Cozumel are scuba divers! Other visitors can observe an extraordinary variety of migratory birds that spend a portion of the year here, visit the Parque Nacional y Jardines Botánicos Chankanaab, go shopping, go fishing, or simply relax on one of the magnificent beaches all around the island.

Located 19km from the coast, the island is flat and shaped like lobster claws. It's about 48km by 16km in size. The centre of Cozumel is overgrown with vegetation. Its periph-ery, though, is a continuous ring of white sand and limestone. Since the east coast of the island is exposed to high winds, tourist establishments and hotels are situated on the west coast. San Miguel, the only city on the island, with a population of about 65,000, is also on the west side.

Some History

Around 300 BC, Cozumel was occupied by Mayas. Between 1200 and 1600 it became an important port of commerce and a pilgrimmage site. Women from the coast would come to Cozumel by pirogue (dugout canoe) to worship Ix-Chel, the goddess of fertility. There are more than 35 archaeological sites throughout the island, but only a few are maintained. Cortez landed here in 1519 before he undertook the conquest of Mexican territory. Cortez was preceded by Juan de Grijalva in 1518 who was seeking slaves.

During the colony's first few decades, the island was the *encomienda* of conquistador Juan de Contreras, who passed it on to his son. Unable to meet his religious obligations toward his Mayan subjects, the latter lost his rights over the island. Moreover, the tributes he demanded from the 60 families of San Miguel and 80 families of Santa María (now El Cedral) became too taxing for them. Little by little, the Maya abandoned Cozumel. But as Spanish (religious or political) rule did not extend to the island, it is not known whether there were permanent residents from 1600 onward.

The island's coves provided refuge to pirates, including the dreaded Jean Lafitte and Henry Morgan, who scoured the seas in the 17th and 18th centuries. In 1848, alarmed by the situation created by the Caste War, governor of the Yucatán Miguel Barbachano offered to sell the island of Cozumel to the Cuban authorities... but to no avail.

A few years later, in February 1862, Mexico's minister of foreign affairs authorized his special envoy to negotiate the sale of the island of Cozumel to the United States, in order for the latter to establish a *negros* colony there. A bill was presented to the U.S. Congress but, after long deliberations, President Lincoln's cabinet resolved that the island was too far from Florida and did not meet the requirement for the establishment of a colony of slaves-turned-freemen. Cozumel thus remained part of Mexico.

In the mid-19th century, the island was once again colonized by Whites and Mestizos fleeing the wrath of the Maya during the Caste War. A good number of present-day families trace their roots back to these "newcomers."

Around the late 19th century, Cozumel's economic mainstays consisted of fishing, agriculture, the gathering of valuable hardwoods and, above all, *benequén* (sisal, a Mexican agave plant) and coconuts, two raw materials exported for processing. *Henequén* yields a fibre used, among other things, for making rope, while coconuts were processed to make oil.

Cozumel's economic revival at the beginning of the 20th century was prompted by the popularity of chewing gum in the United States. The island became an important port for the export to North America of chicle, an extract of the sapodilla tree and the base of chewing gum. This trade declined when a less expensive synthetic product was invented in the 1930s to replace chicle. Later, the United States built an air force base used by the Allies to pursue German submarines during the Second World War. The U.S. Army also trained frogmen (military scuba divers) off Cozumel.

The postwar period was difficult for the inhabitants of Cozumel, as the island experienced a major economic downturn. The decline of coconut and chicle (chewing-gum) exports, as well as the lack of raw materials, due primarily to the overexploitation of valuable hardwoods, created an economic crisis that put the island's very survival at stake. Cozumel's modern economic history began

with this crisis... and the solutions its people found to curb it.

Although the island's first hotel opened in 1928, adventure tourism only took off during the 1950s. Attracted by the island's natural beauty, its history and the proximity of dive sites, a few pioneer investors collected the necessary funds to build the island's tourist infrastructure.

The construction of hotels and attractions has been going on since the 1970s. The current backbone of the local economy is not only diving tourism, which established Cozumel's international reputation, but also, and increasingly, the cruise-ship industry, which—year in, year out—brings a daily contingent of over 6,000 visitors to the island.

Finding Your Way Around

By Plane

Cozumel International Airport

about 3km northeast of San Miguel
☎ *(987) 872-0485 or 872-0923*
The airport has a bar-restaurant, souvenir shops and car-rental and tour operators.

AeroCaribe
☎ *(987) 872-0503*

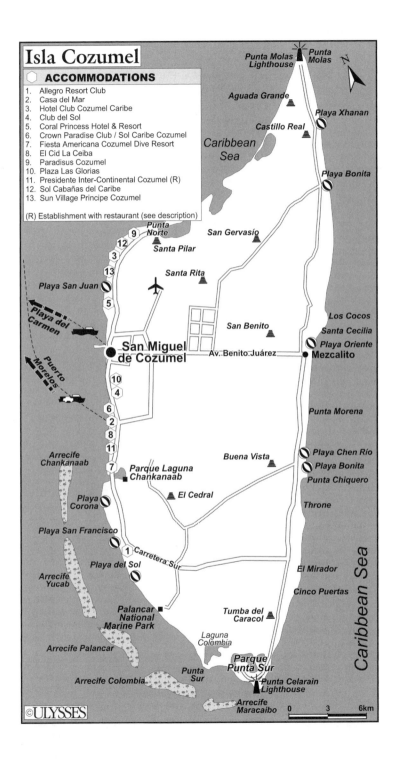

Isla Cozumel

ACCOMMODATIONS

1. Allegro Resort Club
2. Casa del Mar
3. Hotel Club Cozumel Caribe
4. Club del Sol
5. Coral Princess Hotel & Resort
6. Crown Paradise Club / Sol Caribe Cozumel
7. Fiesta Americana Cozumel Dive Resort
8. El Cid La Ceiba
9. Paradisus Cozumel
10. Plaza Las Glorias
11. Presidente Inter-Continental Cozumel (R)
12. Sol Cabañas del Caribe
13. Sun Village Principe Cozumel

(R) Establishment with restaurant (see description)

Punta Molas Lighthouse
Punta Molas
Aguada Grande
Playa Xhanan
Castillo Real
Caribbean Sea
Playa Bonita

Punta Norte
San Gervasio
Santa Pilar
Santa Rita
Playa San Juan
Playa del Carmen
San Benito
Los Cocos
Santa Cecilia
Playa Oriente
Puerto Morelos
San Miguel de Cozumel
Av. Benito Juárez
Mezcalito

Punta Morena

Arrecife Chankanaab
Buena Vista
Playa Chen Río
Playa Bonita
Punta Chiquero

Parque Laguna Chankanaab
El Cedral
Throne

Playa Corona
Playa San Francisco
Arrecife Yucab
Carretera Sur
Playa del Sol
El Mirador
Cinco Puertas

Palancar National Marine Park
Tumba del Caracol
Laguna Colombia

Arrecife Palancar
Parque Punta Sur
Caribbean Sea

Arrecife Colombia
Punta Sur
Punta Celarain Lighthouse

Arrecife Maracaibo
0   3   6km

©ULYSSES

These airlines have daily connections between Cancún and Cozumel (about $40 one way). The flight takes about 20min.

AeroCozumel
☎(987) 872-3456

Mexicana
☎(987) 872-2945
A return trip from Cozumel to Playa del Carmen costs about 150 pesos and the flight takes about 10min. For more information, contact Mexicana. Mexicana also has frequent flights between Cozumel, Miami and San Francisco. Departure tax for international flights is $16.

From the airport you can take one of the frequent shuttles to San Miguel for a reasonable price. Taxis are also available at a fairly good price. This is the most common form of transport.

By Boat

There are around 20 crossings every day between Cozumel and Playa del Carmen.

Between Cozumel and Playa del Carmen
Departures: Playa to Cozumel 5am to 11pm; Cozumel to Playa 4am to 10pm
Fare: 120 pesos return
Trip length: 40min
The ferries dock at the Muelle Fiscal across from Benito Juárez Avenue in San Miguel. Be sure to bring along some motion-sickness medication and to eat only a light meal at least a half an hour before

boarding the ferry. Since the sea is quite choppy, at least a third of the passengers get seasick. On certain ferries you can sit outside on the deck. The following companies travel between these two cities. It is a good idea to confirm departures in advance.

Cozumel
☎(987) 872-1508

Playa del Carmen
☎(984) 873-0067

A car ferry crosses between Cozumel and Puerto Morelos, a small village 36km south of Cancún. It stops at the Muelle Internacional. The crossing takes 3-4hrs and you must get there 3hrs in advance.

By Car

Many hotels in Cozumel have car rental counters. Cars can also be rented at the airport and in San Miguel. A car ferry crosses once a day between Cozumel and Puerto Morelos but it's fairly complicated and expensive (see above).

To reach various places on the island, you have to drive on very rough dirt roads. Insurance included in car rental does not cover damage incurred when not driving on Cozumel's paved road.

The island really has only one paved road which starts from the north point of the island, stretches along the west coast, and then curves around the south point and returns to

San Miguel. A straight road crosses the island in the middle, from the east to the west coast (dangerous at night). When you arrive on Cozumel by boat you will be met by a crowd of people trying to rent you a car or motorcycle. According to the car-rental agencies, it is better to make a reservation in advance from your country, which is less expensive and will save you time upon arrival. Ask for a written confirmation. In Cozumel, car-rentals cost at least $40 a day depending on the model.

Here are a few businesses that rent cars, motorcycles and bicycles in Cozumel:

Aguila Rental
☎(987) 872-0729

Hertz
at the airport
☎(987) 872-3888

By Motorcycle

Although this is a popular way to get around the island, accidents are very common since the roads are rough and traffic is heavy. Also, the roads are often very narrow, which causes some close encounters between cars and motorcycles. Unless you are an experienced rider and familiar with the road signs and driving customs in Mexico, you should take a taxi.

By Taxi

Taxis are available 24 hours a day in Cozumel but there are additional costs between midnight and 6am.

Taxi station

Calle 2 Norte San Miguel
☎(987) 872-0041
There is a taxi stand in San Miguel. At your hotel's reception desk they can inform you of current rates. Please note, that prices are subject to frequent changes.

Practical Information

The area code for Cozumel is **987**

Tourist Information

Be wary of tourist information booths close to the park. Their only goal is to sell time-sharing condominiums, and the tourist information they offer is not reliable.

Direccion Municipal de Turismo

Mon-Fri 9am to 3pm, 6pm to 9pm
Edificio Plaza del Sol, San Miguel
☎872-7563

Cozumel Hotel Association

Mon-Fri 9am to 2pm, 5pm to 8pm
☎872-3132

Post Office

Mon-Fri 8am to 8pm, Sat 9am to 5pm, Sun 9am to 1pm
On Calle 7 Sur, at Av. Rafael Melgar
☎872-0106

Telephone

You can make long distance calls from telephone booths with a calling card.

Banks and Foreign Exchange Offices

Banks are open from 9am to 4pm or 5pm, from Monday to Friday. To change money it is better to arrive before 11am.

Banamex
ATM available
Av. 5 Norte, à la Plaza, San Miguel
☎872-3411

Banco Serfin
ATM available
Calle 1 Sur, between Av. 5 et Av. 10 Sur, San Miguel
☎872-0930

Bital
11 Av. Rafael E. Melgar, San Miguel
☎872-0142

Health

Clinics and Hospitals

Most of the clinics in Cozumel are used to treating minor injuries associated with scuba diving because accidents occur fairly frequently.

Cruz Roja (Red Cross)
☎872-1058

Hospital Civil
Av. 11 Sur
☎872-0140 or 872-5182

Servicios de Securidad Subaquatica (subaquatic safety service)
Calle 5 Sur nº 21B, San Miguel
☎872-2387
This clinic specializes in the pressure-related problems scuba divers can encounter. Open 24hrs a day, it is financed almost entirely by a sort of "levy" imposed on diving excursions *($1/ day)*.

Centro Médico de Cozumel
open 24 hrs, service in English
Calle 1A Sur nº 101, corner Av. 50, San Miguel
☎872-5664 or 872-5370
☎872-3345
This clinic is affiliated with the South Miami Hospital.

Pharmacies

There are six pharmacies in San Miguel. The following two are centrally located:

Farmacia Canto
Av. Pedro Joaquin Coldwell nº 498, at Av. 5 Sur
☎887-7093

Farmacia Paris
24hrs
Av. Pedro J. Coldwell, between Calle 2 and Calle 4 Norte
☎884-0164

Safety

Police
☎872-0490

Miscellaneous

Publications

In many shops and hotels you can get the Blue Guide *(Guía Azul)*, a free English publication that comes out three times a year. It contains a lot of advertising but may be useful.

Gas Station

There is a gas station in San Miguel, at the corner of Benito Juárez Avenue and Avenida 30. It is open every day, 24hrs a day. Avoid going there around 3pm because that is when the staff changes shifts and there is a long wait.

Exploring

San Miguel

This small city is the heart of the island, and the grid-system of streets makes it easy to find your way around. The action centres around the **Plaza San Miguel**, the main park of the city. From approximately 8pm to 10pm on Sunday nights the mariachi bands can be heard, and all the locals gather together to celebrate. Although the selection of craft and T-shirt shops, cafés and jewellery shops is very tourist-oriented in this region, the city has kept its Mexican spirit. Most of the island's restaurants are found in this area,

and many shops line the *malecón* (seaside promenade) which is called Avenida Rafael Melgar.

The **Museo de la Isla de Cozumel** ★★★ *($3; every day 9am to 6pm; Av. Rafael Melgar, between Calles 4 and 6, ☎872-1475)*, located north of Plaza San Miguel, was moved into a stylish hotel built in 1936. This museum comprises four exhibition halls spread over two floors. At the entrance to the first is a small-scale model of the island that spotlights its natural areas and indicates the location of interesting features such as lighthouses and archaeological sites. This gallery also introduces visitors to the island's topography, as well as the origin of local plant and vertebrate species. A diorama of the Cozumel jungle helps visitors understand the evolution of the island's ecosystems.

The genesis, formation and diversity of coral reefs are the themes of the second exhibition hall, while the history of Mayan civilization and the local Maya are the subject of the third hall. On display here are artifacts excavated from local archaeological sites. The gallery devoted to the history of Cozumel introduces visitors to the Spanish castaways who preceded the first Spaniard to set foot on the island, Juan de Grijalva, and the conquistadors.

Large signs explain the historical significance of the mid-19th-century Caste War. Tools and machines

demonstrate the important role played by major crops such as *chicle* and *henequén* in the development of the island's economy.

The 1hr tour of the museum offers a fine overview of the history of Cozumel and will enrich your stay, however short, on the island.

The museum's restaurant, located upstairs, offers a panoramic view of the strait that separates the island of Cozumel from the mainland.

South of the Island

At the southernmost tip of the island, Carretera Costera Sur runs into the **Parque Punta Sur** *(150 pesos, 8am to 4pm; ☎872-2940 or 872-0914)* at Km 27. This park is a 100ha-odd ecological reserve that includes Celarain Point, all of which has recently been carefully planned. The park is designed to promote the conservation of nature and the vestiges of the past, which delineate the different periods of occupation. As such, the great Faro Celarain (lighthouse), built in 1901, borders the Tumba del Caracol (see p 110), a small Mayan monument that once served as a navigational guide.

The recently built Celarain Lighthouse museum is devoted to the history of navigation. The light-keeper's house, occupied by Felix Garcia Aguilar for over 50 years, has

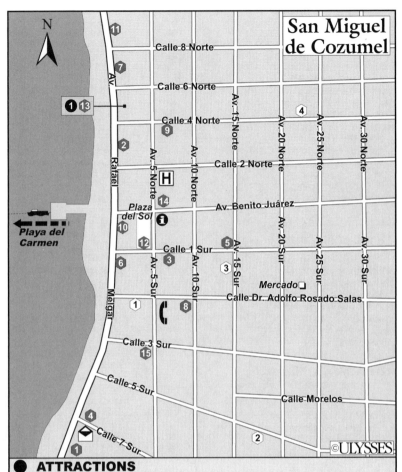

● ATTRACTIONS

1. Museo de la Isla de Cozumel

○ ACCOMMODATIONS

1. Flores
2. Palapas Amaranto
3. Posada Letty
4. Tamarindo Bed & Breakfast

⬡ RESTAURANTS

1. Acuario
2. Carlos 'n Charlie's
3. Casa Denis
4. Costa Brava
5. Diamond Bakery
6. Ernesto's Fajitas Factory
7. Guido's
8. La Choza

9. La Veranda
10. Las Palmeras
11. Pancho's Backyard
12. Plaza Leza
13. Restaurante del Museo
14. Such is Life
15. Tony Romas

been preserved and re-stored.

The park also comprises the Laguna Colombia, where you can rent a bicycle or kayak, swim or simply roam the trails. The amazingly diverse Laguna Colombia is a privileged spot. Observation towers allow more sedentary types to appreciate the surrounding landscape without exerting too much effort.

North of the Island

Although the **Faro Punta Molas** ★ at the north end of the island is difficult to reach, it's worth the trip. A lovely beach awaits those who venture to this se-cluded spot.

Archaeological Sites

The island's 25 archaeo-logical sites illustrate Cozumel's importance as a ceremonial site and centre of commerce. Most of the remains are small, low square buildings. Only a few of the eight major sites are accessible.

Since the semi-destruction of El Cedral (see below), **San Gervasio** ★ *(50 pesos; every day 9am to 4pm)* has become the most impor-tant group of buildings on the island. It is thought that San Gervasio was inhab-ited by Mayans from the year AD 300 to approxi-mately 1500. It was, at that time, the capital of the island. A group of small sanctuaries and temples were erected here to

honour Ix-Chel, the Mayan goddess of fertility. Each of the buildings has an accompanying plaque with text in Mayan, English and Spanish.

Overall, San Gervasio consists of stone struc-tures, lintels and columns, all scattered over a large area, and a few groups of lesser sites that fade into the forest. At the entrance to the site, where you purchase your ticket, there are craft shops and a snack bar. To reach San Gervasio, take the road that crosses the island eastward from San Miguel. A sign will indicate which junction to take, then you will have to drive about 10km north *(1$ for access to the road)*. San Gervasio receives an average of about 285 visitors every day.

South of San Francisco beach, a 3.5km-long paved road leads inland to the small village of **El Cedral** *(free entry; every day 8am to 5pm)*. This village was founded in the mid-19th century by Mes-tizo people from Valladolid who were fleeing the Mayan rebel soldiers. The village comprises, among other things, a small church built next to the only remaining pre-His-panic, and somewhat poorly preserved, Mayan temple. The stones of other Mayan buildings were used for the con-struction of the present village houses.

Not so long ago, this place was home to three groups of buildings erected

around large plazas. Only one structure, whose two rooms were used as a jail for some 20 to 30 years from 1935 on, was spared from demolition. In fact, locals call this building *el carcel* (the prison). The archaeological site dates from the early Postclassic period, that is to say from the time when the great city of Chichén Itzá was the capital of the northern Yucatán.

If you're in the vicinity of El Cedral between May 1st and 3rd, don't miss the Fiestas de la Santa Cruz, an annual festival featuring dancing, *corridas* (bull-fights) and carnival rides. The village then comes to life and takes on the ap-pearance of an island fair.

The vestiges of **Tumba del Caracol** ★, at the south end of the island, get their name from a temple that has a square base with a snail-shaped (in Spanish: *caracol*) dome on it, half of which has been destroyed. It is thought that this site was used as a lighthouse. The shells encrusted in the walls whistle in different tones, according to the wind. On the west side of the temple, over the door, traces of red paint can still be seen.

On the northeast coast of the island there are four temples, including **Castillo Real**, lining the east side of the road. The *castillo* is a square temple which is cracked in the middle and built on a platform. You can still see traces of fres-coes on the inside.

Parks and Beaches

Parks

Ten kilometres south of San Miguel you will find **Parque Chankanaab ★★** *($10; every day 7am to 7pm; Carretera Sur Km 9; ☎872-2940)*, one of the most attractive sites on the island, which features a large **botanical garden**. The Chankanaab lagoon is a natural aquarium supplied with sea water from underground tunnels. Approximately 50 species of fish, crustaceans and corals can be observed here, but scuba diving is not permitted. A winding path leads you through the botanical garden, with its 350 species of plants and tropical trees from 22 different countries. An interesting museum describes the life of the Mayas. Swimming is possible in the calm lagoon off the neighbouring beach. Snorkellers can explore the fascinating caverns and tunnels in the limestone.

The 320m-wide Chankanaab coral reef attracts many scuba divers with its countless colourful species. You have to dive to a depth of between 2 and 18m to examine the sights: the coral, a bronze statue of Christ, a statue of the Virgin Mary, cannons, ancient anchors and a sunken ship.

Scuba-diving equipment can be rented or bought on site. At the entrance to the site, there are changing rooms, beach huts, a snack bar, a bar-restaurant and gift shops. Many lounge chairs and *palapas* (straw parasols) are available for tourists.

Coral Reefs

As earlier mentioned, Cozumel is renowned for the great quantity and tremendous beauty of its coral reefs. Rumour has it that 1,500 scuba divers visit the island every day.

The **Palancar reef**, easily the most spectacular for its size and fabulous schools of fish, alone draws thousands of swimmers every year. Chankanaab park is the ideal place to learn how to scuba dive. There are even stairs you can go down leading to the submerged bronze statue of Christ.

The **Yucab reef**, reserved for intermediate divers, is perfect for underwater photography of species that stay immobile to avoid the current.

The **Santa Rosa** and **Colombia reefs**, famous for their immense size, merit more than a single visit.

The DC-3 airplane that rests at the bottom of the **Ceiba reef** attracts not only scuba divers... but also filmmakers! Sea horses have chosen it as their home.

Finally, the **El Paso del Cedral reef** allows novices to visit a cavern and encounter big hungry fish that don't like tourists who come empty-handed...

West Coast Beaches

Playa San Juan

This beach follows the whole northern hotel zone of San Miguel and ends at Punta Norte. Certified instructors and plenty of diving equipment are available for hire on this quiet beach. Windsurfing is also recommended here. There are many bars and snack bars.

Playa San Francisco

This beach is 5km long and is considered one of the most appealing on the island. Many conveniences (bar, restaurant, changing rooms, boutiques, lounge chairs and *palapas*, diving-equipment rental, volleyball net) are provided. Underwater wonders can be found in the calm waters close to shore. On Sundays, this beach is particularly popular with locals when many of the area's musicians come here to play.

Playa Sol

Just south of Playa San Francisco, this beach is a popular day-trip destination. All the amenities are available: a bar-restaurant, changing rooms and lockers, gift shops and an equipment-rental counter for snorkelling, scuba diving, water skiing and kayaking. Horseback riding outings and fake-iceberg-climbing expeditions are also organized.

East Coast Beaches

Playa Oriente

This beach is slightly north of the road that traverses the island, at the end of the road. The water here is among the choppiest of all the island's beaches, and only experienced surfers should take on these waves. There is a restaurant here.

Punta Chiquero

Tucked in a crescent-shaped cove south of the road, this is one of the most charming beaches on the east coast of the island. It is protected from waves by a reef and is ideal for swimming and surfing. A seafood restaurant named Playa Bonita is located here.

Playa Chen Río

This beach is near the middle of the east side of the island, about 5km north of Punta Chiqueros. The clear, relatively calm waters are suitable for surfing. There is parking, a restaurant and a bar.

Outdoor Activities

Beach Clubs

Beach clubs combine the practical and the pleasant, serving as both a restaurant and sports facility. As you may have guessed, scuba diving is the most popular sport in Cozumel. Most beach clubs are located south of Parque Chankanaab.

Playa Sol
$6
Carretera Costera Sur, Km 15.5
☎872-9030
The Playa Sol Beach Club is well known among hungry divers who enjoy a hearty lunch before heading off to discover Palancar. This beach club offers an outdoor restaurant, a souvenir shop, changing rooms and even a little zoo with alligators, parrots and rabbits. This spot is busier than the two clubs located immediately to the south.

Playa Corona
1km south of Parque Chankanaab
Sponsored by the beer of the same name, Playa

Corona offers diving, deep-sea fishing, refreshments and meals at its restaurant. What makes this site interesting is its proximity to easily observed underwater flora and fauna.

Deep-Sea Fishing

Club Nautico de Cozumel
Zona Hotelera Norte, Km 1,6
☎872-0118
⇄872-1135
This club has organized a world-class fishing tournament in April or May of each year since the 1970s.

Antonio Gonzalez Fernandez
This sports-fishing tournament, which takes place in November from the San Miguel quay, usually has about 30 participants. In 1996, the winner pulled in an impressive 54kg blue marlin and a 6kg red snapper.

Semarnat (Secretaría del Medio Ambiente, Recursos Naturales y Pesca)
Av. Insurgentas nº 445, Col. Magisterial, C.P. 77039 Chetumel, Quintana Roo
☎872-0906
Based in San Miguel, this governmental organization responsible for natural resources and fishing can supply information on upcoming events.

The **Caleta Marina** bay, located steps from the Presidente hotel, is a good spot for fishing excursions throughout the year.

Horseback Riding

It's very pleasant to discover the region on horseback. A 4hr tour usually includes the services of a guide, transport to the hotel and refreshments.

The following organization offers such excursions:

Rancho Buenavista
departures Mon-Sat
☎872-1537

Scuba Diving

Coral reefs (see p 111) are a fantastic sight to see while exploring the sea's depths but coral grows very slowly. Avoid touching it as this causes damage to the coral and you may injure yourself.

Businesses offering scuba-diving services with a guide, equipment and transportation to diving sites abound in Cozumel. Large hotels can also arrange for all necessary outfitting. The cost of a diving excursion may depend on various factors: lessons for beginners, distance to diving sites, excursion-cruise with a meal on a boat, etc. On average, it costs about $60 for a day of scuba diving with a trained guide and two oxygen tanks. Pamphlets and diving magazines abound on the island offering exhaustive list of diving centres. Here are a few specialized businesses in Cozumel:

Aldora Divers
☎872-3397
Aldora Divers has established a significant presence in cyberspace with their Web site. Aldora attracts divers from around the world, who use the Web site to get to know the staff prior to visiting Cozumel. After returning home, divers can visit the Web site again to give an assessment of their expeditions.

Any other questions? Send a short e-mail to this address: *dave@aldora.com*.

Dive Paradise
Av. Rafael E. Melgar n° 601, San Miguel
☎872-1007
Dive Paradise has an impressive team of 58 instructors.

Yucatech Expeditions
144 Av. 15 Sur, near Calle A. Rosado Salas, San Miguel
☎872-5659
In addition to organizing diving trips, Yuchatech can preserve your adventure on video.

It is also possible to take PADI-certification (recognized internationally) courses. For an advanced course, the price is around $700. These courses are spread out over a number of sessions. You can also take shorter courses that cover just the basics.

Cruises

Atlantis Submarines
$72
Zona Hotelera Sur Carretera Chankanaab, Km 4
☎872-5671
Even those who don't scuba dive can now admire the reefs and their inhabitants up close. The *Atlantis* is a specially equipped, 48-passenger submarine that dives to depths of up to 30m to the ocean floor, introducing you to a world all divers dream of. The descent is a once-in-a-lifetime experience: the schools of multicoloured fish, the multi-shaped coral reefs and the feeling of weightlessness provided by the submarine make the adventure worth every penny, and it is sure to become one of your most fantastic memories. Those taking photographs should use high-speed film (ASA 1000), as slower film will cause your photos of the seabed to turn blue. The submarine tour lasts 1.5hrs.

Fury Catamarans
$55
Zona hotelera Sur Km 4, near the Casa del Mar hotel
☎872-5145
Fury Catamarans offers the same type of activities, but also goes to a private beach where you can enjoy volleyball and kayaking among other things. On Tuesdays and Thursdays, Fury Catamarans go to the Palancar reef.

Capitania de Puerto Cozumel
Av. Rafael Melgar n° 601
☎872-2409
If you have your own boat or rent one, it is recommended that you contact the Capitania de Puerto Cozumel, or the office of the Cozumel harbour master before you leave, to find out weather conditions and navigational information.

Accommodations

Hotel Association of Cozumel
Mon-Fri 9am to 2pm and 5pm to 8pm
☎872-3132
⇌872-2809
This association can make hotel reservations for you and provide information. Member establishments are described on their Web site, at
www.islacozumel.com.mx

With respect to lodgings, the island is divided into three areas: San Miguel, the hotel zone north of San Miguel along the waterfront (Costera Norte), and the hotel zone south of San Miguel (Costera Sur). The northern zone, has the most luxurious hotels on the island. The most recent hotels, however, are found in the southern zone as it is developing more rapidly. The southern zone is also conveniently located close to Parque Chankanaab, Cozumel's main attraction.

Flores
$
≡, ⊗
Calle A. Rosado Salas n° 72, San Miguel
☎872-1429
Located in the heart of San Miguel, this small hotel may be modest, but it is certainly practical. The rooms offer a simple comfort. You're better off choosing a room on the third floor where there is less noise from the street.

Posada Letty
$
⊗
Calle 1 Sur n° 29, between Av. 1 et Av. 15, San Miguel
☎872-0257
Posada Letty rents eight simple, economical rooms that look a bit worn, but have humming fans.

Tamarindo Bed & Breakfast
$ bkfst incl.
⊗, ≡
Calle 4 Norte n° 421
☎/⇌872-3614
Run by a friendly Frenchman and his Mexican wife, this bed and breakfast is a good choice in the centre of San Miguel. This charming establishment is a 5min walk from the central park and the ocean. There are three simple rooms, which are quite big, clean, comfortable and decorated in the most genuine Mexican style. The place also offers two air-conditioned rooms, tucked away in the garden. Occupants share a terrace, overlooking the garden, where breakfast is served. The Tamarindo has an attractive shaded courtyard where you can relax in a hammock.

Guests can use the communal kitchen, which has an unlimited supply of purified water. Babysitting service is available upon request.

Palapas Amaranto
$
≡, ⊗
Calle 5 Sur, between Av.15 and Av. 20, San Miguel
☎873-3219 or 872-3614
☎872-6190
Inspired by Mayan architecture, this inn is one of a kind. The Amaranto features three air-conditioned bungalows, a suite and a "penthouse" apartment. Each unit comprises a king-size bed, TV, refrigerator, microwave oven, electric coffee maker and dishes. Guests can also cool off in the small swimming pool and rinse their diving gear in a tank set out for that purpose.

Casa del Mar
$$$
≡, ≈, ℜ
Carretera Chankanaab, Km 4
☎872-1900
⇌872-1855
www.casadelmarcozumel. com
The Casa del Mar's 106 rooms are attractively decorated with local crafts. The rooms overlook either the ocean or the pool. The hotel also has eight *cabañas*, which are a bit more expensive but can accommodate up to four people. The Casa del Mar has a dive shop, a car-rental counter, a restaurant, two bars and a travel agency.

Hotel Club Cozumel Caribe
$$$ all incl.
⊗, ≡, ≈, ℜ

Costera norte, Km 4.5

☎*872-0100 or 872-0255*

The Club Cozumel Caribe makes life easy for its occupants. This is the hotel that first introduced all-inclusive packages in Cozumel. Even though its beach is small, it is excellent for scuba diving. The rooms are large, feature modern decor and provide air conditioning and telephones. Most of them have a view of the sea and a balcony. The hotel has 260 rooms in a 10-storey tower that was added to the original three-story building. There is a medium-sized pool, a dive shop, a tennis court and a shopping promenade.

El Cid La Ceiba
$$$
☉, ≡, ℝ, ≈, ℜ

Costera Sur, Kkm 4.5

☎*872-0844*

⇌*872-0065*

www.elcid.com

A great many scuba divers stay at La Ceiba, many of whom are anxious to explore the remains of an airplane that crashed in the nearby waters. The hotel is located about 3km south of San Miguel, close to the cruise ship docks. The 113 rooms are inviting, with beige tiling and solid wood furniture. They all have an ocean view and a mini-bar. The building is a simple highrise but the gardens are pretty, and from the beach there is open access to an underwater diving site, with all the necessary diving equipment supplied by the hotel. There is also a large square pool with a swim-up bar and a whirl-pool.

Allegro Resort Cozumel
$$$ all incl.
≡, ≈, ℜ

Carretera Costera Sur, Km 16,5

☎*872-3443*

At the edge of Playa San Francisco, close to the Palancar reef, is the Allegro Resort Cozumel, an all-inclusive hotel with 300 rooms in two Polynesian style two-storey pavilions. The rooms are bright, quite big and austerely decorated, and all are air conditioned. The hotel has two pools, two bars, a dining room and four lit tennis courts. Bicycles and motorcycles can be rented here. A small boat takes hotel guests to the Palancar reef and the hotel supplies all the necessary equipment for scuba diving and snorkelling. The hotel organizes regular theme nights (tropical dance, performance by a hypnotist, disco night, karaoke, cabaret, Mexican folklore, etc.).

Club del Sol
$$$
≡, ≈, ℜ

Costera Sur, Km 1.5

☎*872-3777*

⇌*872-5877*

Located 1.5km south of San Miguel, across from the Fiesta Inn, this Mexican-style hotel has 40 rooms, which are clean and modestly furnished. The rooms have tile floors and the bathrooms have shower stalls only.

Sol Cabañas del Caribe
$$$
≡, ≈, ℜ

Costera Norte, Km 5.1

☎*872-0411*

⇌*872-1599*

The intimate and peaceful Sol Cabañas del Caribe is close to a beach that is perfect for sailing and diving. There are 48 rooms and nine private *cabañas* near the beach, as well as a restaurant. All the necessary equipment for snorkelling, scuba diving, fishing and other aquatic sports is supplied. Musicians provide evening entertainment at the small lounge-bar.

Sun Village Principe Cozumel
$$$
⊗, ≡, ≈, ℜ

Costera Norte, Km 3.5

☎*872-0144*

⇌*872-0016*

The Sun Village Principe hotel has 97 comfortable rooms on three floors. They all have telephones and sea views, but only a few have private balconies. The decor is simple, modern and colourful. The biggest pool is bordered on one side by an outdoor restaurant-bar covered with a great *palapa* roof. There is another, smaller pool and a wading pool for kids.

Fiesta Americana Cozumel Dive Resort
$$$-$$$$ bkfst incl.
≡, ≈, ℜ

Carretera Chankanaab, Km 7,5

☎*872-2622*

⇌*872-2154*

www.fiestamexico.com

The Fiesta Americana Cozumel Reef is a 172-room hotel facing a very attractive beach. It is located close to the

Chankanaab lagoon. The establishment also has 56 cottages. The spacious rooms all have balconies and a view of the sea. They are charmingly decorated with wood and rattan furniture and colourful walls. As well as a large pool, this hotel has three restaurants, two tennis courts, a sailing and windsurfing school, two bars (one on the beach), a souvenir shop and a dive shop.

Plaza Las Glorias
$$$$$
≡, ≈, ℜ, ℝ
Av. Rafael E. Melgar, Km 1,5, San Miguel
☎872-2000
⇄872-1937
You can almost touch the water from the Plaza Las Glorias, a Mexican-style hotel that has 170 large, well-decorated rooms, each with a private balcony and a view of the ocean. There are two bars, two restaurants, a dive shop and boutiques. You can rent a moped here. Local bands play here almost every night.

Paradisus Cozumel
$$$$$ all incl.
≡, ≈, ☺, ℜ
Costera Norte, Km 5.8
☎872-0412
⇄872-1599
www.paradisuscozumel.net
The Paradisus Club is a luxurious hotel surrounded by tall trees. There are 150 rooms richly decorated in Mexican style, all of which offer a private balcony and a view of the ocean. Some of them have whirlpools. The hotel has two good restaurants, two pools and two tennis

courts. Fishing, diving, surfing and horseback riding are some of the activities organized at the Paradisus Cozumel.

Crown Paradise Club / Sol Caribe Cozumel
$$$$$ all incl.
≈, ≡, ℝ, ℜ
Playa Paraíso, Costera Sur, Km 3.5
☎872-0700 or 872-1070
⇄872-1301
Crown Paradise Club Sol Caribe Cozumel is a 350-room, nine-storey hotel. The beach, across the street, is accessible by a tunnel. The hotel has an impressive lobby with a large thatched roof. Across from the beach is an arabesque-shaped pool and some large shady trees. The rooms, decorated in pastels, are equipped with wicker furniture, a marble bathroom, a telephone, a minibar and a small balcony. There is also complete dive shop, as well as two lit tennis courts and a private beach.

Coral Princess Hotel and Resort
$$$$$
≡, ⊗, ≈, ℜ
Carretera Costera Norte, Km 2,5
☎872-3200
⇄872-2800
Located north of the city, the recently remodeled Coral Princess has 61 suites. The suites are comprised of either a bedroom and living room, or one or two bedrooms with a kitchen and a living room. There are 39 standard rooms, not forgetting the 37 villas and two penthouses. All the rooms in this luxurious hotel have a ocean view

and telephones. Among other amenities, this hotel offers a restaurant, a pool, a travel agency and a dive shop.

Presidente Inter-Continental Cozumel
$$$$$
ℝ, ≡, ≈, ℜ
Carretera Chankanaab, Km 6.5
☎872-0322
⇄872-1360
www.cozumel.intercontinental.com
Located away from the commotion, the Coral Princess Club is situated close to a beach that is excellent for diving and is surrounded by greenery. The lobby is modern and covered with a thatched roof. The 253 large, comfortable and luxuriously decorated rooms all have a private balcony, and are divided among small one-to four-storey buildings. Most of the rooms have a view of the sea. The hotel has a big square pool, two excellent restaurants including **Arrecife** (see p 118), two bars, a billiard room, everything required for scuba diving, a car and motorcycle rental counter and two lit tennis courts. An interesting bit of trivia: this beautiful hotel was the setting of the film *Against All Odds*, starring Rachel Ward, Jeff Bridges and James Woods.

Restaurants

In general, it is much less expensive to eat at one of the many restaurants in San Miguel than at the hotels. Nevertheless, certain hotels have highly recommended restaurants. Cozumel's cuisine is similar to Cancún's: typically Mexican dishes as well as French, Italian and American food. Large chains such as Dairy Queen, Subway and Kentucky Fried Chicken have arrived in Cozumel over the last few years.

Diamond Bakery
$

Mon-Sat 7am to 11pm, Sun 9am to 11pm
Av. 15 Norte, corner Calle 1A, San Miguel
☎872-5782
Spacious, modern and air-conditioned, Diamond Bakery makes croissants, cookies, cakes and ice-cream. Since its expansion in 2000, the Diamond Bakery has become a café that now serves a variety of dishes. Not to worry, though, as the fresh pasta is still homemade. Vegetarians will have a difficult time chosing and the lunch menu is full of surprises. The ambiance is pleasant and the decor refined, with wrought-iron tables and chairs and a ceiling mural of a star-studded sky. Its panoramic windows provide a good view of the street corner. Friendly service.

Casa Denis
$

7am to 11pm every day
Calle 1 Sur n° 132, corner Av. 10 Sur, San Miguel
☎872-0067
To dine on a terrace overlooking a pedestrian-only street, head to Casa Denis, located across from the flea market. Open since 1945, this eatery prides itself on being the

town's oldest dining establishment. What's more, to judge by the photographs lining the walls, the Casa Denis's traditional Yucatán cuisine has attracted some high-profile guests over the years.

Ernesto's Fajitas Factory
$-$$
Av Rafael E. Melgar n° 141, San Miguel
☎872-3152
Ernesto's Fajitas Factory not only serves fajitas, but the usual assortment of tacos, quesadillas and burritos, as well as some vegetarian dishes. Breakfast costs only $3.

Costa Brava
$-$$
6:30am to 11pm
Av. Rafael Melgar n° 599
☎872-3549
Located south of the lighthouse and Calle 7 Sur, this is one of the best breakfast spots in San Miguel. For less than $3, you get freshly squeezed orange juice, eggs, *frijoles*, bread and jam, salsa and a bottomless cup of coffee. Just what you need to face a long day of diving! For other meals, the Costa Brava serves delicious fresh seafood (try the crab claws for two) and Yucatec specialties like chicken *pibil*. They will prepare your own catch for $2 per person.

🐟 La Choza
$-$$
Calle A. Rosado Salas n° 198, corner Av. 10, San Miguel
☎872-0958
With its *palapa* roof and tasty little dishes, La Choza is one of the best Mexican restaurants on the island. The country's specialties

(*pibil* chicken, *sopa de lima*, *guacamole*, etc.) can be savoured here at very reasonable prices. La Choza is a favourite among local residents. The ambiance is relaxing and the terrace is always pleasant and breezy. Economical breakfasts.

Las Palmeras
$-$$
7am to 11pm
Av. Rafael Melgar, corner Av. Benito Juárez
Las Palmeras is the first restaurant that visitors will encounter as they disembark from the ferry. The dining room is not air conditioned; but is nevertheless quite comfortable. With the sea breezes and a little shade, you may want to linger awhile... The menu is extensive, from fresh fish to steaks, and hamburgers. The food is quite acceptable and attracts many a tourist.

Plaza Leza
$-$$
Calle 1 Sur
☎872-1041
On the south side of San Miguel park, you can eat outside beneath parasols at the restaurant/bar Plaza Leza. Specialties are fish and seafood, steaks and Mexican dishes. It's a simple place that serves good food. Try the delicious Spanish omelette.

🐟 Restaurante del Museo
$-$$
Av. Rafael Melgar between Calles 4 and 6
☎872-0838
Before visiting the Museo de la Isla de Cozumel (see p 108), stop by the Restaurante del Museo,

which serves delicious Mexican food. The breakfasts here are generous, and there is a pretty view of the sea.

Pancho's Backyard
$$

Av. Rafael Melgar no. 27, between Calle 8 Norte and Calle 10 Norte

☎872-2141

Pancho's Backyard is aptly named, because it is literally located in the "backyard" of the Cinco Soles souvenir shop, and there is no sign indicating its location. Once past the sliding doors, you will be immersed in a buccolic interior courtyard, a tranquil spot to relax and have a bite to eat. The white-stucco walls and red-tiled roof evoke the colonial style. Marimba shows liven things up for diners as they savour the classics of Mexican cuisine.

Acuario
$$-$$$

Av. Rafael Melgar n° 778 at Calle 11

☎872-1097

Acuario means aquarium in Spanish and the dining area here is surrounded by aquariums full of fish. The menu also lists plenty of fresh fish, since along with seafood, this is the house specialty. A delicious meal awaits you here.

Carlos 'n Charlie's
$$-$$$
10am to 1am
Av. Rafael E. Melgar n° 11, San Miguel

☎872-0191 or 872-1505

Like the one in Cancún, this restaurant/bar is somewhat of a zoo, with its blaring rock music, constantly flowing beer, ping-pong table, basketball hoop, pool table and busy decor. They serve generous portions of ribs, grilled steak and chicken. Facing the sea, one block north of the port, Carlos 'n Charlie's is easily recognizable by its red exterior.

Such is Life
$$-$$$
Doctor A. Gonzalo Salas n° 764A,
between Calle 5 and Calle 10, San Miguel

☎872-0584

The elegant interior of this restaurant perfectly suits this entirely wooden building. Steak and seafood dishes are served here. The refined decor and discrete service are sure to make your evening an enjoyable one.

Guido's
$$-$$$
closed Sun
Av. Rafael E. Melgar n° 23, between Calle 6 Norte and Calle 8 Norte, San Miguel

☎872-0946

In addition to pizzas cooked in a wood-fired oven, this family-run restaurant offers unique fare. In fact, Guido's daily menu strays from typical Mexican cuisine. Yvonne and Adolfo offer patrons a choice of three starters, four main courses (meat, fish and/or pasta) and dessert. In the interior courtyard, blooming bougainvilleas attract flitting hummingbirds. The decor is simple yet tasteful.

Tony Romas
$$-$$$
Av. 5, between Calle Salas and Calle 3 Sur, San Miguel

☎872-0085 or 872-0084

Tony Romas' large dining room looks like a Mexican sugar shack. The patrons don't seem to care about the decor, but rather about satisfying their appetites with the very simple but filling spare ribs and grilled chicken. All kinds of shows are featured at night with occasional karaoke nights for patrons who aren't afraid of losing their inhibitions.

La Veranda
$$-$$$
Calle 4 Norte, between Av. 5 Norte and Av. 10 Norte, San Miguel

☎872-4132

This restaurant's facade does in fact look a lot like a veranda. The decor is simple, the food is excellent, and the staff is very friendly. When the sun sets over the ocean, the terrace becomes the ideal spot for a romantic dinner. The restaurant serves a good variety of fish and seafood dishes.

Arrecife
$$$$
Carretera Chankanaab, Km 6.5

☎872-0322

Arrecife is located inside the Presidente Inter-Continental Cozumel hotel. Here, you can dine on seafood and Mediterranean nouvelle cuisine while comfortably seated facing large bay windows that overlook the sea. The decor is warm and romantic and there are often musicians performing.

Entertainment

Hard Rock Café
Av. Rafael Melgar, near Benito Juárez
☎872-5271 or 872-0986
As with all the other locations, Cozumel's Hard Rock Café appeals to fans of loud popular rock music. The staff take it upon themselves to liven up customers that are too relaxed.

Joe's Lobster House
Av. 10 Sur nº 29 between Calles A. Rosada Salas and 3 Sur
☎872-3275
To hear reggae and salsa music, the best place in the city is definitely Joe's Lobster. Musicians perform on weekends.

Neptuno Dance Club
Av. Rafael E. Melgar, corner Av. 11, San Miguel
☎872-1537
If you still have energy after a long day of lounging on the beach or underwater exploring, head to Neptuno. With videos, laser lights and booming music, it's *the* nightclub for young people in Cozumel.

Kiss My Cactus
Av. Rafael Melgar nº 161
☎872-0845
Kiss My Cactus, located right near Viva Mexico, is a recent addition to Cozumel's entertainment scene. The building is particularly unusual with its facade in the shape of giant pink and purple sunglasses.

Viva Mexico
Av. Rafael E. Melgar, San Miguel
☎872-0799
At Viva Mexico, the mood is the same as Neptuno's. It has a very large dance floor and usually fills up only on weekends.

Shopping

In Cozumel, many stores and offices close between 1pm and 4pm or even 5pm. Stores on Rafael Melgar Avenue, however, stay open during the high season for the flood of tourists who arrive every day by boat.

As in Cancún, the best buys in Cozumel are crafts, hammocks, silver jewellery and cigars. Do not purchase anything made of black coral, even if they say it is *the* specialty of the island, because this species is threatened with extinction. Take the time to discover the shops in San Miguel, rather than just wandering near the port area, which is less interesting and more expensive. There are dozens of craft boutiques close to the park. Payment is accepted in pesos and in US dollars. Credit cards aren't accepted everywhere, and when they are, there is a surcharge.

San Francisco de Asis
Av. 65, between Calle 25 and Calle 27; Av. 30, corner Av. Juárez, San Miguel
In Cozumel there are large markets that sell everything: oven-fresh bread, clothing, crafts, cosmetics—and alcohol that is significantly less expensive than at the duty-free shop in the port district! San Francisco de Asis is one of the best markets in Cozumel.

Mercado Municipal
Mon-Sat 8am to 5pm
Calle A. Rosado Salas, between Av. 20 Sur and Av. 25 Sur, San Miguel
The municipal outdoor market is alive with the hustle and bustle of *Cozumeleños*.

Los Cinco Soles
Av. Rafael E. Melgar Norte nº 27, San Miguel
☎872-0132
Located in front of Pancho's Backyard (see p 118), this shop is an absolute must for Mexican crafts. There is also a small café inside.

Van Cleef & Arpels
Av. Rafael E. Melgar Norte, in front of the wharf
☎872-6540
This jewellery store sells original, fine-quality gold and silver creations. Compare prices before you buy!

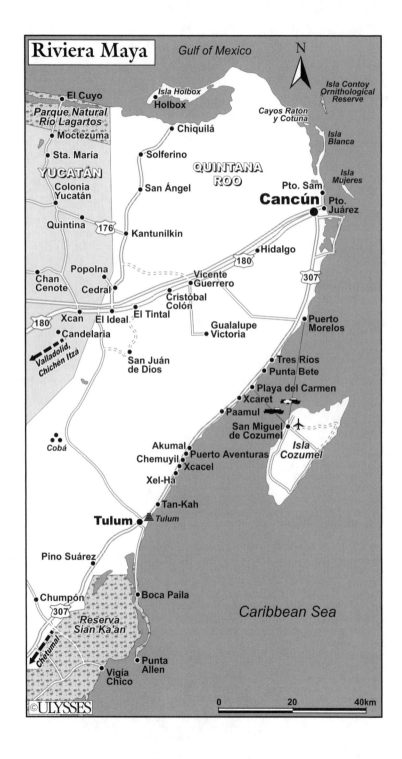

Riviera Maya

The Cancún-Tulum corridor has recently been dubbed the Riviera Maya. This name, evocative of the region's first occupants, refers to the Mexican coast between the port of Puerto Morelos and the village of Punta Allen, located in the Reserva de la Biosfera Sian Ka'an.

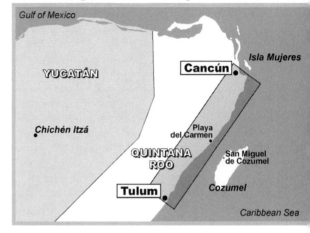

Not so long ago, the Caribbean coast of Mexico consisted of a series of pristine beaches, fish-filled lagoons, unexplored *cenotes*, caves and underground rivers. A generation ago, a secondary road running parallel to the coast linked a few peaceful villages. But things have changed a great deal over the last 25 years.

The region acquired its claim to fame in the 1980s, thanks to scores of organized day trips from Cancún to the archaeological cities of Tulum and Cobá, as well as to the enchanting Xel-Há marine park.

Of course, Cancún remains the ultimate tourist mecca. Nevertheless, the Riviera Maya is worth much more than a simple excursion. It is a destination in itself, and its many attractions are sure to satisfy those in search of natural beauty and outdoor activities. Only a small number of archaeological sites have been restored, but those open to the public offer a very interesting glimpse of how the Maya lived prior to the arrival of the Spanish.

Along the 200km-odd stretch of coastline lie dozens of beautiful beaches, some of which are lined with luxury resorts while others are bordered by rustic *cabañas*. Off the coast, the Great Maya Reef, the world's second-largest coral barrier reef, offers a fantastic view of the seabed.

The remains of ancient Mayan cities share this magnificent landscape with modern buildings erected to satisfy the ever-growing crowd of tourists from Europe and the Americas.

The region's first occupants spoke Yucatec Maya and, though Spanish is now the official language, most descendants of the Maya still speak Yucatec. More recently, French-, German- or Italian-speaking newcomers have given this paradise a cosmopolitan feel. Moreover, English is spoken just about everywhere.

Cancún's immense popularity thus opened new horizons for visitors in search of a more intimate setting. The tourist infrastructure of the Cancún-Tulum corridor took shape in the early 1990s, with the opening of the first major hotels. Although there are no official statistics, it is estimated that the region has more than 15,000 rooms distributed throughout 300 lodging establishments, 225 of which are in Playa del Carmen.

Over the last 10 years or so, the Riviera Maya has become a major tourist destination; the commercial port of Puerto Morelos has retained its look of a sleepy fishing village, but tourist attractions have popped up all around. The once-quiet little town of Playa del Carmen has become a city of over 50,000 inhabitants.Very popular with tourists, it has many "all-inclusive" resort hotels tucked away in the Playacar district. The magnificent beach south of the archaeological site of Tulum is now home to 10 times more hotels and *cabañas* than it was a decade ago.

The village of Tulum Pueblo has not experienced the same transformation as the coast, but now offers all services related to mass tourism (from car rentals and English- or French-speaking doctors to restaurants offering international fare). Tulum Pueblo is not only the starting point for great destinations like Palenque or Tikal, but also a stopover for a growing number of vacationers and globetrotters. Its small hotels and family-run restaurants are every bit as inviting as those in other destinations on the Riviera Maya.

Finding Your Way Around

By Plane

Playa del Carmen

Travellers can reach Playa del Carmen by plane from Cozumel. Situated just south of the town, the small airport receives domestic flights. Travellers must get there 2 hrs ahead of time. From Playa del Carmen, there are two flights a week to Chichén Itzá and Cozumel.

Aerosaab
☎(984) 873-0804

By Car

Driving is definitely the easiest way to cover the region. There are Pemex gas stations every 30 to 40km along Highway 307, also known as Carretera Cancún-Tulum and Carretera Cancún-Chetumal. This newly repaved two-lane highway skirts the coast some 3 to 4km from the beach. A little past Playa del Carmen, it narrows down to one lane and continues to Tulum. From there, Highway 307 runs through inland towns and villages and on to Chetumal, the capital of Quintana Roo.

Side roads and trails off Highway 307 lead to all-inclusive resorts, attractions, villages and natural sights, most of which are located east of the highway. If you're driving in from the north, be careful when turning left as the right of way is not always indicated.

All along the highway are mileage markers that indicate the distance from Chetumal, rather than Cancún. These recently added markers are sure to cause some confusion over the next few years, as hotel and attraction addresses indicate the mileage from Cancún or the international airport, rather than Chetumal. Distances from Cancún are indicated in the box entitled "The Main Exits on Highway 307 from Cancún" (see next page).

Leaving Cancún

To leave downtown Cancún, take southbound Avenida Tulum, which turns into Highway 307.

From the Hotel Zone, take southbound Paseo Kukulcán to Highway 307. Paseo Kukulcán leads to the airport; on reaching the cloverleaf intersection, pay particular attention so as to avoid ending up on the road leading downtown. You must pass over Highway 307 and take the right-hand loop leading south (Playa del Carmen) by this same road.

From the Cancún airport, follow the signs to the exit (some 300m) up to Highway 307 and turn right (heading south).

The army sometimes puts up a roadblock on Highway 307 south of the exit for the airport. They search cars and trucks, but rarely vehicles driven by tourists.

Puerto Morelos

There is a gas station on Highway 307. It is located at the intersection with the road that leads to Puerto Morelos. Because there are not many along the way, drivers would do well to fill up before resuming the trip along the Tulum corridor.

Playa del Carmen

This city is located about 68km from Cancún. It takes 45min to drive from Cancún to Playa del Carmen along the coast.

Car Rental

Hertz
7am to 9pm
Plaza Marina, Playacar
☎*(984) 873-0703*
Carretera Cancún-Tulum, Km 65
☎*(984) 873-1130*

Budget
Hotel Continental Plaza Hotel
Playa del Carmen
☎*(984) 873-0100*

Thrifty
Calle 8, between Av. 5 and Av. 10
☎*(984) 873-0119*

Tulum

To get to Tulum, take Highway 307 south. Some 130km further is the Tulum archaeological site, the village of Tulum (Tulum Pueblo) and Tulum Playa.

Car Rental

Cabañas Playa Mambo
in front of the bus station
☎*(984) 287-2030*

Cobá Archaeological Site

Just south of the ruins of Tulum, turn right and drive 47km to the Cobá archaeological zone. Look out for the speed bumps as they are not indicated.

Reserva de la Biosfera Sian Ka'an

The Carreterra Tulum-Boca Paila, a bumpy and dusty road south of the hotels lining the Tulum beach leads to the Sian Ka'an reserve and continues to the small village of Punta Allen. The reserve is about 16km south of

Tulum. A military outpost is located just after the entrance to the reserve. Tourists are rarely stopped here, but make sure you have the proper identification just in case.

Boca Paila and Punta Allen

If you are going by car, it takes a little over 4hrs to get to Punta Allen from Cancún. The Cancún-Tulum road is in good condition, but it becomes a rocky and bumpy dirt road south of Tulum.

By Bus

Playa del Carmen

Many buses run regularly, about every 15min or so, between Cancún and Playa del Carmen. The fare is $3 and the trip takes 1hr.

The bus station in Playa del Carmen is on Avenida 5, at Avenida Juárez.

A first-class bus departs for Chichén Itzá by bus in first class at 7:50pm. Also, there are a number of departures during the day for Tulum and Xcaret

Tulum

There are two bus stations in Tulum, both of which are the departure points for many destinations. One is near the archaeological zone and another is downtown. The latter is open 24hrs. There are departures for Chichén Itzá on first-class buses at 7:30am and 12:45pm. There are also many

The Main Exits on Highway Mex 307 from Cancún

At Km 14: the airport.

At Km 19: to the resort hotels.

At Km 28.5: to Punta Tanchacte (Bahia Maya Village), near Highway 307, a market and restaurant.

At Km 30: Crococun Crocodile Park, a farm, a zoo; beachfront hotels and restaurants; note that a small road runs along the beach up to Puerto Morelos.

At Km 36: to Puerto Morelos.

At Km 38: Jardín Botánico Dr. Alfredo Barrera.

At Km 40: Rancho Loma Bonita, horseback-riding centre.

At Km 45: to Playa del Secreto.

At Km 49: to the beach and the Carousel hotel.

At Km 51: to Punta Maroma.

At Km 57: to Tres Rios.

At Km 59: to the Le Mandarin hotel.

At Km 62: to the beach; Capitán Lafitte & Kailum hotels and restaurants.

At Km 63.5 and 65: to Punta Bete Xcalacoco.

At Km 66: to the Moxche beach.

At Km 67: to the beach and the Shangri La hotel.

At Km 68, 69 and 69.5: access to the town of Playa del Carmen and Playacar.

At Km 72: to the Motor Jungle Tour.

At Km 73: to the Xcaret marine park.

At Km 77: to Punta Venato or Puerto Calica.

At Km 86: to Paamul

At Km 92: to Puerto Aventuras (resort hotel).

At Km 93 and 94: three exits west of the road to the Katun Chi, Azul and Cristalino *cenotes*.

At Km 94.5: to the Barcelo Maya Beach & Garden Resort.

At Km 95, 96 and 97: to Xpu-Ha (take Route X7 to reach the public beach); the Copacabana hotel has its own private road.

At Km 98: to the Robinson Club Tulum hotel.

At Km 99: to the Le Dorado Resort.

At Km 104: to Kantenah; hotel and restaurants.

At Km 105, 106 and 107: to Akumal; large tourist resort.

At Km 111: to the Bahia Principe Resort.

At Km 112: to the Chemuyil beach.

At Km 113: to the west and the Mayan village of Chemuyil.

At Km 115: to Xcacel.

At Km 117: entrance to the Xel-Há nature park.

At Km 119: to the west and a series of *cenotes* and underground rivers.

At Km 120: an 8km-long road leads to Bahias de Punta de Soliman.

At Km 122 and 125: Tankah, Manati *cenote* and long beach.

At Km 129: to the Sole Resort.

At Km 131: the archaeological site of Tulum, bus station, Pemex.

At Km 132.5: westbound road that leads to Cobá.

At Km 132.5: road to the beach, to the east (2km), with hotels and *cabañas*. This road leads to Carretera Tulum-Punta Allen (which starts just south of the archaeological zone and follows the coast to the Sian Ka'an reserve).

At Km 133: Tulum Pueblo.

Riviera Maya

departures throughout the day for Tulum and Xcaret.

Cobá

Buses run between Playa del Carmen and Cobá, with a stop in Tulum. The trip takes 2hrs and 15min and costs a little over $3.

Boca Paila and Punta Allen

No buses run between Cancún and Boca Paila or Punta Allen. Buses only go to the village of Tulum. From there, take the *collectivo* to Boca Paila or Punta Allen.

By Taxi

You will find taxis in Playa del Carmen, Puerto Morelos, Akumal, Puerto Aventuras and Tulum. Remember to negotiate the fare before setting out.

There is a taxi stand in Playa del Carmen at the

corner of the pedestrian street and Avenida Juárez. Taxis can accommodate up to five people. Having the exact fare is preferable, since drivers never have change. Also, contrary to popular belief, they do appreciate tips.

Playa del Carmen
☎*(984) 873-0032*

Tulum
☎*(984) 871-2029*

By Boat

Playa del Carmen

There are about 15 crossings in both directions every day between Playa del Carmen and Cozumel, aboard modern ferries. The first departure is at 5am, the last at 11pm, and the rest at approximately 2hr intervals. Schedules tend to vary, however. The Playa del Carmen

port is at the southern extremity of the city. Tickets are obtained at the port entrance *(approx. $16 return)*. The crossing takes between 35 and 45min. According to statistics, close to 30% of passengers suffer from seasickness. Eat lightly, not less than half an hour before departure, and bring some plastic bags!

Visitors with cars en route to Cozumel from Puerto Morelos can expect to wait up to 1hr. The crossing takes between 3 to 4hrs, and it is far from cheap: $67 (700 pesos) per car and $6 (63 pesos) per person. The first car-ferry departure for Cozumel is usually at 8am, but schedules change constantly. For accurate departure times, call ☎*(984) 871-0008* (for Puerto Morelos) or ☎*(984) 872-0827* (for Cozumel).

Practical Information

The area code for Playa del Carmen is **984**.

Tourist Information

Like Cancún and Cozumel, Playa del Carmen, Puerto Aventuras, Akumal and Tulum produce tourist information brochures.

Playa del Carmen

At Playa del Carmen, there is counter near the bus station that distributes brochures and maps.

Playa Info
Av. 5, between Calles 10 and 12
☎876-1344

Tourism Bureau
Corner Juárez and Av. 15
☎873-2804

Tulum

In Tulum, **The Weary Traveler** (☎871-2461) is the best source of tourist information.

Health

Clinics

Playa del Carmen

Centro de Salud
Av. Juárez, corner Av. 15
☎872-1230

Cruz Roja (Red Cross)
Av. Juárez, corner Av. 25
☎873-1233

Dr. Victor Macias
Av. 35, between Calles 2 and 4
☎873-0493
☎874-4760 (cell)

Tulum

Dr. Arturo Ventre Manjarrez
Dr. Manjarrez speaks English and French.
Pharmacia Primera
Av. Tulum
☎871-2052

Pharmacies

Puerto Morelos

Farmacia San José Obrero
2 Rojo Gómez
☎871-0053

Playa del Carmen

Farmacia Canto
Av. 30 Norte Mz 34;
Calle 4, corner Constituyenles
☎873-0512

Farmacia Luz de la Aurora
Av. Juárez Sur, corner 30 Av.
☎873-0312

Tulum

La Salud Farmacia
Av. Tulum (in front of the bus station)
☎871-2319

Police

Emergencies: ☎060

Puerto Morelos

☎871-0117

Playa del Carmen

☎873-0291

Tulum

☎871-2055

Banks and Currency Exchange Bureaus

You will find currency exchange bureaus all over the Riviera Maya; banks are rarer.

Puerto Morelos

Mor Ex
southwestern corner of the *zócalo*

Playa del Carmen

Bancomer
Av. Juárez, between Calle 25 et Calle 30, five houses west of Av.5
☎873-0356

Puerto Aventuras

There is an ATM in the shopping centre.

Tulum Pueblo

Banco Bital (*Av. Tulum*) is located north of the police station.

Post Office

Playa del Carmen

Av. Juárez, corner Av. 20
Mon-Fri 8am to 5pm
Sat 9am to 1pm
☎873-0300

Tulum

Av. Tulum

Travel Agencies

Playa del Carmen

Terra Maya Tours
5 Av. corner Calle 4 and 6
☎*873-1385*

Tulum

Sian Ka'an Tours
Av. Tulum
☎*871-2363 or 871-2499*

Internet Cafés

Playa del Carmen

La Taberna
Corner Calle 4 and Av. 18
☎*803-0447*

Atomic Internet Café
Calle 8, corner Av. 5
This Internet café has a modern decor and is air-conditioned. People come here to sip a frothy cappuccino and have a bite to eat while sending e-mail to faraway friends. It costs 1.5 pesos per min to surf the net or 200 pesos for 200 min.

Cyberia Internet Café
Calle 4, between Av.'s 10 and 15
Internet addicts get together at the Cyberia Internet Café to surf the web or read their e-mail from friends back home. The place is not air conditioned, but the fans and a cold beer should keep you cool.

Tulum

The Weary Travelers
☎*871-2461*

Exploring

Puerto Morelos

Thirty-six kilometres south of Cancún, Puerto Morelos is a small fishing village from which car ferries leave for Cozumel. Imported products headed for Cancún and Cozumel are transported in freighters, which pass by Puerto Morelos, the second largest port in the region next to Puerto Juárez, situated a few kilometres north of Cancún. Tourist development here, though not as intense as in Playa del Carmen, is well under way. The beach is beautiful and the village lies only half an hour by car from Cancún. While hotels and condominiums may not be springing up like mushrooms, they are growing at a rapid rate nevertheless. A coral reef just off the coast is ideal for scuba diving and snorkelling. Puerto Morelos is a quiet town where life is simple and people prove to be very gracious.

Puerto Morelos claims to have the largest bookstore (which sells English-language books) on the Riviera Maya. You'll find everything you need in this town for a pleasant stay.

Near Puerto Morelos

The **Jardin Botanico Dr. Alfredo Barrera ★★** (*$3.75; Tue-Sun 9am to 5pm; Hwy. 307, Km 38,*

1km south of Puerto Morelos) is actually a nature trail that allows visitors to discover the region's ecological wealth. In addition to the region's plants, trees and flowers, visitors can see monkeys, iguanas and an interesting little Mayan temple. The garden also includes a lovely collection of orchids.

At Km 30 you'll find **Crococún ★★** (*$15; Mon-Sat 9am to 6pm; Hwy. 307, Km 30*), a large crocodile farm where visitors can observe "Moreletti" crocodiles of all ages and sizes—well screened behind a metal barrier. Guides sometimes open the cages and allow visitors to touch the animals. Lucky visitors also get to see parrots and snakes. This site comprises a little boutique and a restaurant, as well. The journey by bus from Cancún to Puerto Morelos takes half an hour. The driver makes a special stop in Crococún upon request.

Tres Rios

Created at the end of 1998, **Tres Rios** (*$34; every day, 9am to 5pm; ☎887-8077*) is located just 10km (15min) north of Playa del Carmen and 25min south of Cancún. Tres Rios is a private, 150ha ecological reserve that is named for three waterways that empty into the ocean and which draw their source from three *cenotes* (natural pools) on the reserve. After paying the entrance fee, you can take one of the many

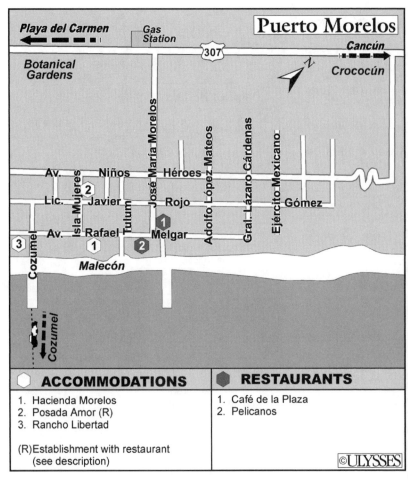

ACCOMMODATIONS

1. Hacienda Morelos
2. Posada Amor (R)
3. Rancho Libertad

(R) Establishment with restaurant
    (see description)

RESTAURANTS

1. Café de la Plaza
2. Pelicanos

©ULYSSES

bicycles parked next to the ostrich farm and ride either to the beach or to the *cenotes*, where you can scuba dive all the way to the sea. Unlike at Xel-Há, where visitors dally about in a giant aquarium next to schools of colourful fish, the waterways at Tres Rios are surrounded by luxurious vegetation, are more isolated and less frequented. You can also kayak down the waterways which wind through forests and mangroves.

Horses can also be rented to gallop on the beach. Finally, scuba divers can't miss the deep-sea wreck not far offshore. The reserve also has a restaurant and a souvenir shop. Towels and lockers can be rented.

Punta Bete/Xcalacoco

Some 65km from Cancún, a bumpy, 3km road leads to Punta Bete/Xcalacoco.

This quiet spot's campsites and beautiful 3km-long beach with few modern facilities make it a popular off-the-beaten-track destination. It is also ideal for swimming and diving. Several families live here from the meagre income derived from a now-decimated coconut plantation. Punta Bete/Xcalacoco has some simple restaurants and hotels as well as *palapas* on the beach.

Playa del Carmen

In Mayan times, this place was known as *Xaman Ha* (Mayan word meaning "Waters of the North"). Today, locals and regular visitors alike simply call it "Playa." The liveliest and most touristy city between Cancún and Chetumal, Playa del Carmen has approximately 50,000 residents. Because of its geographic location, the town is the ideal place from which to begin a tour of the region. Several boats make daily crossings to Cozumel. Cruise ships frequently drop anchor in front of the city; their twinkling lights sparkling on the horizon at night are a beautiful sight. Playa del Carmen is mainly frequented by hikers, archaeology enthusiasts and those who love roaming the outdoors and basking in pleasurable idleness.

On Playa del Carmen's main street, Avenida 5, there is a succession of restaurants, bars and shops, testifying to the pronounced tourist development experienced by this region.

Avenida 5 follows the coastline behind a series of hotels and restaurants. A pedestrian mall, it makes driving on cross streets difficult. In Playa, streets running parallel to the shore are *avenidas* (avenues), and those that are perpendicular are *calles* (streets).

Not long ago, Playa del Carmen was nothing more than a quaint little fishing village with ramshackle huts and dusty, pothole-strewn roads lined with several small, homey, unpretentious restaurants. Sometimes a hen would come out of nowhere and roam through the little village cackling while her owner ran after her to the laughter of children. The beach was devoid of hotels, and you could dip your toes in the water or sling a hammock between two palms and enjoy the *farniente* without being disturbed by a soul. But time marches on, changing everything in its course, and Playa del Carmen is definitely not what it used to be. It is rapidly changing to meet the needs of tourists who flock here year-round. Hotels, restaurants, travel agencies and boutiques are springing up everywhere. Avenida 5, once a bumpy road full of potholes, is now the town's main road. Between Calle 1 and Calle 8, it becomes a pedestrian street closed to traffic and lined with a succession of outdoor cafés, hotels, restaurants, bars and stores with their vendors standing outside yelling "Amigo, cheaper for you, come inside." The beach is as splendid as ever, sunbathing in the nude is still permitted and the sun continues to shine.

Playacar

This major tourist project is located south of downtown Playa del Carmen, on the other side of the airport. The 354ha development is constantly developing and comprises an 18-hole golf course, a tennis centre, several hotels, an arts centre and a shopping mall. All of the major hotel chains are represented here and are all-inclusive.

Visitors must enter the Playacar complex in order to admire the three post-classical Mayan remains at the site. The first group is approximately 300m from the entrance, to the right, easily visible from the road. It consists of a small raised structure whose façade is guarded by a row of stone columns. The two other groups are a few metres away along the same road, and are also very interesting.

The **Aviario Xaman-Ha** ★ *(admission fee; every day 9am to 5pm; Paseo Xaman-Ha, Fracc., ☎/≈873-0593)* is an ornithological reserve for bird species that are found in the Yucatán and elsewhere in Mexico: pink flamingos, toucans, pelicans, ibis, herons, parrots, cormorants and storks, as well as certain species of wild duck. The site is divided into six sections, according to groups of birds. Researchers are studying the breeding habits of about 30 different species in this reserve.

The **Playacar golf course** *(☎873-0624)* is laid out over a vast undulating expanse of greenery. Designed by Robert von Hagge, it is rated one of the best in the country and often hosts international tournaments.

Xcaret

The history of Xcaret (pronounced Ich-ca-rét) begins around the year 600, when it was a city called Pole with a ceremonial centre, a large market and the principal gateway to Cozumel. Francisco de Montejo Sr., the conqueror of the Yucatán, lost several men here during the course of a battle in 1528. This enchanting site comprises a subterranean river, vestiges of Mayan structures, and a *cenote*, which nowadays are supplemented by restaurants, shops, a marina and neighbouring hotels.

Xcaret (a Mayan word meaning "little bay") is now a 40ha property where visitors can dive, sail, horseback ride, swim with dolphins, or just meditate. The site also comprises a museum, a small zoo, an aquarium, a botanical garden and a reconstructed Mayan village. Every night, the "*Xcaret de Noche*" show, a big historical musical production, is presented here. There is so much to do in Xcaret that visitors can easily spend the whole day here.

The popular new watersport in Xcaret is called "snuba." This activity, a cross between scuba diving and snorkelling, involves breathing through a long tube attached to an oxygen tank. With the help of an experienced diver, you can snuba down to the ocean floor and explore the fascinating underwater world.

Every day, buses shuttle back and forth between Cancún and Xcaret. They leave from the head office of the private enterprise that runs the site, in Cancún, at 9am, 10am and 11am (*next to the Fiesta Americana Coral Beach hotel*).

Food, beverages, radios and sun lotion are prohibited in Xcaret. The only accepted lotion is the 100%-natural *Xcaret* lotion.

The site (*www.xcaretcancun.com*) is open from April to October, every day from 8:30am to 10pm.

Admission fee: **$49**
Swimming with dolphins: **$115**

Paamul

Paamul, a well-sheltered little beach, tucked away in a bay, may not seem that heavenly at first glance because of the seashells and pieces of coral strewn about that make it dangerous to walk barefoot. Those who love Paamul mainly come to scuba dive, for the sea is crystal-clear here and a great variety of tropical fish can be observed in its waters.

Every July and August, giant turtles arrive during the night to nest on the beach. Visitors must take particular care not to touch the eggs or shine any lights in their direction so as not to frighten the turtles, who already see half their offspring devoured by predators.

Puerto Aventuras

Puerto Aventuras, 20km south of Playa del Carmen, is undergoing rapid expansion. Formerly deserted, this bay is now the setting of an ambitious, luxury condominium complex, opened in 1987 (see p 143), that extends over 365ha. An additional 600ha are currently under development. Its main attractions are a marina and an 18-hole golf course. Puerto Aventuras comprises private bungalows, condominiums, several hotels, boutiques and restaurants. The "time-share" formula is very popular here.

In 1741, the Spanish galleon *El Matancero* struck the reefs near Akumal. The **Pablo Bush Romero Museum of Submarine Archaeology** ★ (*voluntary donation; Mon-Sat 9am to 1pm and 2:30pm to 6:30pm; ☎873-5129*) exhibits various objects recovered from the wreck such as belt buckles, cannons, coins, pistols and terracotta vases from Mayan ruins in the area.

Xpu-Há

Xpu-há beach, which has been overrun by hotels, is hidden 3km south of Puerto Aventuras. It remains, however, a place where scuba diving and snorkelling are readily enjoyed.

Seven trails lead to the beach. We recommend trail X7. To the north is the Eco-Parc, another hotel/amusement park of the kind that is increasingly common on the Riviera Maya.

Katenah

Before reaching Akumal, you will come across the once deserted Kantenah beach, where a large hotel complex now stand (see p 143).

Akumal

Akumal is a 15km-long crescent beach bordered by the ocean on one side and a long row of palm trees on the other. There is a resort here as well as a residential district. Akumal (Mayan word meaning turtle) was once part of a large coconut plantation. The site was first developed in 1958 by divers who were exploring the submerged wreckage of a Spanish galleon. Akumal's magnificent beaches are sheltered from the open sea by barrier reefs, which have attracted divers from the world over for many years. Quiet Half Moon Bay, measuring approximately 500m in length, is ideal for sailing, surfing and snorkelling. Its quiet serenity is its other major draw. Development has been carried out in harmony with nature so you still get

the impression of being in a wide open space. Akumal also boasts a few good seaside restaurants and bars.

The **Yal-ku lagoon** is situated just north of Akumal, beyond the crescent-shaped bay. This spot is hard to reach and does not get many visitors, but those who take the trouble to get here will be amply rewarded for their pains. Sun lotion is forbidden here. There is a nominal admission fee to gain access to the lagoon.

Founded in 1991, the **Planetary Coral Reef Foundation** (PCRF) (☎874-3484, ≈875-9091), aims to heighten divers' awareness of the fragility of coral reefs and the marine ecosystem. The PCRF works with Akumal's ecological centre, dedicated to the preservation of the environment, to develop a database on the state of Akumal's reef and set up a garbage recycling program.

Chemuyil

Chemuyil's white-sand beach is magnificent. Scuba diving in its crystalline, turquoise waters is a real pleasure. Though several palm trees were ravaged by the violent hurricanes that hit the coast over the last few years, a few still stand near the shore, supplying a bit of welcome shade. Chemuyil boasts a small restaurant, a camping site, a few hotels and a scuba-diving shop.

On the west side of Highway 307 is the Mayan village Chemuyil. Many of the workers who make your stay so pleasant live here. There are some good restaurants here.

Xcacel

Beachside and palm-shaded campsites can be found in Xcacel. It is a lovely spot, but wearing shoes here is essential, for this beach is covered in shells and coral; insect repellent is also a must. There is a restaurant and a small *cenote* here. Bird-watching enthusiasts will enjoy the parrots and *mot-mots* (named for their cry) who inhabit the region. The best time to spot these small creatures is early in the morning. Xcacel's calm and crystal-clear waters are ideal for water sports.

Xel-Há

Xel-Há is really only worth visiting if you like scuba diving. Large schools of blue, yellow and orange parrot-fish, offer a spectacular underwater show. And for $90 more, you can swim with dolphins; these adorable marine mammals will bring smiles to the young and old alike.

Known as the biggest "natural aquarium" in the world, Xel-Há (pronounced Chel-Ha) consists of 4ha of exotic lagoons, coves and creeks naturally furrowed into the crumbly limestone characteristic of the region. Certain creeks, however, have been created by human intervention. Large stretches of calm, crystal-clear water teem with multicoloured fish. Xel-Há is a paradise for experienced divers, but is also suitable for first-timers. Land-lubbers can admire the marine flora and fauna from the promenade overhanging the shores. There are showers and boutiques as well as a seafood restaurant on site. Diving gear can also be rented here.

The site (☎875-6000, www. xel-ha.com.mx) is open every day from 8am to 5pm. Admission fee for adults is $21. It is forbidden to enter the site with food or beverages. It is also forbidden to use sun lotion here, for this product contains ingredients harmful to the underwater fauna. Changing rooms and lockers are available for a fee, as is diving gear.

Tan-Kah

The archaeological site of Tan-Kah lies 9km south of Xel-Há and contains no fewer than 45 ancient Mayan structures in the depths of the forest.

Tulum

The old city of Tulum (Mayan word meaning "wall") reached its peak somewhere between AD 900 and 1540, when the great cities of the interior

declined. These temples and buildings, much smaller than those of Chichén Itzá, are examples of an architectural style that is found all over the Caribbean coast of Mexico. It is the only Mayan port city surrounded by a wall on three sides and one of the ceremonial centres still in use when the Spanish arrived in the 16th century. While on a naval expedition, which skirted the Yucatán coast in 1518, Juan de Grijalva was very impressed by this majestic city set atop a 12m-high cliff. The walls of Tulum's temples were then painted in bright, contrasting colours, few traces of which remain today.

Tulum was originally inhabited by a few thousand people. It was also a major market, linked by paths to several neighbouring cities, Cobá and Xel-Há among them. Though Tulum was abandoned in the 16th century, it served as a refuge for Mayans from Chan Santa Cruz during the Caste War armed conflict between the Europeans and the Mayas. Most of the inhabitants of the village of Tulum (just south of the actual archaeological site) are, in fact, descendants of this proud and independent people.

In 1993, the government launched a massive restoration and conservation program of the Tulum buildings, thus acknowledging their historical significance.

Many tourists staying in Cancún or Cozumel dis-

cover Tulum through one of the numerous guided bus tours organized by almost all tour companies in the region. On the coast, it is the most popular excursion, often combined with a trip to Xel-Há. Tulum receives about a million visitors a year. One can therefore imagine how crowded the place can get, particularly at the height of the tourist season. The most pleasant time of day to visit Tulum is in the late afternoon, when tourists have left and the heat of the sun has abated. The tour lasts about 2hrs.

At the entrance to the site are a covered outdoor souvenir market that includes arts and crafts shops and a few snack bars. Here, visitors can sometimes see *Voladores* performing. It is a very impressive sight, combining acrobatics and music. The village of Tulum, approximately 2km south of El Crucero (the fork that leads to the archaeological site), is also worth a look. The village has all the services you are likely to need.

The Archaeological Zone

In order to preserve the vestiges of Tulum, most of the more interesting attractions are closed to the public as too many tourists were visiting them daily. Due to this restriction, it is no longer possible to go inside the main attraction, El Castillo. Therefore, the structures can only be observed from a distance. But the beauty of the place makes up for this. Tulum

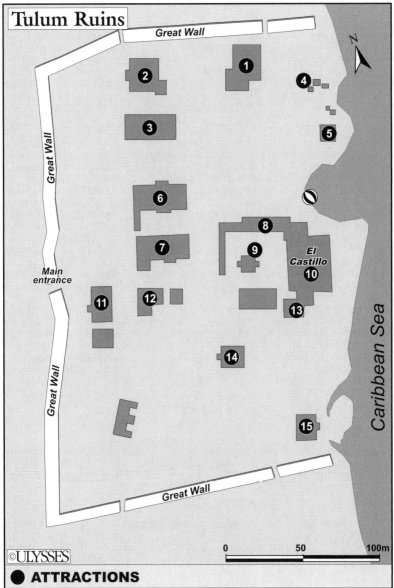

Tulum Ruins

Great Wall

Great Wall

Great Wall

Main entrance

Great Wall

El Castillo

Caribbean Sea

©ULYSSES

| 0 | 50 | 100m |

● ATTRACTIONS

1. House of the Cenote
2. Ruin 34
3. Platform
4. Altars
5. Temple of the Wind (Structure 45)
6. Gran Palacío
7. House of the Columns
8. Temple of the Diving God
9. Interior Courtyard
10. El Castillo
11. Ruin 20
12. Temple of the Frescoes
13. Temples of the Initial Series
14. Ruin 13
15. Structure 54

was built on a cliff overlooking the ocean and surrounded by magnificent countryside. Remember to bring your bathing suit to take a refreshing dip in the sea or in the creek where boats used to dock.

From Monday to Saturday (8am to 5pm), the admission fee for adults is 35 pesos and free for children 12 and under. Admission is free on Sundays (8am to 5pm). The entrance, which was once near the ruins, is now located near the parking lot (*fee applies*), right next to Highway 307, which obliges visitors to cover about 500m on foot or by mini-train (*fee applies*). A guide can be hired at the site's entrance.

Visitors enter the walled area through a narrow passage in the stone wall surrounding the city. The first building you will come upon is the Temple of the Frescoes. When facing the ocean, El Castillo is visible from the highest point. The Temple of the Diving God is right next to it. A few other structures of lesser importance are scattered throughout the grounds.

The Temple of the Frescoes

This two-story temple is composed of a large base, with four stone columns along one of its sides. Visitors cannot enter the temple, but can discern the painted frescoes inside quite well nevertheless; these represent the universe as the Mayans perceived it. Drawings made by the Mayas by dipping

their hands in red dye can be seen on the outside of the temple.

El Castillo

Perched on the edge of a cliff, this temple is unfortunately closed to visitors. Its entrance is flanked by two columns representing serpents and a diving god.

The Temple of the Diving God

Visitors enter this two story-structure through a small door surmounted by a figure carved out of the rock representing the "diving god," that is to say a human form whose feet point toward the sky and whose head points toward the ground. Whether this figure represents a bee or the setting sun is unknown.

Cobá

Cobá is a picturesque little village on Lago Cobá, right near the archaeological zone of the same name. The village has few tourist facilities.

The Archaeological Zone

Silent witnesses to the timeless beauty of the glorious Mayan empire, gone forever but not forgotten, the **old city of Cobá** (*about $3; every day 7am to 6pm*) is located 47km west of Tulum, amidst luxuriant vegetation under a blazing sun. According to archaeologists, only a small percentage of the structures is visible,

and if the funds were available to restore the whole site, Cobá would be one of the largest Mayan cities ever discovered. It is believed that Cobá was at its peak between AD 300 and 1000, with a population of about 50,000, and rivaled the splendid city of Tikal, Guatemala in prestige. But unlike Chichén-Itzá, which is a mix of Mayan and Toltec architecture, the architecture of Cobá is similar to the Peten style found at Tikal. Cobá's buildings, however, do not have the splendour of Tikal, Chichén-Itzá or Palenque. Few structures have been uncovered and those that have been are very far away from each other, so we strongly suggest that you wear a hat, bring a bottle of water and insect repellent to visit the ruins. If you want to get more than a quick look at the ruins and to learn more about the site's architecture, it is best to hire a guide at the entrance to the site.

The first group of structures, called the Cobá group, is about 100m from the entrance on your right. The second largest pyramid (22m) of the site, called **Iglesia**, is located here. There is also a small but well-restored, *juego de pelota* (ball court) near the pyramid.

A little further is a second group of ruins called **Las Pinturas** because of the colourful frescoes on its facade.

Just after Las Pinturas is **Xay-be**, which means "at the crossroads" in the

Mayan language. The circular pyramid stands about 12m high and has three levels. It seems that these ruins stood in the middle of four Mayan roads and were used strategically as a watchtower and an astronomical observatory.

The site's main attraction, **Nohoch Mul**, is located about 1km from the entrance and at 42m high, is the tallest pyramid in the Yucatan. There are 120 stairs going up to the top of the pyramid. A cord is used as a ramp to help visitors with vertigo get back down. Next to the pyramid is a 4m-high, 4-tonne **stele** inscribed with hieroglyphs that bear the date November 30, 780.

Numerous *sacbeob* (white paths) criss-cross the region, contributing to the theory that Cobá played an important role in the region. To avoid getting lost, stay on the marked path, but briefly take one of the many *sacbeob* that cross it. The *sacbeob* pass some scattered, partially visible Mayan structures that are shrouded in mystery in the middle of exuberant vegetation. These ruins possess a definite charm and gazing upon them, it is not hard to believe that these vestiges of a prosperous

and long-gone era were once, even more spectacular than what you see now.

Reserva de la Biosfera de Sian Ka'an

In the Mayan language, Sian Ka'an means "the place where the sky was born." This reserve covers 1.3 million acres of land along the coast, south of Tulum. The Sian Ka'an reserve is made up of tropical forests, *cenotes*, savannahs, dunes, lagoons, and a coral reef that stretches along the coast about 100m offshore. There are also many small Mayan ruins scattered about. This fascinating mix of luxuriant vegetation, both on land and in the ocean, serves as a natural habitat for a very diverse fauna and flora. For example, the reserve contains 300 species of birds fluttering about. Among the most popular are the toucan, the ara and the pink flamingo.

Listen to the wind gently caress the leaves of the trees and rustle their branches where a flock of colourful birds sometimes perches. Though the larger animals tend to flee at the slightest hint of

human presence, you may be able to catch sight of a puma or a jaguar swiftly leaping through the green foliage, monkeys chasing each other from branch to branch, crocodiles slowly gliding on the water in pursuit of their prey in the dissipating morning mist, or sea turtles frolicking about in the lagoons.

Though it might be more interesting to travel without any itinerary or time constraints, it is not such a bad idea to go with a travel agency. In fact, the best way to visit the reserve is with **Amigos de Sian Ka'an** (*Crepúsculo 18, Amanecer, SM 44, ME 13, Cancún, www.amigosde siankaan.org, www.cancun.com /siankaan,* ☎880-6024), an organization whose goal is to promote and protect the reserve's splendid natural environment. The excursion leaves fromthe hotel Cabañas Ana y José (see p 145) and lasts 6hrs. Half of the excursion is by boat. It costs $58 per person if you get to Boca Paila in your own vehicle, otherwise it costs an additional $10 if you leave from Cabañas Ana y José.

The travel agency **Sian Ka'an Tours** (*Av. Tulum, Tulum Pueblo,* ☎871-2363) organizes tours.

Boca Paila and Punta Allen

Boca Paila and Punta Allen are two picturesque villages whose main activities are fishing and tourism. They are located on a small peninsula in the

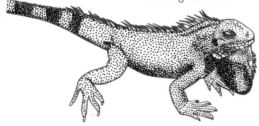

Reserva de la Biosfera de Sian Ka'an. Here, electricity is supplied by generators and there are hardly any tourist facilities.

Boca Paila is bordered by a pretty white-sand beach on one side and by a bay full of fish called Bahía de la Ascensión on the other. Most tourists come here to fish. The **Casa Blanca** *(www.casablancafishing.com)* is a hotel made up of *cabañas* that are very clean, covered with palm-thatched roofs and have private bathrooms as well as a terrace looking out to sea. The hotel offers guided fishing trips with professional guides who will show you the best spots. The area includes such species as bonefish, tarpon and snapper. Visitors can also go sea kayaking, scuba diving or just lounge on the beach with a good book.

Founded in the middle of the 20th century for lobster fishing, the quaint little village of Punta Allen is located on the Bahía de la Ascensión and has a population of 1,000. Further south is Bahía del Espíritu Santo, which, at 120,000ha, is the second-largest lobster reserve in Mexico. Tourist facilities are limited at Punta Allen, but the small restaurants serve the catch of the day. The beaches are long and a bit rocky. The hotels offer spartan comfort and camping is permitted.

Outdoor Activities

Apart from surfing, virtually every water sport is enjoyed along the Riviera Maya. The major hotels generally rent out the necessary equipment. They also offer introductory scuba-diving lessons as well as shuttle service to the Playacar or Puerto Aventuras golf club. Equipment-rental shops are also found in urban areas as well as on the major beaches of the Riviera Maya.

Moreover, there are a surprising number of specialized agencies catering to adventure lovers' every need, including riding in all-terrain vehicles, hiking the trails of the tropical forest and boating excursions through the mangroves. Scores of nature parks have also been created and rank among the region's finest tourist attractions.

Scuba Diving and Snorkelling

Two hundred metres from the shores of Puerto Morelos is a coral reef much prized by divers. Since March 1997, it has been protected by Mexico's department of the environment. It is the longest reef in the northern hemisphere. Numerous ships have run aground in the area since the beginnings of Spanish colonization, including a Spanish galleon that attracts many divers. The **Bahía Maya Village** hotel (see p 138) rents out diving gear and also organizes excursions to Puerto Morelos and to the very beautiful Dos Ojos *cenote (90km inland)*. This centre also offers day or half-day deep-sea fishing expeditions.

Punta Bete

La Posada del Capitán Lafitte
Carretera Cancún-Tulum, Km 62
☎**800-538-6802 or 873-0214**
www.capitanlafitte.com
In Punta Bete, the Posada del Capitán Lafitte houses a dive shop called **Buccaneer's Landing**, which offers full-service. All the necessary diving and snorkelling gear can be rented here. Horseback riding excursions are also organized.

Playa del Carmen

Several enterprises rent snorkelling or scuba diving gear and organize excursions. Here are a few:

Seafari Divers
Av. 5, between Calle 2 Norte and Av. Juárez
☎**873-0901**

Club Naútico Tarraya
Calle 2 Norte, near the beach
☎*873-2040*
gmillet@prodigy.net.mx

Phocea Caribe
Av. 5, between Calles 12 and 14
☎/≈*873-1210*
This outfitter offers one-day introductory diving courses as well as longer, more extensive courses.

Puerto Aventuras

Golf, deep-sea fishing, scuba diving, snorkelling, sailing and kayaking are all possible here. One kilometre south of the complex is the **Azul Cenote** *(entrance on Highway 307)*, where visitors can swim in clear and refreshing water.

Mike Madden's CEDAM Dive Center
☎*873-5129*
mmadden@cancun.rce. com.mx
This outfitter offers diving certification courses, rents all the necessary equipment and organizes excursions to neighbouring *cenotes*. Mike Madden is a world-famous expert diver who has explored many *cenotes* in the region. The company runs five dive centres, all staffed with PADI-certified guides.

Akumal

Dive Center Akumal
On the beach
☎/≈*875-9025*
www.akumaldivecenter. com

Horseback Riding

Puerto Morelos

Rancho Loma Bonita
Carretera Cancún-Tulum, Km 40
before Punta Bete
☎*887-5423 or 887-5465*
This ranch has been offering visitors the chance to ride through wild jungle or along kilometres of beach for over 25 years now. You can even play polo on donkeys while armed with a broom! Twice a day, a bus shuttles back and forth between Cancún and the ranch. Departures are from the OK Maguey restaurant *(Plaza Kukulcan)*. Rates, which vary according to the activity, include accident insurance. There is also a restaurant here.

Accommodations

Puerto Morelos

Posada Amor
$
⊗, ℜ
Av. Xavier Rojo Gómez
☎*871-0033*
This establishment has 20 small, simple and comfortable rooms decorated in Mexican style, distributed throughout dwellings that surround a small, shaded interior courtyard. Some rooms have a

private bathroom with a shower. It is also possible to rent a *cabaña* for four people.

Hacienda Morelos
$$
⊗, ≈, ℜ
Av. Rafael Melgar, on the beach near Quay 8
☎*871-0015*
This hotel has 15 studios with large beds. The rooms are spacious and charmingly decorated in Mexican style. The swimming pool is surrounded by *palapas*. Slightly elevated, it offers a lovely view of the sea.

🐟 **Rancho Libertad**
$$ bkfst incl.
⊗, ≡
Prolongacion Rafael Melgar, south of the port
☎*871-0181*
www.rancholibertad.com
This property is run by Americans. The main building houses a large, ground-level room whose floor is covered in sand, where guests can play checkers, gaze at the stars through a telescope, strum the guitar or play the drum. A well-equipped communal kitchen is open to all. The 12 rooms have ceiling fans and some have beds suspended from ropes. Or, if guests prefer, there are hammocks. The hotel's beach is very lovely. Turning in early and sleeping late are *de rigueur* here. Scuba-diving courses are offered and guests can pay to rent a kayak, but bicycles and snorkelling gear are available free of charge.

Bahía Maya Village
$$$ all incl.
⊗, ≡, ℝ, ≈, ℜ
Carretera Cancun-Tulum, Km 28.5, on the Punta Tanchacte beach
☎*800-695-8284*
The Bahía Maya Village, located 7km north of Puerto Morelos, has 100 rooms, each with a minibar and a fan. Some have air conditioning. This hotel consists of several buildings surrounded by gardens. The swimming pool is large and surrounded by *palapas*, hammocks and deckchairs. The hotel boasts an Italian restaurant, a nightclub, a boutique, a diving centre and a car-rental counter.

Punta Maroma

 Maroma
$$$$$ bkfst incl.
≡, ⊗, ≈, ℝ, ☉, ✪
Hwy 307, Km 51
☎*872-8200*
www.maromahotel.com
The Maroma hotel is located right on magnificent Playa Maroma, a 3km-long white-sand beach south of Puerto Morelos, about a 15min drive from Playa del Carmen. Unquestionably the most luxurious resort hotel on the Riviera Maya, this exceptional hideaway offers only 36 rooms or villas, set in heavenly surroundings. The architecture of the buildings and the layout of the surrounding garden are enchanting. The Maroma prides itself on being a favourite with "the Beverly Hills crowd." And no wonder! Afficionados of New Age disciplines such as aromatherapy, reflexology

and *Temazcal* (Mayan sauna) will be taken in hand by skilled "artisans" who will acquaint them with muscles they never knew they had.

Punta Bete

 La Posada del Capitan Lafitte
$$$$$ ½b
⊗, ≈, ℜ
☎*873-0212 or 800-538-6802*
www.capitanlafitte.com
This establishment is an institution in Punta Bete. Its units distributed throughout a series of thatch-roofed cottages, each comprise a bedroom and a terrace with a view of the ocean. A few of the units have two bedrooms. The bathrooms are only equipped with showers, however. Toward the end of the day, mariachis perform near the pool. The Posada rents horses and organizes scuba-diving and fishing trips.

Playa del Carmen

Most of the hotels in Playa del Carmen are located on the beach, just a few steps away from the ocean. Some of them rent *cabañas*. The pricier and more comfortable ones are situated at the northern and southern extremities of the city.

Urban Hostel
$ bkfst incl.
sb
Av. 10, between Calle 4 and Calle 6
☎*879-9342*
Like all towns on the Caribbean coast of Mex-

ico, Playa del Carmen offers backpackers low-priced accommodations. This downtown youth hostel offers beds set out beneath large *palapas* for $10 a night, breakfast included. The hostel can accommodate some 20 travellers, who have access to a lounge as well as a kitchen in which to prepare their own meals. Bathrooms and showers are shared. Guests are also provided with mosquito nets and lockers. No membership card required.

Mom's
$
≈, ℜ, ⊗, ≡
Calle 4, corner Av. 30
☎/≈*873-0315*
www.momshotel.com
Built somewhat like a hacienda with a central courtyard and a small swimming pool, Mom's is rather secluded, since it is about a 5min walk from the pedestrian street. The rooms are clean, comfortable, large and cool, with private bathrooms. Some offer air conditioning. The proprietor has a very interesting library and will be delighted to lend you a few books, which you can peruse on the terrace upstairs.

Villa Deportiva Juvenil
$
Av. 30, corner Calle 8
Undoubtedly one of the least expensive places to stay in Playa del Carmen, this is a youth hostel for all, with 200 beds distributed throughout 10 dormitories and five *cabañas*. The latter, equipped with fans and private showers, can accommodate three or

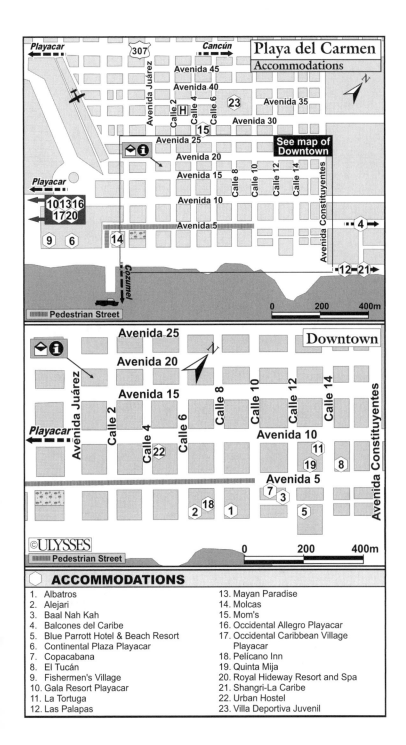

Playa del Carmen
Accommodations

Playacar · 307 · **Cancún**

Avenida 45
Avenida 40
Avenida Juárez
Calle 2
Calle 4
Calle 6
23 · Avenida 35
Avenida 30
15
Avenida 25
Avenida 20
Avenida 15
Calle 8
Calle 10
Calle 12
Calle 14
See map of Downtown
Avenida 10
Avenida Constituyentes
4
Avenida 5
10 13 16
17 20
9 6
14
12 – 21
Cozumel

0   200   400m

Pedestrian Street

Downtown

Avenida 25
Avenida 20
Avenida Juárez
Avenida 15
Calle 2
Calle 4
Calle 6
Calle 8
Calle 10
Calle 12
Calle 14
Avenida 10
Avenida Constituyentes
Playacar
22
11
19   8
Avenida 5
7
3
2 18   1
5

©ULYSSES

0   200   400m

Pedestrian Street

ACCOMMODATIONS

1. Albatros
2. Alejari
3. Baal Nah Kah
4. Balcones del Caribe
5. Blue Parrott Hotel & Beach Resort
6. Continental Plaza Playacar
7. Copacabana
8. El Tucán
9. Fishermen's Village
10. Gala Resort Playacar
11. La Tortuga
12. Las Palapas
13. Mayan Paradise
14. Molcas
15. Mom's
16. Occidental Allegro Playacar
17. Occidental Caribbean Village Playacar
18. Pelícano Inn
19. Quinta Mija
20. Royal Hideway Resort and Spa
21. Shangri-La Caribe
22. Urban Hostel
23. Villa Deportiva Juvenil

four people. By sharing the cost of these modest dwellings with a few other people, you can pay even less than you would for a bed in the dormitory. Men and women sleep in separate dormitories and *cabañas*, which are all relatively clean. Ideal for no-fuss travellers.

Albatros
$-$$ bkfst incl.
≡, ⊗, ℜ
On the beach, at Calle 8
☎873-0001
Only 20m from the beach, this hotel with 38 rooms is composed of beige, thatch-roofed cottages. Every room has a private balcony with a hammock. They are painted white and soberly decorated with ceramic-tiled floors. Coffee and croissants are served in the morning. The hotel organizes scuba diving excursions and rents all the necessary diving gear.

El Tucán
$$ bkfst incl.
≈, ≡
Ave. Norte, no. 5A
between Calles 14 and 16
☎873-0417
⇌873-0668
The El Tucán has 65 rooms that are clean and comfortable but somewhat small. There is, however, a refreshing little private garden with waterfalls and a small *cenote* next to the hotel near the reception.

Alejari
$$ bkfst incl.
≡, ⊗, ℜ, ℝ
On the beach corner Calle 6
☎873-0372
⇌873-0005
This small, seaside, family hotel attracts visitors for its

clean rooms, smiling service and prices that won't dig too deep into your budget.

La Tortuga
$$ bkfst incl.
≈,⊗, ℜ, ≡
Av. 10, corner Calle 14
☎873-1484
⇌873-0798
www.hotellatortuga.com
La Tortuga is located only two streets away from the beach, but far enough from the bustle of Avenida 5. The rooms are quiet and well-decorated. All the suites are equipped with whirlpool baths. Good value for your money.

Baal Nah Kah
$$-$$$ bkfst incl.
⊗, ≡
Calle 12, corner Av. 5
☎873-0110
⇌873-0050
www.cancunsouth.com/ baalnahkah
Comfort and a warm welcome await at Baal Nah Kah, a cute little bed and breakfast. Up to six rooms are available for rent, and though each is a different size, all are charmingly decorated in a simplistic but refined Mexican style. Two rooms have balconies, but all visitors can use the kitchen. The beach is a 30-second walk away, and the service is friendly.

Copacabana
$$-$$$
≡
Av. 5 between Calle 10 and Calle 12
Next to 100% Natural restaurant (see p 148), the Copacabana is very close to the beach and has pretty rooms that are clean, colourful and laid out around an interior

courtyard. There is an outdoor whirlpool bath to relax in after a day at the beach. The hotel also rents bicycles and organizes scuba-diving and deep-sea fishing excursions.

Balcones del Caribe
$$$
⊗, ≡, ≈, ℜ K
Calle 34, between Av. 5 and Av. 10
☎873-0830
⇌873-0831
This all-inclusive hotel has 72 two-bedroom suites. Each is pleasantly decorated and equipped with a kitchenette, a dining room and air conditioning. They are distributed throughout two modern, four-storey buildings. The Balcones also has a tennis court and a car-rental counter. There is shuttle service to the beach.

Molcas
$$$ bkfst incl.
≡, ℜ, ≈
Calle 1, corner Av. 5
☎873-0070
⇌873-0138
Molcas has managed to adapt to the recent hotel boom and still looks good after all these years. Located two steps away from the pier where boats leave for Cozumel, this establishment has simple, clean and modern rooms.

Quinta Mija
$$$-$$$$
K, ⊗, ℜ, ≈
Av. 5, between Calles 12 and 14
☎873-0111
info@quintamija.com.mx
A short distance from the frenzy south of Avenida 5, but only a block and a half from the ocean is the charming Quinta Mija. The simple, pleasant and quiet

rooms surround a bucolic interior courtyard and come with kitchenettes. The pool is good for a dip after a long day visiting the nearby ruins under the blazing Yucatán sun, or after tanning yourself on the hotel's patio, where there is an excellent view of the ocean. Several computers with Internet access are also available, for an additional charge.

Pelicano Inn
$$$$ bkfst incl.
⊗, ℜ, ≡
on the beach, corner Calle 8
☎873-0997
This is a 38-room hotel, surrounded by a tropical garden. The rooms have either two queen-size beds or one king-size bed. At breakfast, guests serve themselves from the buffet table. The hotel has a fishing and diving shop.

Blue Parrott Hotel & Beach Resort
$$$$
⊗, ≡, ℜ, K, ℝ
On the beach, corner Calle 12
☎888-854-4498 or 873-0083
www.blueparrot.com
Very popular because of the many services it offers, the Blue Parrot organizes a variety of water activities (kayaking, scuba diving, snorkelling, fishing, etc.). Every one of its 32 rooms is air conditioned.

Las Palapas
$$$$ bkfst incl.
≈, ℜ, ≡, ⊗
Av. 34 Norte
☎873-0584 or 873-0616
⇌873-0458
www.laspalapas.com.mx
With a total of 75 rooms, Las Palapas is located approximately 2km north of Playa del Carmen, on the beach. The hotel's propietor is Swiss. The rooms consist of circular, one- or two-storey bungalows with thatched roofs. Each has a bathroom, fans or air conditioning, double beds and a balcony. Breakfast and dinner are included in the price of the room. The complex includes a bar, a boutique and two restaurants; it also organizes excursions.

Shangri-La Caribe
$$$$$ all incl.
ℜ, ≈, ≡, ⊗
About 2km north of downtown Calle 38, between Av. 5 and Zona Playa
☎873-0611
⇌873-0500
www.shangrilacaribe.net
The Shangri-La Caribe is a little away from the downtown area right next to Las Palapas. This chic hotel is just the place to get away from it all and has everything to make your stay as pleasant as possible. The spacious *cabañas* have comfortable beds and balconies with hammocks slung between palm trees, two steps away from a

calm, sandy beach. The services and facilities include a car-rental office, taxi service, scuba-diving shop, professional massage service, two pool tables, a ping-pong table, three excellent restaurants (see p 149) and a fresh-water pool. Impeccable service with a smile.

Playacar

Mayan Paradise
$$$$ all incl.
K, ≡, ℜ, ≈, ⊛
☎873-0933
This is another big hotel complex that offers the "all-inclusive formula." The air-conditioned rooms are located in colourful buildings that are attached together all the way to the pool. In this luxury hotel where every demand is met, guests will find everything they need, so they never have to leave the property.

Gala Resort Playacar
$$$$
≡, ⊗, ≈, ℜ, ℝ, ⊘, ❋
☎873-1150
⇌873-1154
This is a large, all-inclusive complex with a modern decor in quintessentially Mexican colours; most of its 300 rooms have a view of the ocean. Guests can enjoy a host of sports activities here, and there are holiday camps for children. This hotel is the third of its kind in Mexico; the first and second of this chain's establishments are in Huatulco and Manzanillo.

Royal Hideway Resort and Spa
$$$$$
≈, ℜ, ≡, ⊗, ♻, ☺
Lote Hotelero 6
☎*873-4500*
⇄*873-4506*
www.royalhideaway.com
If money is no object and you want to immerse yourself in absolute luxury, the Royal Hideway is a sparkling grand hotel with a somewhat pompous decor. The Royal Hideaway offers a unique all-inclusive package: unlike other hotels that prefer quantity to quality, it offers a more personalized service and is the only all-inclusive hotel in Cancún that belongs to the Preferred Hotels and Resorts Worldwide. The moment you arrive, you will be greeted with a glass of champagne. Freshly cut flowers adorn the rooms along with a basket of fresh fruit. The rooms are in small colonial-style villas where a concierge takes care of your dinner reservations and your every desire. Each room is equipped with a VCR, a stereo system with a selection of CDs, as well as a modem hookup for portable computers. The bathrooms are clad in marble. There is also a 220-seat theatre where guests can dine while watching folk shows. A pool, bar, gym, travel agency, tennis court, health club and the usual services and water sports are offered at this high-class establishment.

🌴 Occidental Allegro Playacar
$$$$$
≡, ≈, ℜ, ⊗
www.occidentalhotels.com
Formerly known as the Diamond Resort, the Allegro is also an all-inclusive hotel. Its 300 rooms are impeccably furnished with palm-thatched roofs and slope gently down toward the ocean. In front of each room is a hammock where guests can read or casually observe the different kinds of birds flying about. This hotel is ideal for romantic couples or families. Children can play in the game room or swim in the kiddie pool. There is another pool for adults who just want to lounge about and mind their own business. The beach is clean and quiet.

Occidental Caribbean Village Playacar
$$$$$
⊗, ≡, ≈, ℜ
☎*873-0506*
⇄*873-1047*
This all-inclusive hotel complex is located near the Playacar golf course and contains 300 large, modern and comfortable rooms with two queen-size beds, a television and a telephone. There are two swimming pools and three tennis courts in the gardens surrounding the hotel. The establishment also has a car-rental counter and a dive shop. The cost of a room includes a daily round of golf.

Continental Plaza Playacar
$$$$$
⊗, ≡, ≈, ℜ
Av. Espíritu Santo
☎*873-0095*
⇄*873-0105*
The 188 rooms and 16 suites at this hotel each provide a television and private balcony, and are decorated in Mexican fashion. The hotel faces one of the loveliest beaches in the area, and is within walking distance of downtown Playa del Carmen. There is a car-rental counter, tennis courts and a dive shop on the premises. Guests can enjoy a host of activities, including water-skiing and sailing. This is the only hotel in Playacar that is not all-inclusive.

Fishermen's Village
$$$$$ all incl.
Bahía del Espíritu Santo no. 9
☎*873-1390*
⇄*873-1393*
The Fishermen's Village is located next to the Continental Plaza and offers the "all-inclusive formula." All the rooms are comfortable and have a lovely view of the ocean. The pool is the perfect place to relax after taking a dip in the ocean or before the evening buffet is served.

Paamul

Cabañas Paamul
$ bkfst incl.
⊗, ℜ
Hwy 307
☎*875-1051*
⇄*875-1053*
www.paamulcabanas.com
This modest hotel is run by a friendly Mexican family. The establishment is plain, but guests eat well

here. This same family also runs the only camp site in Paamul, situated quite close to the hotel. Guests will find a dive shop and a laundromat at the hotel.

Puerto Aventuras

Aventura Spa Palace
$$$
⊗, ≡, ≈, ☺, ℜ, ☮, ✪
On the beach, north end of the marina
☎*800-695-8284*
⇄*875-1101*
Aventura Spa Palace comprises 582 spacious rooms, with balconies and a magnificent view of the ocean. Guests can play for free at the Puerto Aventuras golf course. The hotel also has several restaurants and bars, as well as a dive shop.

Club Oasis Puerto Aventuras
$$$$ all incl.
≈, ≡, ⊗, K, ℜ, ☮
on the beach, north of the marina
☎*872-3333*
⇄*872-3332*
www.oasishotels.com
The Club Oasis Puerto Aventuras houses 275 rooms, some of which have a whirlpool bath and a kitchenette. This hotel has adopted the "all-inclusive" formula and organizes numerous activities for its guests. Transportation to the marina is also included in the price of the room.

Barcelo Maya Beach Resort
$$$$ all incl.
≡, ⊗, ≈, ℝ, ☺
Carretera Cancún-Tulum, Km 94.5
☎*875-1500*
www.barcelo.com
Definitely the largest resort hotel on this part of the coast, the Barcelo Maya Beach Resort is set right on an isolated beach located 5min south of Puerto Aventuras and 50min from the airport. This first-class resort boasts large rooms distributed throughout the main building and among several three-storey buildings with elevators.

Xpu-há

Hotel Copacabana
$$$$ all incl.
≡, ⊗, ≈, ℝ, ✪
Carretera Cancún-Tulum
☎*875-1800*
⇄*875-1818*
www.hotelcopacabana.com
Located on Xpu-há beach, the Hotel Copacabana is a huge all-inclusive resort set amidst a garden that extends from the main road to the beach. The rooms offer all the perks expected of a hotel of this class: air conditioning, ceiling fan, king-size bed or two double beds, bathroom with shower, hair-dryer, telephone, cable or satellite TV, minibar, in-room safe, balcony or terrace. This self-sufficient "village" also offers a range of services, including shops, a car-rental counter, currency-exchange bureau, laundry and

dry-cleaning service, massage shop, as well as all water-sports equipment.

The Xpu-há Ecopark, which features an assortment of natural attractions, is located north of the beach. The park comprises a network of *cenotes* linked by underground rivers, as well as an aviary, a botanical garden and bike paths. A plethora of water sports are practised here.

Robinson Club Tulum
$$$$$
⊗, ≈, ≡, ☺, ℜ
Carretera Cancún-Tulum, Km 98
☎*881-1010*
South of Xpu-há, the Robinson Club offers 300 lovely rooms decorated in pastel shades. Despite its name, this hotel is several kilometres north of Tulum.

Kantenah

El Dorado Resort
$$$$$ all incl.
⊗, ≡, ≈, ℜ
Carretera Cancún-Tulum, Km 99
☎*872-8030*
⇄*872-8034*
www.eldoradosparesorts.com
The El Dorado Resort occupies a large part of Kantenah beach. This complex consists of 135 large suites with marble floors and satellite televisions. The hotel also features two swimming pools, two restaurants, three bars and vast gardens. All meals and sports activities are included in the above-mentioned rate.

Akumal

Club Akumal Caribe & Villas Maya
$$$
≈, ⊗, *K*, ℜ
☎*800-351-1622 or 875-9011*
www.hotelakumalcaribe. com
This large resort offers different types of accommodations, ranging from large, fully equipped *cabañas* to one- or two-bedroom condominiums to small hotel rooms. There are tennis and basketball courts, but scuba diving is the activity of choice, what with the complex's two dive shops.

Club Oasis Akumal
$$$
☉, ⊗, ≈, ⊛, ℜ, ≡
☎*873-0843*
www.oasishotels.com
The 180 spacious rooms of the Club Oasis all have a large balcony with a view of the ocean or the gardens, and most offer air conditioning. This *U*-shaped hotel, with its quintessentially Mexican architecture, is located on a very lovely beach. Club Oasis has a tennis court, a travel agency, a car rental counter and a diving club, the Oasis, run by CEDAM.

Hacienda la Tortuga
$$$
⊗, ≡, *K*, ≈, ℜ
A 10min walk from the Club Akumal Caribe
☎/⇌*875-9068*
www.haciendatortuga.com
This is a small hotel situated on the beach; it encompasses nine condominiums, each of which has one or two rooms, a kitchenette and a sizeable bathroom.

Bahía Príncipe Tulum
$$$$ all incl.
≡, ⊗, ≈, ℝ, ⊛, ☉, ℜ
Carretera Chetumal-Cancún, Km 250
☎*875-5000*
⇌*875-5001*
www.bahiaprincipe.com
Bahía Príncipe Tulum is located on a long white-sand beach south of the village of Akumal. Built on extensive landscaped grounds, this huge resort is a village in itself, with first-class rooms distributed throughout several three-storey buildings. Located at the entrance to the hotel, the small Hacienda Doña Isabel shopping centre encompasses a dance club, restaurant, dairy bar, beauty salon, massage shop, car-rental agency, cybercafé and a small clinic that provides basic medical services.

Tan-Kah

Sole Resorts
$$$$$ all incl.
≡, ⊗, ≈, ℝ, ☉, ✿
Riviera Maya, Km 234, Tulum
☎*871-3333*
www.soleresorts.com
The Sole Resorts is located right on Tan-Kah beach, about 5min north of Tulum and 25min from Playa del Carmen. It offers rooms and suites distributed throughout several buildings modelled after a 19th-century Mexican hacienda, all of which are surrounded by lush tropical vegetation. The architects have successfully made use of the ochre so characteristic of the build-ings of the town of Izamal, in the Yucatán; the tone is sober and the spaces open. The resort offers all the requisite services as well as shuttle service to the Playacar golf course. What's more, guests can practise water sports such as sailing, windsurfing, snorkelling, kayaking and scuba diving, as well as deep-sea fishing.

Tulum Playa

There are a few hotels at the El Crucero junction, but these are not close to the ocean. South of the archaeological zone, on a road that leads to Boca Paila, a series of *cabañas* is spread out on a long stretch of beach, bordered by palm trees. Some provide simple comfort and a place to eat. A few of these *cabañas* do not even have running water, while others are quite luxurious. The Tulum-Boca-Paila road is bumpy, dusty and runs along the beach south of the Tulum archaeological zone until the Sian Ka'an reserve.

Cabañas Don Armando
$
sb, ℜ
On the beach, 650m south of the archaeological zone
☎*871-2417*
This establishment is very popular with globetrotters without much cash. The rooms are spartan, but ideal for those looking for a hut on the beach. When the sun goes down, everyone heads to the bar for a pitcher of sangria and a good time.

Tulum (translated as "the wall") is the only Mayan port city that is surrounded with a wall on three sides.

In the archaeological site of Tulum, El stillo, sits atop an cliff, looking out at the Caribbean Sea.

A fruit market in Playa del Carmen attracts passers-by with its bright colours and tempting fragrances.

Handmade terracotta reproductions of Mayan gods are often found in the stands of *mercados*.

Acuario
$$
≈, ⊗, ℜ, ≡
El Crucero, Carretera Cancún-Tulum, Km 131
☎*871-2195*
Opened in 1990, the Acuario has 27 large and comfortable rooms with colour televisions and private bathrooms. Buses to Playa del Carmen leave from this hotel's parking lot.

El Paraíso
$$
ℜ, ⊗
Approximately 1km from the archaeological zone
☎*871-2006*
By continuing south, travellers will come across the El Paraíso hotel. The rooms each include two large beds and a private bathroom. The hotel has a very satisfactory restaurant and the beach here is magnificent.

Piedra Escondida
$$
ℜ
Carretera Tulum-Boca Paila, Km 3.5
☎*809-8155*
⇄*871-2217*
www.piedraescondida.com
The Piedra Escondida has simple *cabañas* with tiled floors. The balcony is strung with a hammock that will take the shape of your body the moment you lay in it. Smiling staff.

Cabañas Ana y José
$$-$$$
ℜ, ≈, ⊗
Carretera Tulum-Boca Paila, Km 7
☎*887-5470*
⇄*887-5469*
www.anayjose.com
This charming establishment has 15 rooms two steps away from the beach, but only five have ocean views and are obviously more expensive. However, all the rooms are charming, ultra-clean, decorated in a Mexican style and have mosquito screens. The pool is pleasantly located in the middle of a peaceful garden. There is also a car-rental office, and you can pick up your car either at the airport or at the hotel. Free parking for guests.

Tropical Padus
$$-$$$
ℜ
Carretera Tulum-Boca Paila, Km 9
☎*876-2088*
⇄*871-2092*
Run by a friendly Italian couple, the Tropical Padus is primarily known for its quality restaurant Da Orazio (see p 150), but the establishment also rents clean, comfortable and spacious *cabañas*. It is also possible to rent fishing, scuba-diving or snorkelling equipment. Private parking is available for guests.

Posada Dos Ceibas
$$-$$$
≡, ⊗, ℜ
Carretera Tulum-Boca Paila, Km 10
☎*877-6024*
⇄*871-2335*
www.dosceibas.com
The Posada Dos Ceibas is prized by California yogis and meditation buffs. The owner offers classes in a room designed just for that purpose. He has also taken an interest in the sea-turtle conservation program ever since he discovered, one fine morning, an egg-filled nest on the stairway leading to the beach. At the Posada Dos Ceibas, guests stay in one of 8 luxurious round "bungalows" perched atop a promontory. The in-house restaurant serves varied, Italian-influenced fare.

Tulum Pueblo

Tulum Pueblo offers accommodations in all categories. The only drawback is the cost of transportation to the beach, located some 2km from Highway 307. Cab fare, of course, varies according to the distance (30 pesos for the first 2km, 100 pesos to the Posada Dos Ceibas).

The Weary Travelers
$
⊗, ℜ
across from the ADO bus station
Av. Tulum (Route Mex 307)
☎*871-2461*
The Weary Travelers is much more than the best youth hostel on the Riviera Maya. In fact, it also serves as an information office, cybercafé and used-book shop, and features a garden laid out in the interior courtyard. The dorms are designed to provide as much intimacy as possible while staying true to the hostel format. The owners are globetrotters who are well acquainted with travellers' needs.

Maya Tulum
$$$$
ℜ, ⊗, ✪
Carretera Tulum-Boca Paila, Km 5
☎/⇄*877-8638*
www.mayantulum.com
Formerly known as the Oslo Tulum, the Maya Tulum attracts visitors

seeking relaxation, since yoga and meditation sessions are held on the beach. The establishment is located two steps away from the beach, near the Sian Ka'an reserve, and rents *cabañas* spread out in the middle of a lush palm grove. Some *cabañas* have splendid sea views, while others are a little bit removed from the beach. The beds are covered with mosquito netting to protect guests from these pests and other blood-sucking insects. The atmosphere is rather soothing and restful.

Cobá

Hotel El Bocadito
$
ℜ, ⊗
☎876-3738
Located on the right as you enter the village, the El Bocadito rents clean rooms with the basic comforts that are perfect for adventurers who want to stay as close as possible to the Cobá archaeological zone.

Villas Arqueologicas
$$
≈, ℜ, ⊗, ≡
on Lago Cobá
☎/≠874-2087
Obviously in a higher price category, this former Club Med is suitable for those with a bigger budget who also want to be close to the Cobá archaeological zone. The main building is on the lake and the entire property was built exactly like the Club Med near the Chichén-Itzá ruins. The 40 rooms were completely renovated in 2000 and surround an interior court-

yard where the pool is located. The hotel also has a pool room with a small library that guests can use after spending a day at the ruins.

Restaurants

Puerto Morelos

Kab Meyah
$
Calle Tulum, south of Plaza Morelos
This establishment is both a handicraft shop and an Internet café. It costs 25 pesos to surf the net.

Cafe de la Plaza
$
Plaza Morelos
This establishment is located inside a simply decorated space that can barely fit five tables. Healthy, homemade food is served in a casual and bohemian ambiance.

Pelicanos
$-$$
Av. Rafael Melgar, by the ocean
☎871-0014
Here, fresh fish, seafood and Yucatec specialties are served in a warm and inviting ambiance and at very good prices.

Posada Amor
$$$
Av. Xavier Rojo Gómez
☎871-0033
Delicious, hearty breakfasts are served at the restaurant of the Posada Amor hotel (see p 137). There is even real maple syrup to go with the pancakes! On Sundays, very

generous buffets featuring Mexican and North American dishes are served.

Punta Bete/Xcalacoco

Los Pinos
$-$$$
on the beach, Km 63.5
Popular with globetrotters, this is a small, unpretentious restaurant. The menu features fish and seafood and changes according to the catch of the day.

Frederiko
$-$$$
on the Xcalacoco beach
Right next to Los Pinos, the Frederiko restaurant offers a menu similar to that of its neighbour.

Playa del Carmen

Andale
$-$$
8am to 2am
Av. 5, between Calles 6 and 8
☎873-2928
Refreshing ice-cream, crispy pizzas, strong coffee and smiling service await at Andale. This small restaurant has a terrace used as a sort of lookout station to watch the activity on the main street of Playa del Carmen.

Sabor
$-$$
Av.5, between Calles 2 and 4
Sabor is very popular for its salads, tofu burgers, sandwiches and delectable desserts. It is the favourite haunt of vegetarians in Playa del Carmen.

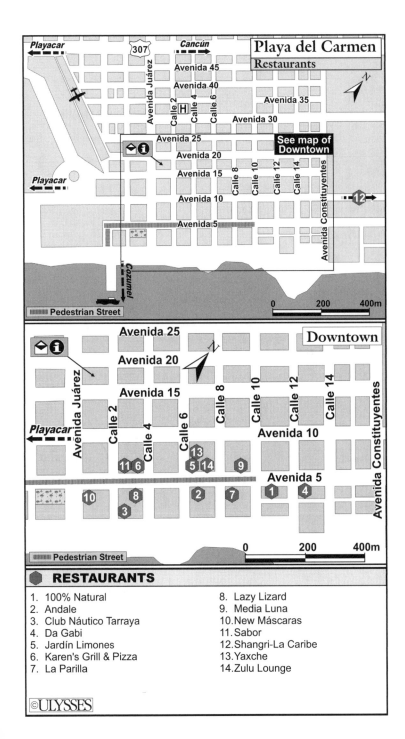

Playa del Carmen
Restaurants

Playacar
307
Cancún
Avenida 45
Avenida 40
Avenida Juárez
Calle 2
Calle 4
Calle 6
H
Avenida 35
Avenida 30
Avenida 25
See map of Downtown
Avenida 20
Playacar
Avenida 15
Calle 8
Calle 10
Calle 12
Calle 14
Avenida 10
Avenida Constituyentes
12
Avenida 5

Cozumel

0   200   400m

Pedestrian Street

Downtown

Avenida 25
Avenida 20
Avenida Juárez
Avenida 15
Calle 8
Calle 10
Calle 12
Calle 14
Calle 2
Calle 4
Calle 6
Avenida 10
Playacar
13
11 6
5 14
9
Avenida Constituyentes
Avenida 5
10
8
2
7
1
4
3

0   200   400m

Pedestrian Street

⬡ RESTAURANTS

1. 100% Natural
2. Andale
3. Club Náutico Tarraya
4. Da Gabi
5. Jardín Limones
6. Karen's Grill & Pizza
7. La Parilla
8. Lazy Lizard
9. Media Luna
10. New Máscaras
11. Sabor
12. Shangri-La Caribe
13. Yaxche
14. Zulu Lounge

©ULYSSES

Club Náutico Tarraya
$-$$
Calle 2 Norte
☎*873-2040*

Club Náutico Tarraya's beachfront restaurant is located near the town square. Specializing in fish and seafood since it opened in 1968, this family restaurant is much appreciated by local families, who mainly gather here on weekends. Of course, with such a name, it goes without saying that the place rents out kayaks and diving gear—something confirmed by the decor.

Karen's Grill & Pizza
$-$$
Av. 5 between Calle 2 and Calle 4
☎*873-2743*

Pizza and hamburgers share the menu with traditional Mexican dishes at Karen's Grill & Pizza. The ambiance becomes quite festive when South American folk music shows liven up *muy caliente* evenings.

Lazy Lizard
$-$$
Av. 5, between Calles 2 and 4
☎*873-1201*

Lazy Lizard's shady, attractive terrace attracts many tourists who come to satisfy their appetite with homemade pasta, juicy hamburgers, grilled shrimp or Mexican specialities. Most decide to linger like lazy lizards in the sun, washing down their meal with a cold beer.

Zulu Lounge
$-$$
Av. 5, between Calle 6 and Calle 8
☎*873-0056*

Zulu Lounge is a bar-restaurant whose African

motifs provide an eclectic atmosphere to the dining room. The chef prepares Thai food with Mexican influences for a casual, bohemian clientele. There are also several pool tables where you can distract yourself, engage in conversation, or simply enjoy a cocktail or a cold beer.

100% Natural
$-$$$
Av. 5 between Calle 10 and Calle 12

For good, healthy Mexican cuisine, 100% Natural is located in the Copacabana hotel (see p 140), more specifically in a splendid interior courtyard shaded by tall trees and covered with a thatched roof. An excellent assortment of fruit juices is served, as well as lighter fare for those watching their diets.

Da Gabi
$-$$$
6pm to11pm
Calle 12, corner Av. 1 Norte
☎*873-0048*

This popular Italian restaurant offers fish and seafood dishes, fresh pasta and, to top off your meal, a very good espresso. The dining room is large, well-decorated and ventilated by ceiling fans.

New Máscaras
$$
Av. Juárez, facing the park
☎*873-1053*

At the New Máscaras bar-restaurant, guests can enjoy delicious pizzas baked in a wood-burning oven (the three-cheese pizza is outstanding). The restaurant refers to itself as

the only genuine Italian restaurant in town. The terrace overlooks the town's playground.

Jardín Limones
$$-$$$
Av. 5, between Calle 6 and Calle 8
☎*873-0848*

Venture into Jardín Limones and savour the delicious fish and steaks prepared here. Indeed, the restaurant, open since the 1980s, prides itself on cooking the best steaks in town. What's more, there's an impressive yet affordable wine list, as well as a unique decor.

Yaxche
$$-$$$
Calle 8, between Av.5 and 10
☎*873-2502*

On crossing the threshold of the Yaxche restaurant, you'll enter a Mayan temple like those that must have existed in ancient times. But what is truly to be discovered here is modern Yucatec Maya cuisine, with over 20 dishes alternately bearing the name of a Mayan god, ruler or place. Yucatec cuisine such as this is seldom found on the east coast of the peninsula. The decor is inspired by the imagined interior of a Mayan royal palace, while frescoes made of plant-based paint depict the walls of various ancient, now-abandoned cities. At night, be sure to tour Yaxche's garden, which features an amazing light show and fountain.

Media Luna
$$-$$$
Av. 5, between Calle 12 and
Calle 14
☎*873-0520*
The restaurant Media Luna
serves copious breakfasts
and a reasonably priced
table d'hôte menu. At night,
the restaurant is illumi-
nated by candles in wall
recesses, giving it a pleasant, romantic ambiance.
There are some vegetarian
dishes on the menu, but
we suggest the marvel-
ously prepared filet of fish.
The decor, however,
leaves something to be
desired.

Shangri-La
$$-$$$
2km north of Playa del Carmen,
on the beach
☎*873-0611*
It is very surprising that the
restaurant of the Shangri-
La hotel is not one of the
more popular in the re-
gion. Although it might be
a little expensive, the quality of the food is unparal-
leled. The menu changes
according to the whim of
the chef who successfully
mixes Mexican and classic
international cuisine.
Clearly, his goal is to tanta-
lize your tastebuds! Every
Sunday night, a lavish
Mexican buffet is served
and entertainment is pro-
vided by mariachis. The
restaurant is airy, and the
service is impeccable and
discrete.

La Parilla
$$-$$$$
Ave. 5, corner Calle 8
☎*873-0687*
Like Cancún, Playa del
Carmen has a branch of
this restaurant where
pizzas baked in a wood-
burning oven, seafood as

well as Mexican and Italian
specialties are served. The
restaurant prepares break-
fast, lunch and dinner.
Every night, around 7pm,
musicians come by and
play for the enjoyment of
diners.

Puerto Aventuras

For a good meal at a low
price, there is a **small
market** facing Aventura
Spa Palace. You can enjoy
delicious tacos while
comfortably seated at one
of six tables inside. You
can also wash this meal
down with a local beer.
Every night, on the little
island across from the
market, you can witness
the amazing sight of the
birds returning to their
nests.

Cafe Ole International
$
A few minutes' walking distance
from the Aventura Spa Palace
This restaurant offers
reasonably-priced Mexican
specialties, topped off by
good coffee. The fixed-
price menu is the best bet
here.

Papaya Republic
$-$$
Behind the golf course
At Papaya Republic pa-
trons sit right on the sand!
Surrounded by palm trees,
this restaurant serves
appetizing fish and seafood
dishes in a relaxed ambi-
ance.

Carlos 'n Charlie's
$$
in the shopping centre
That's right, the links of this
chain have reached all the
way to Puerto Aventuras.

Generous portions of
grilled meats and Tex-Mex
food are served here.

Akumal

Dining in Akumal proves to
be a pleasant experience.
There are few restaurants,
but those that are here
offer variety and, espe-
cially, a warm ambiance
and an enchanting setting.
Local and foreign cuisine
can be enjoyed here.

Near the city's main en-
trance, is the **Super
Chomak** store. Adjacent to
this market, a little snack
bar, Loncheria Akumalito,
sells good little tacos for a
pittance.

Buena Vida
$-$$
on the beach road, north of
Akumal, Half Moon Bay
This bar-restaurant offers a
lovely view of the bay.
Guests can lazily sip a
cocktail here with their
toes in the sand. Its breakfasts will not disappoint.

La Lunita
$-$$
Hacienda Las Tortugas, Half
Moon Bay
☎*875-9070 or 875-9068*
Patrons can sit inside or
out on the beach at La
Lunita. Here, they can
enjoy contemporary and
creative Mexican dishes, a
great variety of desserts
and good coffee. The
restaurant is open every
day for lunch and dinner,
and for breakfast during
the winter months.

Riviera Maya

Lol-ha
$-$$$
Playa Akumal
☎*875-9011 or 875-9012*
This popular restaurant serves fresh fish, seafood and tacos for dinner. It is a lively and very colourful place. It is also open for huge breakfasts, but closes for lunch.

Que Onda
$$
Near the Yal-ku lagoon
☎*875-9101 or 875-9102*
Que Onda is an Italian restaurant that serves fresh home-made pasta. It has a good selection of Italian wines, a lounge bar, a lovely terrace and a pool that is illuminated at night.

Tulum Playa

At the entrance to the Tulum archaeological zone, there are a handful of **snack bars** where you can have something to eat for under 50 pesos.

Maya Tulum
$-$$
Carretera Tulum-Boca Paila, Km 7
☎*877-8638*
This is a vegetarian restaurant, but since the sea is right nearby, fish and seafood, including lobster, are available on the menu.

Christina
$-$$
El Crucero
☎*884-4856*
The restaurant inside the Acuario hotel, Christina offers typically Mexican dishes, prepared with care. Copious breakfasts.

Cabañas Ana y José
$$-$$$
7km south of the ruins
☎*887-5470*
⇄*887-5469*
The restaurant of this hotel is a feet-in-the-sand kind of place that comes highly recommended.

Da Orazio
$$-$$$
Carretera Tulum-Boca Paila, Km 9
☎*876-2088*
If you are craving home-made pasta and other well-prepared Italian dishes, head to this charming restaurant inside the Tropical Padus hotel (see p 145). The chef/owner concocts delectable culinary creations that will literally melt in your mouth and satisfy your taste for exoticism.

Tulum Pueblo

Most hotels in Tulum Pueblo feature an in-house restaurant. On the main street, Avenida Tulum, are restaurants without signs, some of which offer barbecued fare that is messy but very delicious. Others, with a more traditional decor, feature local and international fare. To the great pleasure of visitors, the many Italian restaurants here reflect the size of this community in the village.

Il Basílico
$$
Av. Tulum, corner of Beta Norte
☎*875-3352*
Il Basílico is definitely one of the most esteemed Italian restaurants in the village. Served here are thin-crust pizzas and tradi-

tional Italian dishes. The appetizers prove to be more refined and the wine list features a few good European vintages. Flawless service.

Cobá

Bocadito
$-$$
next to the bus stop
The Bocadito hotel's (see p 146) restaurant offers family-style cuisine that is simple and tasty and sure to suit everyon's budget.

Villa Arguelogicas
$$$
on Lago Cobá
Those looking to treat themselves can go all out at Club Med's restaurant. The menu lists a fine assortment of international and local offerings. The service is impeccable.

Entertainment

Playa del Carmen

Bars and Nightclubs

Capitán Tutix
on the beach, corner Calle 4
Friday nights after 11pm, when other bars are closing their doors, locals get together with fun-seeking tourists to party at Capitán Tutix. The bar looks sort of like the hull of a ship and the dance floor fills up when the musicians start to play. There are tables and chairs outside in the sand, where you can drink a beer on the beach while

listening to top-40 music. The bar is frequented by local performers and artists providing guests with an alternative form of entertainment.

La Rana
On the beach, next to Capitán Tutix
For those of you who want to get away from the Latin beat, La Rana is a bar that plays mostly techno music. Since it is next to Capitán Tutix, (see above) you have to use the beach to access the secluded patio and beyond the dark and smoky interior. If you can put up with the smoke, and find your way, head upstairs to the second floor, which is usually empty.

Beer Bucket
Av. 5, between Calles 10 and 12
The Beer Bucket is a small but friendly place that serves the cheapest beer in town. The beer is served in an ice-bucket containing five bottles for about 35 pesos. Come here especially if you like Corona. This open-air bar with mellow music is perfect for conversing while watching the passersby on Avenida 5. There are few seats, so get there early.

Cabalova Sports Bar
Av. 5, corner Calle 16
Sportsfans can watch their favourite games here on the second floor of the Mosquito Blue hotel. Games are broadcast on a giant screen hooked up to a satellite. If you are not interested in watching a match, or there is no more room at the Beer Bucket (see above), you

can always take in the night-time entertainment on the third floor.

Karen's Grill & Pizza
Av. 5, between Calles 2 and 4
This is a restaurant with a large dance floor where Latin folk musicians perform at night.

Pez Vela
Av. 5, corner Calle 2
Pez Vela advertizes what you're in for right at its door: food, drinks and rock'n'roll. Come nightfall, amateur bands burn down the house with old rock classics.

La Tequilaría
Av. 5, between Calles 4 and 6
Find for the flagpole flying the Mexican standard and you will be right in front of the lovely orange facade of La Tequilaría. Four small tables and as many chairs are set up on the patio, where passersby can stop and have a drink and a bit of conversation. Or, if you can't deal with the heat, go inside and sit upstairs in front of the open window and quench your thirst with one of the 269 different kinds of tequila or several kinds of mescal. At night, guitar-playing mariachis serenade tourists.

Shopping

Puerto Morelos

Kab Meyah
Calle Tulum, Plaza Morelos
☎/≈*871-0164*
The boutique of this Internet café features local arts and crafts. Hand-painted terracotta vases, finely-crafted silver bracelets and lovely drawings are made and sold here. You can see the artists at work in the back of the shop.

Playa del Carmen

The dozens of boutiques all along pedestrian Avenida 5 sell *huipiles*, hand-woven wool blankets, terracotta vases and masks as well as a variety of art pieces. Playa del Carmen also has good beachwear and dive shops.

Mexican Amber
Av. 5, between Calles 4 and 6
☎*873-2357*
This boutique stocks beautiful amber jewellery.

Fuente
50m from the port
facing Cicsa Money Exchange
This jewellery store sells hand-made silver bracelets, rings and earrings. To ensure that a silver piece is authentic, check to see if it bears the inscription "925."

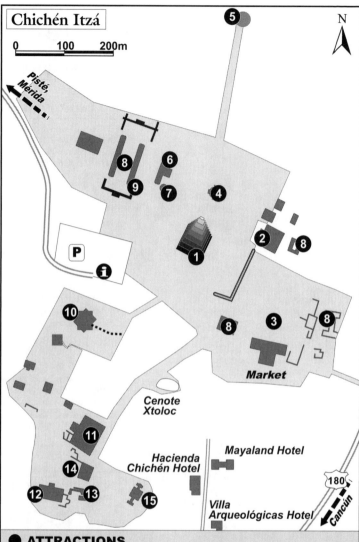

Chichén Itzá

0   100   200m

N

Pisté, Mérida

P

Market

Cenote Xtoloc

Hacienda Chichén Hotel

Mayaland Hotel

Villa Arqueológicas Hotel

180

Cancún

● ATTRACTIONS

The North Group
1. El Castillo (Temple of Kukulkán)
2. Templo de los Guerreros (Temple of the Warriors)
3. Grupo de las Mil Columnas (Group of the Thousand Columns)
4. Plataforma de Venus (Tomb of Chac-Mool)
5. Cenote Sagrado (Sacred Cenote)
6. Tzompantli or Plataforma de los Craneos (Platform of the Skulls)
7. Plataforma de las Aguilas y de los Jaguares (Platform of the Eagles and the Jaguars)
8. Ball Court

9. Templo de los Jaguares (Temple of the Jaguars)

The South Group
10. El Osario ou Tumba del Gran Sacerdote (Tomb of the High Priest)
11. El Caracol (Observatory)
12. Edificio de las Monjas (Nunnery)
13. Iglesia (The Church)
14. Templo de los Tableros (Temple of the Wall Panels)
15. Akab Dzib (Temple of Obscure Writing)

©ULYSSES

Excursion to Chichén Itzá

Chichén Itzá lies
in the heart of a vast plain in the north of the peninsula, where the only sources of water to be found are a few randomly dispersed *cenotes*.

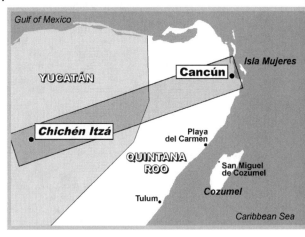

The trees, though numerous, are somewhat stunted. Major restorations have resulted in the preservation of the temples and palaces, which were once overgrown by vegetation. From Cancún, the site may be reached by car or bus on a smooth road, or even by plane. The archaeological zone is located 179km from Cancún.

The village of Pisté, located a few kilometres from the site, is something of a commercial extension of Chichén Itzá. The village includes arts and crafts boutiques, restaurants, hotels, a campsite, a Pemex petrol station and a bank.

Finding Your Way Around

The area code for Chichén Itzá and Pisté is **985**.

By Car

From Cancún, take Highway 180 to Chichén Itzá and the small village of Pisté. The trip takes approximately 2hrs.

If you plan to go it alone and rent a car to visit Chichén Itzá, there are some additional expenses involved. There are two toll booths en route: the first costs 120 pesos, and the second, which is located closer to the site, costs 30 pesos. Don't forget to double these amounts because you will have to pay again on the way back. Finally, on top of the entry fee of 70 pesos and the cost of food, you will need 10 pesos for parking plus money for gas.

Arriving from Cancún, take the turnoff approximately 0.5km south of the entrance to the archaeological site. Follow the road signs from there.

By Plane

Aerocaribe
☎*884-2000*
⌨*884-1364*
This airline offers same-day return flights from Cancún to Chichén Itzá for $120. The flight takes about 20min; there are approximately three return flights per day. The airport is located close to the taxi stand from which drivers take travellers to the site.

By Bus

Cancún

Bus Station
corner Tulum and Uxmal
From Cancún, first- and second-class buses leave every hour during the day for Chichén Itzá. The trip costs about 30 pesos, and, depending on the type of bus, can take from 2 to 3hrs. The last night bus from Chichén Itzá to Cancún leaves at 11pm. Check the schedule because it is subject to frequent changes.

Pisté

Bus Station
in front of the Pirámide Inn

Exploring

Chichén Itzá

Travellers to the Yucatán Peninsula cannot in good

Popul Vul

The *Popul Vul* was the Mayan bible. It is an incredible reference tool on the Mayan civilization because it contains their customs, beliefs, traditions and knowledge. When the Spanish took control of the Yucatán Peninsula, Catholic priests, who wanted to propagate the Christian faith and convert the pagan Amerindians, burnt copies of the *Popul Vul* before startled and helpless Mayans. Only four copies of the book survived the autodafé and continue to be studied by specialists who have unravelled some of the mysteries left by this brilliant civilization, which is gone forever.

conscience fail to visit the large archaeological town of Chichén Itzá. Covering close to 15km², numerous temples and buildings bear witness to a bygone era, when Chichén Itzá reigned over the entire northern peninsula.

Chichén Itzá has been ranked a World Heritage Site by UNESCO. It is one of the best-restored sites on the peninsula, as well as one of the biggest, even though some of its build-

ings remain buried beneath a thick blanket of vegetation.

Chichén Itzá is a very popular spot; there are simply hordes of people here during the day. The best time to discover the charms of this ancient city is early in the morning, before the intense heat of midday and, above all, before the tour buses arrive *(around 11am)*. Getting here early will also give you greater freedom to admire the sumptuous Castillo, the large ball court or the Group of the Thousand Columns. If you're passing through during the spring or autumn equinox (March 21st and September 21st, respectively), you can observe the descent of the serpent (see inset).

The Chichén Itzá site is open every day from 8am to 5pm; admission costs 90 pesos *(except Sundays, when admission is free)*. At the entrance to the site, there is a restaurant *($$)*, a free cinema, a small museum, a book shop and many souvenir shops. There is also a free check room *(8am to 5pm)*, bathrooms and a large parking lot *(10 pesos for the day)*. Those who prefer to use a guide will have to keep up a quick pace. Video cameras may be rented for 30 pesos.

A sound and light show is presented every night in Chichén Itzá *(25 pesos in English at 9pm, or in Spanish at 5pm)*. Major events, such as tenor Luciano Pavarotti's performance in December 1996, are sometimes organized. Because the site is mostly out in the open, a hat or a cap, sunscreen lotion, bottled water and sunglasses are essential. Good walking shoes are also a must.

History

Chichén Itzá is unquestionably the most impressive archaeological city in the Mayan world. A small village first known as Uucyl Abnal, Chichén Itzá remained a place of pilgrimage until the arrival of the Spanish in the 16th century. For three centuries, from AD 900 to 1200, it was the centre of power of a city-state that ruled the entire region.

Its Mayan-language name means "Place of the Well of the Itzá." The first term, "Chichén," refers to the sacred *cenote*, a large, natural well like those scattered throughout the peninsula. The term "Itzá" refers to the powerful semi-historical, semi-mythical men who ruled the city in its heyday.

Despite much conservation and restoration work, Chichén Itzá has yet to reveal most of its secrets, particularly thoses of its inhabitants. In fact, there are several theories regarding the origins, influences and conquests of the Itzá. The mural paintings and the columns' basreliefs have time and again confirmed an interpreta-

tion of the past that was later refuted. The writings left behind by the Maya contradict the current interpretation of the hieroglyphs carved into the buildings' lintels.

The standard interpretation holds that Chichén Itzá was conquered by the Toltec of Tula, the ancient Toltec capital in central Mexico, who influenced the architecture and layout of Chichén Itzá. But dissenting voices argue that the opposite is true. The head archaeologist of the latest research on the site has concluded that it is highly possible that several different peoples had a hand in the political, military and economic control of Chichén Itzá.

These numerous interpretations lead to confusion for visitors to this archaeological site. Moreover, the nomenclature used for the different structures often comes down to us from the first Spanish colonists, and attributes such as Maya, Toltec or Old Chichén (Chichén Viejo) are still used to date the different groups of structures.

Situated halfway between the east and west coasts of the Yucatán peninsula, Chichén Itzá covers over 15km^2. Its geographical position gave it access to the large salt marshes on the north coast; from its seaport on Isla Cerritos, boats sailed between the Gulf of Mexico and the Caribbean Sea. Its military and political supremacy allowed it to extend its control over the plain's

The Serpent's Descent

During the spring and autumn equinoxes (March 21st and September 21st), the shadow cast by the sun forms a sinuous shape resembling a serpent slowly slithering its way down one of the corners of El Castillo. This phenomenon lasts approximately 15 min. The rays of the sun gliding over the steps create the illusion that an animal is actually in the process of moving. Moreover, there is an enormous stone serpent head with gaping mouth at the foot of each of the four corners of the temple, which leads one to believe that, if the phenomenon were merely a coincidence, the Mayans knew full well how to exploit it and turn it into a dramatic event. Because the Mayans were keen observers of the stars and sky, it would hardly be surprising if the temple plans were, in fact, conceived with the particular intention of creating this effect.

fertile land and, in its heyday, Chichén Itzá controlled major overland routes.

Town Planning

Most public buildings are distributed throughout a network of large plazas. The vast Plaza del Caracol (Observatory Square), which occupies the southern part of the site, comprises the Edificio de las Monjas (the Nunnery) and its annex, the Templo de los Tableros (Temple of the Sculptured Panels) and the Akab Dzib (Temple of the Obscure Writing). An intermediate plaza known as El Osario (the Ossuary) or the Tomb of the High Priest comprises all structures inside the platform located east of the Xtoloc Cenote. The third is the huge Plaza del Castillo, which encompasses the Group of the Thousand Columns, the Mercado (Market), the Templo de los Guerreros (Temple of Warriors), the large ball court, the Sacred Cenote and the small structures north of the Castillo.

In addition to these three central plazas, there are other public buildings of more modest size located 200m to 700m south of the administrative and religious centre. These structures are surrounded by hillocks on which houses were built of perishable materials, like those that still exist in the Yucatán. Some 20 *sacbeob* ("white roads") ranging from 2m to 8m wide linked these structures in the city centre.

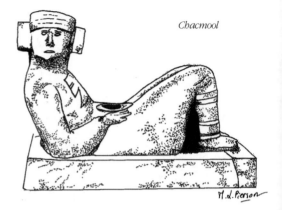

Chacmool

M.d. Pierson

Architectural Styles of Chichén Itzá

At least two styles of public architecture can now be discerned at Chichén Itzá. The first is a local variant of the Puuc style, which evolved in the eighth and ninth centuries in the hills of the Yucatán. This style is characterized by masonry facades and, above all, by stone mosaic reliefs on the upper part of the facades of temples and palaces. Several temples are built on high, round-cornered platforms with open stairways.

The principal motif of the mosaic decorative elements consists of superimposed masks of the rain god Chac and geometric designs like Persian and Greek borders that form representations of stylized serpents.

The second style, known as Maya-Toltec, is also derived from the Puuc style but greatly enriched by elements and techniques of Mexican and, more particularly, Tula origin. Structures of this style at Chichén Itzá include features such as tiered pyramids with sloping walls, and panels with geometric designs or figurative reliefs on each level. Maya-Toltec-style buildings harbour large rooms with supporting columns or pillars and half-open porticos.

Relief ornamentation is omnipresent, with bas-reliefs of plumed serpents, moving or seated jaguars, eagles, animated scenes and endless processions of warriors and dignitaries.

Integrated with this architectural ensemble is a series of sculptures, including Chacmool figures at the entrance to the temples; small and large Atlantean figures supporting altars, lintels or beams; jaguar-shaped thrones; human heads emerging from the mouths of serpents; as well as serpentine friezes, lintels, columns or banisters.

Visiting the Site

In order to allot visitors enough time to tour the

most important structures, we have divided the site into two sections: the North Group comprises Maya–Toltec-style buildings, and the South Group, which includes the Plaza del Osuario and the Plaza del Caracol, features Maya–Toltec- and Puuc-style buildings.

The North Group

El Castillo
(Temple of Kukulkán)

Situated more or less in the middle of the north group, this pyramid, topped with a temple, dominates the others because of its height (30m). El Castillo, a pyramidal temple, combines elements of Mayan and Toltec cultures and displays several cosmological symbols. The Mayas intimately linked the study of stars and mathematics with religion. As such, El Castillo comprises 365 steps on each of its four sides (corresponding to the number of days in the solar year), 52 paving stones (the number of years in a Mayan century) and 18 terraces (the months of the sacred year).

Many tourists scale El Castillo for the stunning view its summit offers of the surrounding area. This is no easy task, however, for the steps are

at a 45° angle. Moreover, the descent is harder than the ascent.

El Castillo harbours another pyramid with a smaller temple, reached by a narrow flight of steps. The entrance to this staircase is at the base of the temple, under the stairs on the north side.

Templo de los Guerreros
(The Temple of Warriors)

Surmounted by a sculpture of Chacmool and two serpent-shaped columns, this temple could be an imitation of the morning star temple in Tula, only bigger. It is an imposing structure, surmounting a tiered platform, surrounded by stone columns. There is another older, more modestly sized temple inside.

Grupo de las Mil Columnas
(The Group of the Thousand Columns)

Precisely aligned the length of the Temple of Warriors, these imposing stone columns include several buildings used for administrative purposes and for large meetings.

Plataforma de Venus
(Platform of Venus)

North of El Castillo, on the road that leads to the Sacred Cenote, stands a small square platform decorated with numerous sculptures in bas relief. Visitors can reach this temple's summit by climbing one of the staircases going up each of its four sides. At the summit, a large platform may have served as a place for sacred dances.

Cenote Sagrado
(The Sacred Cenote)

From the Platform of Venus, a 300m-long *sacbeob*, or white path, surrounded by towering trees leads to the Sacred Cenote. Almost perfectly round, this natural well measures 55m in diametre and 25m in depth and holds greenish, opaque water. On the right, a small temple overhangs the *cenote*. About 50 skeletons (mostly men and children), and gold, copper, jade and obsidian artifacts as well as rubber dolls have been brought to the surface in searches of the *cenote*. There is a little snack bar nearby where visitors can enjoy refreshments.

Tzompantli or Plataforma de los Craneos
(Platform of the Skulls)

This is a large square platform with stone walls adorned with skulls carved in bas relief, full-face or in profile, each one with its own unique personality.

Excursion to Chichén Itzá

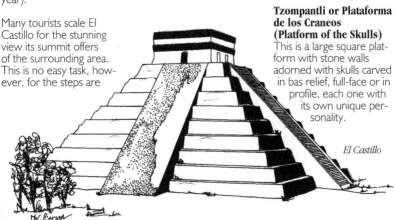

El Castillo

**Plataforma de las Aguilas
y de los Jaguares
(The House of Eagles)**
Close to Tzompantli is a
platform whose walls are
adorned with images of
eagles clutching human
hearts in their talons. The
stairs are flanked by stone
serpents on either side.

**Juego de Pelota
(The Ball Court)**
At the northwestern ex-
tremity of the north group
extends the largest pelota
field ever discovered in the
Mayan world. Measuring
145m by 37m, the field is
lined on either side by two
8m-high stone walls. Both
these walls have a stone
hoop through which play-
ers were to toss a rubber
ball. The ball, symbolizing
the sun, had to stay off the
ground at all times. The
way sound reverberates

inside the playing field is
impressive.

At the right entrance to
the site, the Temple of
Jaguars (Templo de los
Jaguares) is adorned with
many bas reliefs and a
large mural. A jaguar sculpture also faces the House
of Eagles.

The South Group

**El Osario or Tumba del
Gran Sacerdote
(The Tomb of the High
Priest)**
At the South Group's
entrance stands this 10m-
high pyramid. Skeletons
and precious artifacts have
been discovered inside.

**El Caracol
(The Observatory)**
Further south stands a
round, two-storey struc-

ture, which undoubtedly
served as an observatory.
Narrow windows that let
the sun in enabled the
Mayan priests to measure
time.

**Edificio de las Monjas
(The Nunnery)**
Continuing south, visitors
reach this building whose
facade is richly adorned
with masks that depict the
god of rain, Chac.

**Iglesia
(The Church)**
Right next door, this small
building in the Puuc architectural style presents a
façade of geometric motifs
and animals, notably the
four bearers of the sky as
they are represented in
Mayan mythology: a crab,
a snail, an armadillo and a
tortoise.

Juego de pelota

The *juego de pelota* or
the *pok-ta-pok*, was
first practised by the
Olmecs and later by
the Mayas. This game
was a cross between
fútbol and rugby,
where all kinds of
shots were permitted,
and had a religious
significance. Nobody
knows exactly how
many players were in
the game or exactly
what the rules were,
but we know that
matches were played
on fields that had a
particular shape and

various dimensions.
Two long stone walls
bordered the field, in
the middle of which
was a huge stone ring.
The opponents wore
protective gear on
their knees and hips
and without using
their hands or legs,
had to pass around a
ball, probably made of
rubber and about
10cm in diametre,
without dropping it
until someone scored
by throwing it through
the ring. Clearly, the
games were long and

difficult. And the out-
come of the game?
During the Mayan
period, it is believed
that the winner was
allowed to offer sacri-
fices to the gods.
Another explanation is
that after the despotic
and war-like Toltecs
were integrated into
Mayan empire, the
game took on a whole
new meaning. Someti-
mes the losers were
decapitated, and some-
times the winners
were sacrificed to the
gods.

In this same area, the following attractions should be highlighted: the **Templo de los Tableros** (Temple of the Sculptured Panels) and **Akab Dzib** (the Temple of the Obscure Writing).

Accommodations

Chichén Itzá

Hacienda Chichén
$$$
≡, ≈, ℜ
Carretera Mérida-Cancún, Km 120
☎*924-2150 or 851-0045*
⇌*924-5011*
Built in the 17th century, this property is located on an old agave plantation. The explorers John Lloyd Stephens and Frederick Catherwood stayed here during the first archaeological digs in the Yucatán, around 1840. It later belonged to the American consul Edward Thompson, while he studied Chichén Itzá. It is now a picturesque inn with 18 rooms, a delightful garden and a large swimming pool. Simply decorated in the colonial style, the rooms all offer verandas and private bathrooms. The lobby and the outbuildings are full of artifacts and Mayan arts and crafts. The hacienda also rents cottages comprised of two simply furnished rooms, with exposed ceiling beams. The hacienda is open from November to April.

Mayaland
$$$ bkfst incl.
⊗, ≈, ℜ, ≡, ⊛
Carretera Mérida-Cancún, Km 120
☎*851-0027*
⇌*851-0129*
www.mayaland.com
Quite close to the archaeological zone, this modern complex is built around a main building with colonial-style architecture. The hotel has 65 rooms surrounded by lush vegetation. The Mayaland offers all the amenities of a luxury hotel, notably four restaurants, four bars and three swimming pools. Guests can stay in one of 50 thatched-roofed cottages or 24 colonial-style rooms in the main building.

Villas Arqueológicas
$$$
≈, ℜ, △, ⊘, ⊛
100m east of the Mayaland
☎*851-0034 or 851-0018*
This property has white stucco walls with a red-tile roof. Each of its small rooms contains twin beds and a bathroom with shower facilities. The hotel itself has a library well-stocked with books on Mayan culture, as well as a restaurant and a pool surrounded by gardens. Though the establishment is affiliated with Club Med, it is possible to simply rent a room for a night or two.

Pisté

Dolores Alba
$ bkfst incl.
⊗, ≡, ≈, ℜ
Carretera Mérida-Cancún, Km 122
☎*858-1555 (in Mérida)*
☎*928-5650*
⇌*928-3163*
www.doloresalba.com
This is a "budget" hotel with 40 rooms that are modest but clean and comfortable. Not all of the rooms are air-conditioned, so visitors must ask for this amenity if they want it. The hotel also offers free transportation to the ruins. There are two pools and free parking.

Pirámide Inn
$
≈, ℜ
Calle 15A No.28, corner Calle 20
☎*851-0115*
⇌*851-0114*
www.piramideinn.com
This property consists of two buildings housing 50 modern rooms with white walls and floors. The hotel boasts a garden, a swimming pool and a good restaurant. Guests can also pitch tents on a small campsite adjacent to the hotel. Campers have access to the pool, and hot water showers have been installed for their use. The hotel is situated at the eastern extremity of Pisté. Free parking.

Hotel Chichén Itzá
$
≡, ≈, ℜ
Calle 15A No.45
☎*851-0022*
⇌*851-0023*
www.hotelchichenitza.com
Located 2km from the ruins of Chichén Itzá, in the village of Pisté, the

Hotel Chichén Itzá offers comfortable rooms. It is a little set back from the main road, but easily accessible.

Restaurants

Chichén Itzá

There is a small cafeteria ($) as well as an air-conditioned restaurant ($$) at the western entrance to the archaeological site. The latter serves simple, decent food. Another option is to go to one of the restaurants of the hotels described above.

Hacienda Chichén
$$
Carretera Mérida-Puerto Juárez, Km 120
☎*851-0045 or 924-2150*
This restaurant serves delicious Yucatán special-ties at very reasonable prices.

Mayaland
$$-$$$
Carretera Mérida-Puerto Juárez, Km 120
☎*924-2099*
At this hotel, there are four restaurants that serve different specialties. The food is rather expensive, but patrons can admire the hotel's beautiful gardens.

Villas Arqueológicas
$$$
100m east of the Mayaland
☎*851-0034 or 851-0018*
This hotel houses a very elegantly decorated restaurant offering French and Mexican cuisine. Whether for lunch or dinner, the fixed-price meal is a better choice than the more expensive *à la carte* menu.

Pisté

This small village a few kilometres from Chichén Itzá is home to a few establishments offering up a more local cuisine than those in Chichén Itzá.

Route 180 passes a multitude of small restaurants that have fixed-price menus and serve local dishes.

In Pisté itself, facing the Misión Chichén hotel, is the **Sayil** restaurant, where diners can eat very well for under 50 pesos.

Visitors can enjoy the buffet in the comfortable, air conditioned dining room of the **Xaybe** restaurant, right near the Sayil. The food is quite good and the all-you-can-eat lunch buffet costs about 50 pesos. The dinner buffet is slightly more expensive.

Glossary

Consonants

b   Is pronounced **b** or sometimes a soft **v**, depending on the region or the person: *bizcocho* (biz-koh-choh or viz-koh-choh).

c   As in English, *c* is pronounced as **s** before *i* and *e*: *cerro* (seh-rroh). When it is placed in front of other vowels, it is hard and pronounced as **k**: *carro* (kah-rroh). The *c* is also hard when it comes before a consonant, except before an *h* (see further below).

d   Is pronounced like a soft **d**: *dar* (dahr). *D* is usually not pronounced when at the end of a word.

g   As with the *c*, *g* is soft before an *i* or an *e*, and is pronounced like a soft **h**: *gente* (hente). In front of other vowels and consonants, the *g* is hard: *golf* (pronounced the same way as in English).

ch   Pronounced **ch**, as in English: *leche* (le-che). Like the *ll*, this combination is considered a single letter in the Spanish alphabet, listed separately in dictionaries and telephone directories.

h   Is not pronounced: *hora* (oh-ra).

j   Is pronounced like a guttural **h**, as in "him".

ll   Is pronounced like a hard **y**, as in "yes": *llamar* (yah-mar). In some regions, such as central Colombia, *ll* is pronounced as a soft **g**, as in "mirage" (*Medellín* is pronounced Medegin). Like the *ch*, this combination is considered a single letter in the Spanish alphabet, and is listed separately in dictionaries and telephone directories.

ñ   Is pronounced like the **ni** in "onion", or the **ny** in "canyon": *señora* (seh-nyo-rah).

qu   Is pronounced **k**: *aquí* (ah-kee).

r   Is rolled, as the Irish or Italian pronunciation of **r**.

s   Is always pronounced **s** like "sign": *casa* (cah-ssah).

v   Is pronounced like a **b**: *vino* (bee-noh).

z   Is pronounced like **s**: *paz* (pahss).

Vowels

a   Is always pronounced **ah** as in "part", and never *ay* as in "day": *faro* (fah-roh).

e   Is always pronounced **eh** as in "elf," and never *ey* as in "grey or "ee" as in "key": *helado* (eh-lah-doh].

i   Is always pronounced **ee**: *cine* (see-neh).

o   Is always pronounced **oh** as in "cone": *copa* (koh-pah).

u   Is always pronounced **oo**: *universidad* (oo-nee-ver-see-dah).

All other letters are pronounced the same as in English.

Stressing Syllables

In Spanish, syllables are differently stressed. This stress is very important, and emphasizing the right syllable might even be necessary to make yourself understood. If a vowel has an accent, this syllable is the one that should be stressed. If there is no accent, follow this rule:

Stress the second-last syllable of any word that ends with a vowel: *a***mi**go.

Stress the last syllable of any word that ends in a consonant, except for **s** (plural of nouns and adjectives) or **n** (plural of nouns): *us***ted** (but *a***mi**gos, **ha**blan).

Frequently Used Words and Expressions

Greetings

Goodbye	*adiós, hasta luego*
Good afternoon and good evening	*buenas tardes*
Hi (casual)	*hola*
Good morning	*buenos días*
Good night	*buenas noches*
Thank-you	*gracias*
Please	*por favor*
You are welcome	*de nada*
Excuse me	*perdone/a*
My name is...	*mi nombre es...*
What is your name?	*¿cómo se llama usted?*
no/yes	*no/sí*
Do you speak English?	*¿habla usted inglés?*
Slower, please	*más despacio, por favor*
I am sorry, I don't speak Spanish	*Lo siento, no hablo español*
How are you?	*¿qué tal?*
I am fine	*estoy bien*
I am American (male/female)	*Soy estadounidense*
I am Australian	*Soy autraliano/a*
I am Belgian	*Soy belga*
I am British (male/female)	*Soy británico/a*
I am Canadian	*Soy canadiense*
I am German (male/female)	*Soy alemán/a*
I am Italian (male/female)	*Soy italiano/a*
I am Swiss	*Soy suizo*
I am a tourist	*Soy turista*
single (m/f)	*soltero/a*
divorced (m/f)	*divorciado/a*
married (m/f)	*casado/a*
friend (m/f)	*amigo/a*
child (m/f)	*niño/a*

husband, wife	*esposo/a*
mother, father	*madre, padre*
brother, sister	*hermano/a*
widower widow	*viudo/a*
I am hungry	*tengo hambre*
I am ill	*estoy enfermo/a*
I am thirsty	*tengo sed*

Directions

beside	*al lado de*
to the right	*a la derecha*
to the left	*a la izquierda*
here, there	*aquí, allí*
into, inside	*dentro*
outside	*fuera*
behind	*detrás*
in front of	*delante*
between	*entre*
far from	*lejos de*
Where is ... ?	*¿dónde está ... ?*
To get to ...?	*¿para ir a...?*
near	*cerca de*
straight ahead	*todo recto*

Money

money	*dinero / plata*
credit card	*tarjeta de crédito*
exchange	*cambio*
traveller's cheque	*cheque de viaje*
I don't have any money	*no tengo dinero*
The bill, please	*la cuenta, por favor*
receipt	*recibo*

Shopping

store	*tienda*
market	*mercado*
open, closed	*abierto/a, cerrado/a*
How much is this?	*¿cuánto es?*
to buy, to sell	*comprar,* vender
the customer	*el / la cliente*
salesman	*vendedor*
saleswoman	*vendedora*
I need...	*necesito...*
I would like...	*yo quisiera...*
batteries	*pilas*
blouse	*blusa*
cameras	*cámaras*
cosmetics and perfumes	*cosméticos y perfumes*
cotton	*algodón*
dress jacket	*saco*
eyeglasses	*lentes, gafas*
fabric	*tela*
film	*película*
gifts	*regalos*

gold	*oro*
handbag	*bolsa*
hat	*sombrero*
jewellery	*joyería*
leather	*cuero, piel*
local crafts	*artesanía*
magazines	*revistas*
newpapers	*periódicos*
pants	*pantalones*
records, cassettes	*discos, casetas*
sandals	*sandalias*
shirt	*camisa*
shoes	*zapatos*
silver	*plata*
skirt	*falda*
sun screen products	*productos solares*
T-shirt	*camiseta*
watch	*reloj*
wool	*lana*

Miscellaneous

a little	*poco*
a lot	*mucho*
good (m/f)	*bueno/a*
bad (m/f)	*malo/a*
beautiful (m/f)	*hermoso/a*
pretty (m/f)	*bonito/a*
ugly	*feo*
big	*grande*
tall (m/f)	*alto/a*
small (m/f)	*pequeño/a*
short (length) (m/f)	*corto/a*
short (person) (m/f)	*bajo/a*
cold (m/f)	*frío/a*
hot	*caliente*
dark (m/f)	*oscuro/a*
light (colour)	*claro*
do not touch	*no tocar*
expensive (m/f)	*caro/a*
cheap (m/f)	*barato/a*
fat (m/f)	*gordo/a*
slim, skinny (m/f)	*delgado/a*
heavy (m/f)	*pesado/a*
light (weight) (m/f)	*ligero/a*
less	*menos*
more	*más*
narrow (m/f)	*estrecho/a*
wide (m/f)	*ancho/a*
new (m/f)	*nuevo/a*
old (m/f)	*viejo/a*
nothing	*nada*
something (m/f)	*algo/a*
quickly	*rápidamente*
slowly (m/f)	*despacio/a*
What is this?	*¿qué es esto?*

| when? | *¿cuando?* |
| where? | *¿dónde?* |

Time

in the afternoon, early evening	*por la tarde*
at night	*por la noche*
in the daytime	*por el día*
in the morning	*por la mañana*
minute	*minuto*
month	*mes*
ever	*jamás*
never	*nunca*
now	*ahora*
today	*hoy*
yesterday	*ayer*
tomorrow	*mañana*
What time is it?	*¿qué hora es?*
hour	*hora*
week	*semana*
year	*año*
Sunday	*domingo*
Monday	*lunes*
Tuesday	*martes*
Wednesday	*miércoles*
Thursday	*jueves*
Friday	*viernes*
Saturday	*sábado*
January	*enero*
February	*febrero*
March	*marzo*
April	*abril*
May	*mayo*
June	*junio*
July	*julio*
August	*agosto*
September	*septiembre*
October	*octubre*
November	*noviembre*
December	*diciembre*

Weather

It is cold	*hace frío*
It is warm	*hace calor*
It is very hot	*hace mucho calor*
sun	*sol*
It is sunny	*hace sol*
It is cloudy	*está nublado*
rain	*lluvia*
It is raining	*está lloviendo*
wind	*viento*
It is windy	*hay viento*
snow	*nieve*
damp	*húmedo*
dry	*seco*

storm	*tormenta*
hurricane	*huracán*

Communication

air mail	*correos aéreo*
collect call	*llamada por cobrar*
dial the number	*marcar el número*
area code, country code	*código*
envelope	*sobre*
long distance	*larga distancia*
post office	*correo*
rate	*tarifa*
stamps	*estampillas*
telegram	*telegrama*
telephone book	*un guia telefónica*
wait for the tone	*esperar la señal*

Activities

beach	*playa*
museum or gallery	*museo*
scuba diving	*buceo*
to swim	*bañarse*
to walk around	*pasear*
hiking	*caminata*
trail	*pista, sendero*
cycling	*ciclismo*
fishing	*pesca*

Transportation

arrival, departure	*llegada, salida*
on time	*a tiempo*
cancelled (m/f)	*anulado/a*
one way ticket	*ida*
return	*regreso*
round trip	*ida y vuelta*
schedule	*horario*
baggage	*equipajes*
north, south	*norte, sur*
east, west	*este, oeste*
avenue	*avenida*
street	*calle*
highway	*carretera*
expressway	*autopista*
airplane	*avión*
airport	*aeropuerto*
bicycle	*bicicleta*
boat	*barco*
bus	*bus*
bus stop	*parada*
bus terminal	*terminal*
train	*tren*
train crossing	*crucero ferrocarril*
station	*estación*
neighbourhood	*barrio*

collective taxi	*colectivo*
corner	*esquina*
express	*rápido*
safe	*seguro/a*
be careful	*cuidado*
car	*coche, carro*
to rent a car	*alquilar un auto*
gas	*gasolina*
gas station	*gasolinera*
no parking	*no estacionar*
no passing	*no adelantar*
parking	*parqueo*
pedestrian	*peaton*
road closed, no through traffic	*no hay paso*
slow down	*reduzca velocidad*
speed limit	*velocidad permitida*
stop	*alto*
stop! (an order)	*pare*
traffic light	*semáforo*

Accommodation

cabin, bungalow	*cabaña*
accommodation	*alojamiento*
double, for two people	*doble*
single, for one person	*sencillo*
high season	*temporada alta*
low season	*temporada baja*
bed	*cama*
floor (first, second...)	*piso*
main floor	*planta baja*
manager	*gerente, jefe*
double bed	*cama matrimonial*
cot	*camita*
bathroom	*baños*
with private bathroom	*con baño privado*
hot water	*agua caliente*
breakfast	*desayuno*
elevator	*ascensor*
air conditioning	*aire acondicionado*
fan	*ventilador, abanico*
pool	*piscina, alberca*
room	*habitación*

Numbers

1	*uno*	12	*doce*
2	*dos*	13	*trece*
3	*tres*	14	*catorce*
4	*cuatro*	15	*quince*
5	*cinco*	16	*dieciséis*
6	*seis*	17	*diecisiete*
7	*siete*	18	*dieciocho*
8	*ocho*	19	*diecinueve*
9	*nueve*	20	*veinte*
10	*diez*	21	*veintiuno*
11	*once*	22	*veintidós*

23	*veintitrés*	102	*ciento dos*
24	*veinticuatro*	200	*doscientos*
25	*veinticinco*	300	*trescientos*
26	*veintiséis*	400	*quatrocientoa*
27	*veintisiete*	500	*quinientos*
28	*veintiocho*	600	*seiscientos*
29	*veintinueve*	700	*sietecientos*
30	*treinta*	800	*ochocientos*
31	*treinta y uno*	900	*novecientos*
32	*treinta y dos*	1,000	*mil*
40	*cuarenta*	1,100	*mil cien*
50	*cincuenta*	1,200	*mil doscientos*
60	*sesenta*	2,000	*dos mil*
70	*setenta*	3,000	*tres mil*
80	*ochenta*	10,000	*diez mil*
90	*noventa*	100,000	*cien mil*
100	*cien*	1,000,000	*un millón*
101	*ciento uno*		

Index

Index

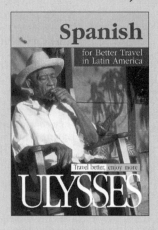
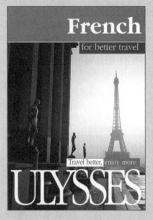